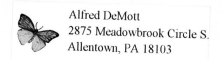
Alfred DeMott
2875 Meadowbrook Circle S.
Allentown, PA 18103

D1311618

Alfred DeMott
2875 Meadowbrook Circle S.
Allentown, PA 18103

We Remember The Fabulous '50s

The music on the jukebox has softened and the rumble of distant hot rods muffled, but the memories of those Fabulous '50s are as fresh as yesterday.

R from the readers of Reminisce magazine

H. Armstrong Roberts

PROSPERITY REIGNS. As folks got their lives back together following World War II, many married, raised families and bought houses. The 1950s was a decade of amazing growth, based in solid family values.

Editor: Lee Aschoff

Contributing Editor: Clancy Strock

Assistant Editors: Deborah Mulvey, Kristine Krueger, John Schroeder, Bettina Miller, Mike Beno

Art Director: Niki Malmberg

Art Associates: Bonnie Ziolecki, Maribeth Greinke

Photo Coordinator: Trudi Bellin

Editorial Assistants: Blanche Comiskey, Melody Trick, Jack Kertzman, Mary Ann Koebernik, Jean Steiner

Production Assistants: Ellen Lloyd, Catherine Fletcher

Publisher: Roy J. Reiman

©2001 Reiman Publications, LLC
5400 S. 60th St., Greendale WI 53129

Reminisce Books
International Standard Book Number:
0-89821-314-2

Library of Congress Control Number: 2001132089

On the Cover: A guy, a gal and their music combine for a timeless picture. But in the Fabulous '50s, the music took on a whole new rhythm and volume as rock 'n' roll reverberated across the country. Hairstyles, hot rods and clothing were all chronicled in—and sometimes inspired by—the music. (Photo: H. Armstrong Roberts)

For additional copies of this book or information on other books, write: Reminisce Books, P.O. Box 990, Greendale WI 53129-0990; call toll-free 1-800/558-1013 to order with a credit card; or visit our Web site at **www.reimanpub.com**.

Contents

Corbis

THE WORLD IN OUR LIVING ROOM. Television brought us together when it first arrived on the scene in the 1950s. The whole family gathered around that glowing tube, much like an earlier generation had circled around the radio. You'll find plenty of early-day TV memories starting on page 27.

Prologue

By Clancy Strock, Contributing Editor

"SOME DAYS, there is just more news than a fellow can use," my dad occasionally complained.

The same thing could have been said about the 1950s. It seemed like something momentous came along every week...and sometimes every day. The so-called "American Decade" was chock-full of news, both good and bad.

To be honest, I had forgotten about many of the things that rated headlines and changed our lives. But then readers began to flood us with material for this book. Letter after letter contained rich memories of that fabulous decade.

Here are just a few of the headlines generated during those event-packed 10 years: *Eisenhower Sends Troops to Little Rock*
> *Quiz Shows Rigged, Admits Big Winner*
> *Kefauver Exposes Mafia*
> *Elvis Shakes and Shimmies*
> *Home Bomb Shelters Are Big Sellers*
> *MacArthur Fired by Truman*
> *Hydrogen Bomb Test Awes Scientists*
> *McCarthy Hearings Televised*

What a time to be a journalist! Dad was right—sometimes there truly was more news than a person could use.

Most of the servicemen and women had taken advantage of the GI Bill of Rights to learn trades or earn college degrees during what was left of the '40s. The dawning of the '50s found them ready to start careers and families. There was a feeling of urgency, bred by trying to make up for those "lost" years spent in the military.

What's more, all those factories that had produced tanks and bombsights and military uniforms had finished retooling for peacetime and began to produce a flood of beguiling new consumer products.

But the new decade was barely under way in June of 1950, when President Truman sent troops to Korea. Here was some of that news we really didn't need. We'd barely finished celebrating the end of World War II, and now the cannons were firing again.

Within weeks, my policeman neighbor across the street—a veteran of combat in the European theater and father of two small youngsters—was called back to duty. Good grief! They even pulled in Ted Williams, the best baseball player of his era and a certified Air Force hero. If they grabbed him again, surely no one was safe.

Somehow I didn't get the call, possibly because I had two kids and a third on the way. Or, more likely, it was just another of the mysterious accidents that had no logical explanation when you dealt with the military.

War or no war, the Fabulous '50s astonished us at a fast and furious pace. I doubt there's ever been another 10-year period that brought such changes in how we lived, worked, amused ourselves and raised our families.

We also had an oversupply of heroes and villains, ranging from a feisty, no-nonsense president from Missouri who dared fire an insubordinate war hero...to a modest revolutionary named Rosa Parks, who made Americans finally face the disgrace of bigotry. We had a hip-shaking redneck who scandalized even Ed Sullivan...and a Tennessee senator who dared name names as he unmasked the Mafia.

A doctor named Spock impacted an entire generation of kids with his radical theories on raising babies...and a physician named Salk found the magic bullet that ended polio, the country's most paralyzing, terrifying health problem.

Lives were changed in both trivial and profound ways... socially, economically, vocationally and morally. Our ideas of right and wrong were being challenged. Our amusements and our life goals took on new dimensions.

To begin with, all those newly formed families needed places to live and raise children. That meant lots of new housing, which in turn meant finding new land for the homes.

The answer was in a concept someone dubbed "suburbia"—not urban living and not rural living, but something out on the edges of cities and towns where land was cheap and the air was fresh. The bad news was there were no schools, no corner grocery, no theaters and no relatives just down the street. The best description of the new lifestyle came from a neighbor lady of mine who, looking back on those years, said, ⚲

IN LEVITTOWN, New York (right), an assembly-line process quickly built scores of houses in the '50s with waves of workmen—first concrete men, then carpenters, then electricians and plumbers, followed by plasterers.

Ewing Galloway

"I devoted my life to keeping our new grass wet and our new babies dry." Yup, that was life in suburbia.

Instead of apartment houses, suburbia featured homes with yards and crab grass and sandboxes and swing sets, but no front porches. Sales of lawn and patio furniture nearly tripled during the '50s, as did sales of power mowers.

Suburbia also spawned millions of commuters, who jammed the streets and highways morning and evening during what became known as "rush hour". Car pools substituted for mass transportation but created new aggravations of their own. Someone was sure to be late in the morning, and someone else had to stop at the store on the way home.

So the two-car family was born, and the two-car-garage home became a fixture of suburban architecture.

For better or worse, "teenage" became an official life stage, and teenagers became an important advertising target. When hula hoops were introduced, kids snapped up 30 million of them in just 6 months.

Teens Voiced Their Displeasure

But suburban teenagers were generally an unhappy lot. They had no place to hang out. There were no YMCAs or community swimming pools, not even sidewalks for boy-girl saunters. "There's nothing to do," was the oft-heard wail, and it wasn't unreasonable, either.

Meanwhile, things weren't going well in Korea. Harry Truman and Gen. Douglas MacArthur had substantially different views on how the war should be fought. MacArthur misjudged his clout and defied his boss and Truman fired him.

On the home front, things were lively, too. Senator Estes Kefauver (with help from a young attorney named Robert Kennedy) held lengthy hearings that unmasked the widespread clout of something called the Mafia. A friend of mine was astonished to learn that his amiable next-door neighbor was the boss of the Milwaukee Mafia "family".

One by one, the top gangsters appeared at the televised hearings, refusing to testify under the protection of the Fifth Amendment. The FBI's J. Edgar Hoover sturdily maintained there wasn't any such thing as a Mafia, no matter what evidence Kefauver dug up.

As profound an effect as suburbia had on American life, something vastly more far-reaching was turning the United States upside down. In 1955, Rosa Parks became the spark

that lit a powder keg Americans had tried to ignore for a hundred years.

Soon the name Martin Luther King Jr. appeared almost daily in the headlines, as did the initials NAACP. Police in Montgomery, Alabama turned their attack dogs and fire hoses loose on black "freedom marchers".

There were restaurant sit-ins, church bombings and lots more of that news we really didn't need.

In the midst of this turmoil, I unthinkingly drove from Milwaukee to New Orleans on a vacation. My Wisconsin license plates made me an item of keen interest to every law enforcement officer south of the Missouri state line. I was pegged as another Yankee troublemaker, and nothing I could say changed many minds.

Elvis' gyrations were big news in the '50s.

A stubborn governor decided to stand in a Little Rock schoolhouse doorway to personally bar black children from entering a segregated school. But President Dwight Eisenhower trumped his move by sending part of the battle-toughened 101st Airborne to restore peace and order.

Look, Up in the Sky

Then one day we discovered that the Russians had arrived—out in space. Something called *Sputnik* was whizzing over us as it orbited the Earth several times a day.

This dazzling and frightening achievement came on the heels of Nikita Khrushchev's warning that "We will bury you" and an earlier notice that America no longer had a monopoly on hydrogen bombs.

One consequence was a national outcry that we somehow had dropped behind the Russians in the technology department. Why weren't our kids and teachers more interested in science? Our national survival was at stake. Science education became a matter of urgency.

So did survival. As the hysteria grew, the building of backyard bomb shelters became a growth industry. But so, too, did a new moral dilemma. If you had a bomb shelter and your neighbors didn't, would you let them share yours in the event of attack? And even if you survived, what was the point if you emerged into a nuclear-devastated world? Great fodder for the coffee klatch or weekend patio barbecue.

Meanwhile, something that would change our lives forever quietly took root: Television. At first it consisted mostly of test patterns, Milton Berle, wrestling and boxing matches. Truly nice neighbors might not invite you into their bomb shelter, but who cared, as long as they asked you over on Friday night to watch the fights?

Dad was right. There really was more news than we could use. There's no way anyone could cram it all into a single book. But this volume does a remarkably good job, describing a turbulent decade through the eyes of those who lived it. I'm sure you will enjoy every page. ❧

HAPPIER TIMES. President Harry Truman views a medal on World War II hero Gen. Douglas MacArthur. During the Korean War, MacArthur challenged Truman and was relieved of his command.

Chapter One

Fads & Fashions

Fads & Fashions

YOU HAD TO be there to understand the mood of the nation as the '50s dawned. There has been nothing quite like it since.

It was like coming out of a dark tunnel and walking into golden sunlight and trees full of singing birds.

The '40s had been filled with fear and frustration, frantic days and lonely nights and shortages of nearly everything. When World War II ended, there was still a scramble to finish educations, regain good jobs and play catch-up for those lost years.

But the '50s freed most of us from all that. The economy was booming as factories tried to satisfy America's demand for new cars, toasters, shoes, houses, food products, tractors...you name it. New families were starting up faster than wedding licenses could be printed.

Given all that, you can understand and hopefully forgive people for going a little bit nuts. Lots of us do that when we are happy. And it was most certainly a joyous time.

Fads Became Daily Events

Strange fads appeared overnight and spread across the country between breakfast and sunset. Yesterday boys wore their hair in conventional styles, but today they began sporting something called "duck-tails".

Not to be outdone, young women hacked off their cherished tresses and styled their hair in "poodles". My wife says they were influenced by Mary Martin, who sang in *South Pacific* about how she would "wash that man right out of my hair" and did every night on stage.

High school girls decided they weren't properly dressed without huge skirts that looked like lamp shades on steroids. The trick was to have several heavily starched petticoats underneath the skirt.

Even dignified grown-ups got caught up in the hula hoop fad, which involved gyrating your hips in an attempt to keep a large plastic ring swirling around your waist.

Television fostered and spread many of the dizzy fads, which is why elementary school boys suddenly appeared in coonskin caps. Blame it on shows about Davy Crockett. It was great to be a boy, but a perilous time to be a raccoon.

One of the daffiest—and shortest-lived—fads had to do with chlorophyll... the green stuff in grass. It was promoted as the antidote for everything from foot odor to bad breath.

But the excitement ended as fast as it had begun. Personally, I attribute the

> *"Television fostered and spread many of the dizzy fads..."*

end of the craze to a brief piece of doggerel that appeared in the letters section of *The Saturday Evening Post*:

"Why reeks the goat on yonder hill,
 Who feeds all day on chlorophyll?"

Another craze was trading stamps. Customers received stamps for every dollar's worth of groceries they bought, then redeemed them for a wide range of merchandise. To the customer, the stamps meant getting "free" household things that weren't affordable on a tight family budget.

Eventually trading stamps lost their appeal, and major store chains dropped them, announcing they would cut prices instead of giving out stamps. It was okay with us. We could only use so many sets of steak knives.

—*Clancy Strock*

She Was Model for a Day

Runway turned career girls into Cinderellas.

By Dorothy Stanaitis, Gloucester, New Jersey

WHEN YOU LOOK at today's ultrathin fashion models, it's hard to believe that girls and women of normal size once strolled the runways, but it's true. I know, because I was one of them.

In 1952, I was one of a group of eight young women chosen to present a career-girl fashion show called "From Taffeta to Tweeds" for Bonwit Teller, an exclusive women's shop in Philadelphia.

All of us were tall brunettes, but none of us were reed-thin or professional models. We weren't gluttons, but we ate whatever we wanted, as much as we wanted, whenever we wanted. We didn't diet or obsess about food.

Our fitting and dressing rooms were well stocked with sodas and snacks to "keep up our energy", and we were nothing if not energetic. Our runway walks were rapid and perky. No slouching or moping for us.

Each girl was very serious about doing a good job, but there was no envy or competition among us. Everyone helped one another, knowing that the show's success depended on a good group effort. We shared our combs, brushes…even our makeup.

Makeup Was Primitive and Minimal

Our makeup seems quaint compared to today's sophisticated products. We started with a foundation of pancake makeup that seemed to come in one consistency (thick) and two colors (orange and deeper orange).

We all used eyebrow pencils to darken and extend our natural brows. Mascara came in a black cake and was dampened and rubbed with a brush before applying. Instead of blush, we had rouge—the redder, the better. The same rule applied to our lipstick.

Our hair was tightly curled, either with pin curls or metal clip rollers used on slightly gelled hair. We didn't brush it out very vigorously, hoping to keep the curl as long as possible. Hair spray hadn't hit the market yet. For a sleek look, some of the girls used lacquer to hold every hair in place. Many of us had to wear hats, so we used bobby pins and hatpins to keep them at just the right angle.

There was a lot of giggling and chatter in the fitting and dressing rooms as we buttoned, snapped and pinned each other into our outfits.

Happiness Was Genuine

We were cheerful on the runway, too. We looked as if we were enjoying ourselves and Bonwit Teller's beautiful clothes. We wanted the audience to feel that if they bought some of these lovely outfits, they'd be just as happy.

For the most part, we truly were delighted with the clothes, though we had no role in selecting them. The fashion coordinator chose what she thought would suit us best. She really knew her fashions. She put styles and clothes on us that we never would've thought to select for ourselves, and they seemed perfect.

I had a beautiful green woolen dress to wear for one runway trip. It was the only green garment I'd ever worn, out-

FASHIONABLY ATTIRED. Author (left) was a clerk in a Philadelphia insurance office when the opportunity to participate in a department store fashion show "just popped up".

side of a few St. Patrick's Day sweaters. I'd never been fond of the color, but as soon as I put on the dress, I saw how flattering it was. In this outfit, the audience was told, a career girl could go "from the office to dinner or a tea dance" without changing.

A Shimmery, Glittery Group

Each of us modeled a basic black dress. All of them were so classic, they could still be worn today.

The holiday or "occasion" dresses were much fancier, with frills, ruffles and extravagant full skirts supported by stiff crinoline petticoats. We were a shimmery, glittery group as we assembled for the show's grand finale.

The audience applauded loudly—for the clothes, I'm sure—but we accepted the applause for ourselves. The runway had turned our group of career girls into Cinderellas.

Some of the models accepted the generous discounts the store offered its employees and bought their holiday dresses at Bonwit's. Since I had few holiday engagements and absolutely no tea dance invitations, I put my lovely garments back on the dress racks in the fitting room.

Then I sat down with a bottle of soda and a plate of cheese and crackers to celebrate my participation in the "From Taffeta to Tweeds" fashion show.

SOCK HOPS were popular school dances in the '50s. This picture was taken in 1958 at the Canton (New York) Junior-Senior High School. "On the night of the sock hop, the music room became the 'shoe check' room, with each pair of shoes getting a numbered slip," remembers Phyllis Snyder Shimmel of Hannawa Falls, New York (far right). "The rows also were numbered to make it easier to find a dancer's shoes when they turned in their half of the slip at the end of the night. Notice the shoe styles—white bucks, blue suede, penny loafers and saddle shoes."

Prized Blue Suede Shoes Still Kicking After 45 Years!

I GREW UP in a large family, the last of nine children. All of us learned early on to appreciate what we had.

In the fall of 1953, my senior year of high school, what I had was a brand-new pair of blue suede shoes! My parents bought them to go with my new blue graduation suit.

The shoes came with a small wire brush that was used to keep the suede looking new. It was a constant challenge to avoid getting the shoes dirty or scuffed.

I wore my blue suede shoes on and off until 1998, when I donated them to the State of Michigan Museum.

—*Charles Wing*
Okemos, Michigan

WELL-HEELED. "I was so proud of my first pair of high heels," writes Ellie Mahlman Davis of Brighton, Colorado. "Mom took me to the Red Cross shoe store to buy them when I was 14. I didn't care much for the shoes later on, when I realized we'd gone to the store where 'old ladies' bought their shoes! Mother's shoes were quite pretty and feminine." Ellie and her mother put their best feet forward here on Easter Sunday 1957 outside their home in Crown Point, Indiana.

Girls' Vinegar Diet
Ended on a Sour Note

MY GIRLFRIEND Gail and I weren't overweight when we were 16, but for some reason we didn't think we were thin enough. After trying several diets, we came up with a surefire way to slim down: Drinking vinegar.

We'd heard that vinegar shrank things, so we decided to have a spoonful before every meal, hoping to shrink our stomachs so we wouldn't eat so much.

I took my teaspoonful first and was appalled at how bad it tasted. Gail took her spoonful, and then a second one.

We did this only once that I recall. I can't even remember if it affected our appetites. All we knew was that we never wanted to try the "vinegar diet" again.

One thing I do remember: I was 5-foot-9 and weighed about 110 pounds. Did I really need to lose weight?

—*Irene Gehring, Seattle, Washington*

New Outfit Showed
Mom's True Colors

WHEN I ATTENDED Sundeen Junior High School in Corpus Christi, Texas in the 1950s, the PTA decided we should start wearing the school colors, blue and gold, every Friday.

When Friday rolled around, I was in a panic. I had nothing in those colors. I complained to Mom that the closest thing I had was a floral print dress and told her I wanted to stay home. She suggested I look again, "in the whole closet".

Hanging there in the back was a blue jumper with a gold blouse. Mom had been sewing it for me secretly all week. I was so proud of that outfit. I wore it happily every Friday.

The next school year, we moved to Pasadena, Texas, and I wore the blouse and jumper on my first day at the new school. Much to my embarrassment, I discovered blue and gold were our rival school's colors!

—*Sharon Tallon*
Tomball, Texas

Green Stamps Stretched
Family's Modest Budget

WHEN OUR CHILDREN were young, we collected Top Value and S&H Green Stamps for many of our purchases. We had a modest budget, but with four young mouths to feed, we accumulated stamps rapidly and put them in books.

After spending the first few books on baseball gloves, cooking utensils and the like, we decided to save for something big.

Many months and filled books later, we looked over the catalog to consider our redemption possibilities. We finally agreed to order a table—the first piece of a beautiful walnut dining room set.

When the table arrived, we were all excited and immediately started saving for the matching chairs. Many months passed as we closed in on the needed number of books. Then, to our great disappointment, we learned the dining room set was no longer available through the cat-alog. Now we'd have to save money to buy those chairs.

Interestingly, the table is still being used today by one of our sons, while every chair but one has bitten the dust.

—*Paul Brandt, Auburn, Alabama*

Those Pink Flamingos
Have Come a Lawn Way

EVER WONDER who hatched the first pink flamingo lawn ornament?

Don Featherstone was fresh out of the School of the Worcester Art Museum in 1957 when he signed on at Union Products in Leominster, Massachusetts.

His first project was sculpting a flamingo out of clay to then be transformed into a plastic lawn ornament.

Don went on to own Union Products, the nation's largest producer of pink flamingo lawn ornaments, before retiring recently. Forty-four years after the bird's creation, the company sells roughly 500,000 of them a year.

Union Products

Pop Beads Were Tops For Fashionable Teens

NO GIRL was in fashion in the '50s without pop beads.

In our pre- and early teen years, my sister Brenda and I were always delighted when our mother brought us another string. The beads came in a rainbow of colors and a variety of sizes, and we loved to mix and match them.

Each plastic bead had a head that fitted into an opening in the bottom of another bead. When taken apart or put together, the beads made a popping sound.

Some of our teachers didn't allow girls to wear the beads, lest we disturb the class by popping them. If we happened to bring them to school, they would disappear in the teacher's desk, never to be seen again. —*Donna McGuire Tanner*
Ocala, Florida

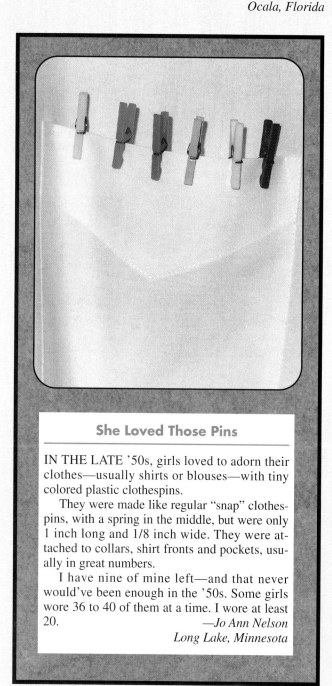

She Loved Those Pins

IN THE LATE '50s, girls loved to adorn their clothes—usually shirts or blouses—with tiny colored plastic clothespins.

They were made like regular "snap" clothespins, with a spring in the middle, but were only 1 inch long and 1/8 inch wide. They were attached to collars, shirt fronts and pockets, usually in great numbers.

I have nine of mine left—and that never would've been enough in the '50s. Some girls wore 36 to 40 of them at a time. I wore at least 20. —*Jo Ann Nelson*
Long Lake, Minnesota

BEAUTY PAGEANT. Dolores Warlaumont posed for this photo in the mid-1950s when the General Electric Co. in Cincinnati, Ohio staged a beauty contest for female employees in its Jet Engine Division. "Most of the ladies wore outfits similar to Mom's—short shorts, sleeveless blouses and flats," says Deb Mulvey of Greendale, Wisconsin. "The shorts had rings that were used to adjust the leg openings. My mom kept them for years."

Girls Were Uniform in Dislike of Gym Outfit

I STILL REMEMBER the physical education uniform for girls at our northeast-Ohio junior high school. It was a short white dress with a collar, buttons down the front to the waist, a self-fabric belt and a short A-line skirt over bloomers with elastic at the waist and legs.

The skirt and knotted belt always got in the way when we had activities like climbing a rope up to the gym ceiling.

And since the uniform was white, it got dirty very fast and had to be washed and ironed for every class. I don't remember anyone liking that uniform.

—Dorothy Saurer
Santee, California

Counting Convertibles Foretold Girls' Fate

THIS CRAZE was fun for predicting a girl's future. In summertime, we'd count convertibles until we got to 100. The first boy to talk to a girl after she'd reached 100 was the boy she was destined to marry.

—Janice Korpela
Cornucopia, Wisconsin

Pogo Stick Kept Big Sis Hopping

MY FATHER was stationed at Fort George Mead in Maryland in 1956 and '57.

We lived in a large apartment complex for officers' families. There were lots of concrete sidewalks connecting the buildings—just right for me and my pogo stick. I went everywhere on it.

When my brother was born, my sister and I were expected to help Mom any way we could. When my baby brother was old enough, I loved volunteering to take him for walks in his carriage. It got him out of my mother's hair every day during the spring and summer.

What I really wanted to do, though, was jump on my pogo stick. Finally I decided that I could combine the two.

With a little practice, I was able to push the carriage and jump on my pogo stick at the same time. Those are such sweet memories.

I had a pogo stick until I was 40 years old and still used it. My husband bought me the last one because he knew how much I loved it.

—Cathi de Hermida-Ifft
Everson, Washington

GO FOR POGO? A pogo stick was a ticket to fun and adventure, if you had the stomach—and balance—for it.

HATS OFF. When Camilla Miller's youngest sister, Ila (in nurse's uniform), graduated from nurses' training in 1957, all the nurses in the family donned their finest hats for the celebration. "The family joke has always been that they raided the neighborhood for garbage can lids," chuckles Camilla, of Leeds, Alabama. Her aunt (far left) and four sisters all graduated from St. Joseph's Hospital in Mitchell, South Dakota. Also pictured is Camilla's mother, Kate Sottlob (seated at right).

ONE COOL CAT. Scarlett Beach, an employee at Grants Store in Geneva, New York, donned a Halloween costume in October 1958 to pitch a new product—hula hoops. "Hula hoops had only been out for a short time," recalls co-worker Elizabeth Lannon of Geneva, who sent the photo. "Scarlett went out on the sidewalk to demonstrate. We did sell a few that night."

Double "Wham-y" for Toy Manufacturer

LIGHTNING STRUCK TWICE in 1958 at the Wham-O toy company with two blockbuster toys, the Frisbee and hula hoop.

According to Wham-O history, a building inspector named Fred Morrison puttered with and refined a plastic flying disk that he sold to Wham-O in 1955. The company introduced it in 1957 as the Pluto Platter, inspired by the country's obsession with unidentified flying objects.

In 1958, it was modified and renamed the Frisbee.

Also in 1958, Wham-O's two founders, Arthur "Spud" Melin and Richard Knerr, heard about Australian children who used a bamboo ring for exercise and fun. They created the plastic hula hoop. They demonstrated the rings on California playgrounds, then gave them away to children to foster interest in the product.

The hula hoop became a classic fad. Some 25 million were sold in 4 months.

Ship 'n' Shore Blouses Ruled Girls' Wardrobes

BACK IN 1952, we girls just had to wear Ship 'n' Shore blouses. Our big skirts were cinched with wide elastic belts, with layers of crinoline stuffed underneath.

Colored nylons came out during this time, but they didn't last very long.

When girls were just "hanging out", we liked to wear our fathers' long-tailed white shirts over our blue jeans, which had to be turned up about 4 inches at the bottom. White socks and white sneakers completed the look.

I remember wearing sweaters a lot, too. Some days I'd wear them buttoned in the front, and on other days I'd turn them so the buttons were in back.

Boys' fashion fads included white buck shoes, pegged pants, ducktail haircuts, zippered black suede shoes and leather jackets with lots of zippers.
—*Beth Harmon*
Holiday, Florida

Fashion Set the Tone For High School Proms

PROM NIGHT in 1956 meant shoulder corsages, choker necklaces and full-skirted dresses with yards of netting.

The net was scratchy, but it was very popular at the time.

I was 15 that year when I attended my first prom. My family was living in Orwell, Vermont then.
—*Jean Boice*
Chesapeake, Virginia

FOREVER FASHIONABLE. "This permanently pleated Black Watch plaid skirt was given to me by my parents for Christmas in 1952, when I was in the seventh grade in West Seneca, New York," says Carol Fornoff of Mesa, Arizona. "I've worn it ever since, even though I'm a mother of seven and grandmother of 16. I don't have much use for it in Arizona, but I just can't get rid of it."

Billowing Skirts Congested Hallways

REMEMBER CIRCLE SKIRTS? We used to wear as many tulle petticoats as we could under them so they'd stand out as close to horizontal as possible.

Our skirts were so enormous that the school administrators often chastised us for causing congestion in the hallways. But that didn't stop anyone I knew.

The starched tulle was scratchy and hurt our legs, but that didn't stop us, either. We'd just wear a slip under the tulle.

Even the work of starching the tulle every week didn't deter us. I helped my mother dilute the starch, then I hung the petticoats across the clotheslines so they'd stand out more.

Interest in some new fads must have ended this one…along with the congestion in the school hallways.
—*Marjorie Schoenfeld*
Fairfield, California

Keeping Crinoline Stiff Was a Sticky Business

ONE FASHION that caught my attention was a crinoline slip worn under a gathered skirt.

To keep the crinoline crisp so the layers would hold the skirt up, someone recommended dipping it into thick sugar water and letting it drip-dry. That made the crinoline crisp, all right—but it also scratched my legs. Even worse, if it got moist, all that sugar turned the crinoline sticky!
—*Iris Doksansky*
Fremont, Nebraska

Bus Seats Bustled With Big Petticoats

WHEN I WAS in high school in Nampa, Idaho in the '50s, we girls wore huge skirts, broomstick-gathered or circular, with as many petticoats as we could afford. We stiffened the petticoats with sugar water.

On the long bus ride to school, I always sat with another girl, as we never sat with boys. We must have made quite a sight, with our skirts and petticoats and zippered notebooks all piled up.

I still have a couple of those petticoats, which make my grandchildren scream with laughter about "how weird Grandma used to dress".

I haven't had the nerve to tell them about the short-short curly Italian haircuts and ballerina shoes.
—*Veva Howell Enghouse*
Portland, Oregon

"Cancan Slips" Got Weekly Starch Baths

EVERY WEEKEND, we girls dipped our "cancan slips" in cooked starch and spread them out on the clothesline to dry. The more cancans you could get, the better your skirt would stick out.

We never washed these slips until we absolutely had to. When you started with a clean, limp slip, it took forever to firm it up again.

In my senior yearbook picture of the choir, the robes of all the girls in the front row are sticking out because of the cancans underneath.

Traveling with those slips was a chore. I don't know which was worse, trying to pack the yards of stiff net, or wearing them on the bus or in the car. They took up a lot of seat room.

The slips were a lot of trouble, but we never would have considered not wearing them, because they were the fashion. Personally, I was glad when they went out of style and I could throw them away.
—*Dolores Adams*
Gentry, Arkansas

TIERED SKIRTS were a favorite for Shelley Jamieson and her best friends during their teen years in the mid-'50s in Chalybeate, Mississippi. "We sang as a trio for church, club meetings and school events," recalls Shelley, now of Brentwood, Tennessee. "We had a lot of fun harmonizing and making our own arrangements of popular tunes like Patti Page's *Butterflies.*

"Because we were giggly teenagers, there were several times when we just about lost it while singing. Once, in church, we stood close with our arms clasped around each other. A stubborn fly came along and landed on each of our noses. That time we had a perfect excuse to laugh, but we made it through the song."

Shelley's on the left; Nancy Hollis Duncan, now of Chattanooga, Tennessee, is in the middle; and Martha Ellen Harrison Prophett of Fairfax, Virginia is on the right.

Trip to Grocery Store Was "Howdy Doody Time"

ALMOST ANY CHILD of the 1950s remembers the *Howdy Doody* TV program—and all the products associated with it.

We drank Ovaltine from our Howdy Doody mugs and ate Rice Krispies squares because we'd seen a Howdy Doody ad for them in *LIFE* magazine. When we got a cut, imagined or not, we wore Howdy Doody bandages.

We preferred Royal pudding to Jell-O (Howdy's face was on the package), Blue Bonnet margarine to butter (Howdy cutouts were on the back of the box), and Welch's grape juice to orange (our favorite puppet was on the bottle).

Only Hostess bread and cakes would do, because Howdy said so. Howdy Doody ice cream was our treat, and we'd walk a mile in his favorite Poll Parrot shoes. Our young lives were under a magical spell, and we loved it.

When Welch's started selling jelly in Howdy Doody glasses (see the photo above right), I just had to have one. The bottom of each glass was etched with a Doodyville character's face, which you could see whenever you took a sip.

My mother made most of our jams and jellies, and I knew she didn't see the point in buying them from the store. Besides, if I had a glass, my sister Brenda would want one, too. To my surprise and delight, one Saturday I found not one, but two jelly glasses in the grocery bag. I quickly checked the bottoms and claimed the yellow one with the Howdy Doody face.

My sister wasn't disappointed, though. Hers featured her favorite character, the Flub-A-Dub. Brenda and I ate peanut butter and jelly sandwiches several times a day until our glasses were empty. Those glasses served us well into our teens.

To this day, whenever I see a product that was associated with Howdy Doody, I fondly remember our freckle-faced friend.
—*Donna McGuire Tanner*
Ocala, Florida

PEDAL PUSHERS, sleeveless blouses and sneakers were fashionable choices when Peggy Nemec and her friends visited Riverview Amusement Park in Chicago in 1954. "We were juniors at Providence High School," writes Peggy, of Hinsdale, Illinois. "What a great time we had! As far as we were concerned, Riverview was the best amusement park in the world." Peggy's on the right; from left, her friends are Florence Klein, Nancy Kaval and Nancy Trant.

Mixing Marshmallow Coke Required a Steady Hand

WHEN MY CLASS had its 40th reunion, I was amazed to learn that few of my classmates remembered the marshmallow Coke. It's one of my most vivid memories of the 1950s.

Cherry and chocolate Cokes were the favored beverages at our local soda fountain. But one summer an acquaintance from another area introduced us to a glass of Coca-Cola topped with marshmallow creme. I'll never forget the stir this caused when we first tried it!

First-timers invariably plunged the drinking straw into the middle of the marshmallow creme. This made the soda foam over the edge of the glass and onto the table—quickly followed by everyone trying to scramble out of the soon-to-be-wet booth.

Marshmallow Cokes became a favorite with my friends. To this day I'm not certain why. Was it the taste, or the challenge of carefully maneuvering the straw so the two ingredients would mix without causing a mess?
—*Nancy Winters, Huron, South Dakota*

Kentucky Cheerleader Left Her Mark On Playing Field

By Wally Windscheffel, Grand Junction, Colorado

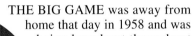

THE BIG GAME was away from home that day in 1958 and was being broadcast throughout central Kentucky on radio station WHIR.

The Admirals from Danville (Kentucky) High School were having a good year, and the cheerleaders did a good job keeping up the spirit and enthusiasm.

Parents, friends and fans who could not attend the game were glued to their radios as the kickoff approached. Beverly Rae Lawhorn, captain of the cheerleaders (right), waited for the signal to race out onto the muddy field at the 50-yard line to form the first letter of the big "HELLO" formation.

Totally enthused as always, Beverly ran onto the field, dug in the heels of her saddle shoes, skidded a short distance, then lifted into the air and plopped flat on her back.

The WHIR announcer, already set to call the game, announced in his booming voice, "Admirals' cheerleader down…"

I return to Danville to visit occasionally, along with my wife, Beverly, the cheerleader from that game. No one remembers the game, but many enjoy telling me about Beverly's dramatic fall.

Nearly 40 years later, Beverly accepted the stage role of a cheerleader in the first Grand Junction Senior Follies, performed in the historic Avalon Theater.

Out of the cedar chest came the old Admirals sweater, a little snugger perhaps, but the enthusiasm of the wearer was still intact (see photo above left).

Starch Put Pal's Ducktail on Hold

MY BEST FRIEND Jack and I were always striving for the perfect ducktail. With a fair amount of Brylcreem, I could comb my dark wavy hair up on the sides, curve it toward the front and comb the back into a near-perfect ducktail (right).

Jack, on the other hand, had coarse straight hair. Even with large quantities of Brylcreem, he had a difficult time getting his sides and ducktail to hold in place. His hair stuck out all over.

But Jack was a pretty ingenious fellow. He found the solution to his problem under the kitchen sink, in the form of Niagara Liquid Starch. He wet his hair down, then started dipping his comb into that nasty starch and combing it through his hair. It worked.

Jack came to school with a perfect ducktail, and when he went home that afternoon, not a hair had moved. As a matter of fact, not a hair moved for 2 days. When Jack got up the next morning, his hair looked just as it had the night before.

Toward the end of the second day, things started to change. The starch started flaking off Jack's hair. Soon his desktop and shoulders were covered with what looked like the worst case of dandruff imaginable. Jack never used starch again. —*Mike Brophy*
Elma, Iowa

She Wished That She'd Ducked This Trendy Haircut

I WAS 13 or 14 when the ducktail fad started—with boys mostly, but a few girls, too. I thought it was a pretty neat hairdo, with the pointed little "tail" in back. My own hair was beautiful and black, naturally curly and waist-length.

I decided I was going to be "in style" and surprise my friends and family with my new look. With my baby-sitting money in hand, I went downtown and got the famous ducktail haircut.

The minute I looked in the mirror and saw my hair, I was horrified. I hurried home as fast as I could, hoping no one would see me, and covered my hair with a scarf.

When my mother got home from work, she asked why I was wearing a scarf. I broke down crying and showed her my hair. Mom never said a word, but the look on her face made it clear what she thought.

It took forever to get my waist-length hair back, and it was years before I had another haircut.

—*Bea Anne Taylor*
Gordon, Nebraska

Sewing Project Got Her Goat

DURING HIGH SCHOOL in central Wisconsin in 1953, I took home economics. For our class sewing project, I decided to make a dress for myself.

My mother took me shopping for material, and we found a lovely dark green cotton sateen. I chose white buttons and a white belt for trim.

Using an old Singer treadle sewing machine, I struggled over the seams, tucks and sleeves. When I finally finished, wearing the dress gave me great satisfaction. I was proud of accomplishing a difficult task.

One day, our family's pet goat, "June", got out of her pen. No one noticed she was out until she'd sampled most of the laundry hanging on the clothesline.

June had a fine time tasting many of the items, but she seemed to like my dress most of all. It was shredded to pieces, and I'd only worn it a couple of times.

I was heartbroken, but I couldn't stay angry with June very long. She was our pet and gave us lots of good milk.

—Mary Foster, Hancock, Wisconsin

CLASSY DRESS. Mary Foster made this pretty shirtwaist for her high school home economics class. The cinched waist, full skirt and three-quarter-length sleeves were all in vogue in the early 1950s.

Saddle Shoes? Only Spauldings Would Do

BEING LIKE everyone else was so important to a 15-year-old girl in 1955. My cry was, "But *everybody* wears Spaulding saddles. Why can't I?"

I got two pairs of saddle shoes each school year, at $4.95 a pair. But Spauldings were $10.95. That's paying for the name, I was told.

When my parents finally agreed to look at the Spauldings, I was so happy. I finally got my first pair—and they lasted so long that I only needed *one* pair per school year!

I got to be like everyone else, so I was happy, and the price was the same, so my parents were happy, too. Oh, how I wish I had a pair of those shoes now!

It was so much fun growing up in the '50s.
—Bonnie Holland
Shawboro, North Carolina

Late-Blooming Colonel Had a Way with Chicken

WHEN WE fell in love with fast food in the 1950s, someone already had a leg up and was waiting in the wings.

Harland Sanders (left), born in 1890, was a streetcar conductor, justice of the peace, steamboat ferry operator and insurance salesman before he started serving folks fried chicken from his own table while operating a service station in Corbin, Kentucky in 1930.

Curious by nature, he experimented with herbs and spices for his chicken and also tried cooking it under pressure to serve folks faster.

His fame grew, and in 1935, he was made an honorary Kentucky Colonel in recognition of his contributions to the state's cuisine. When a new highway bypassed his restaurant in the early 1950s, he sold his operation and lived briefly on Social Security checks.

Confident of his product, the Colonel began franchising his chicken business in 1952, entering into handshake agreements with restaurant owners who paid him a nickel for each chicken they sold.

When he sold the operation in 1964, there were more than 600 franchised outlets. By 1971, there were more than 3,500 KFC restaurants around the world. He remained a public spokesman for KFC until his death in 1980, traveling 250,000 miles a year visiting the empire he founded.

Coonskin Caps Were Hot For First Day of School

SCHOOL STARTED on a boiling-hot September day that year in Springfield, Massachusetts.

The children lined up for their teachers on the playground, with boys and girls in separate rows. I had about 40 children in my sixth-grade class, most of them boys.

Although it was intensely hot and uncomfortable, all the girls were dolled up in their new dresses—a pretty sight indeed. Then I turned to the boys.

Imagine my surprise when I beheld a long row of coonskin caps, with all the tails hanging in exactly the same position. It was a whole row of Davy Crocketts!

I never had another class like that one, but it was certainly a memorable sight.
—*Adele Jacobson*
Bridgeport, Connecticut

Everett /CSU Archives

Dish Made a Mockery of Chicken Drumsticks

OUR FAVORITE "FAD" FOOD when we were growing up in the '50s wasn't hamburgers, hot dogs or even pizza. It was mock chicken legs!

Made of seasoned ground beef and pork, they were shaped into drumsticks and placed on sticks before cooking, then eaten like chicken legs.

We loved that treat and requested the dish at least once a week. Sometimes we enjoyed our mock chicken legs while our parents ate liver or something else we really disliked.

You don't see them anymore these days, but I would love to find a recipe for mock chicken legs so I could taste them once more and share them with my own family.

Several years ago while I was working in a hospital, our 3-to-11 shift was encouraged to finish off the mock chicken that had been served in the cafeteria that day.

The meat was chopped and mixed with a white sauce. While it was delicious, somehow it lost something in not being on a stick and looking like a chicken leg!
—*Sharon Tallon*
Tomball, Texas

His Coonskin Cap Proved Too Lifelike

OUR SON, Chris, was about 3 when the Davy Crockett fad started. I was able to find him a genuine coonskin cap, complete with tail down the back, for a dime at our church rummage sale.

Chris was delighted. He wore that thing, earflaps down, everywhere he went—even on the Fourth of July.

One sunny summer day, my husband, Dale, was working outside when he heard Chris shriek. Suddenly Chris rounded the corner of the barn, running as fast as his chubby little legs would carry him—with our rooster on his back, attacking the cap!

Dale caught up to them, grabbed the rooster and wrung its neck. He later said it was the first time he'd killed a chicken with no regret whatsoever.
—*Joan Moat Knochel*
Kentland, Indiana

TRUE BLUE. High-school sweethearts Carol Frankovitch and Dick True made a fashionable pair at their senior prom in Copley, Ohio in 1954. "The argyle socks, blue suede shoes, flat-top haircut and crinolines were all typical of the mid-1950s," says Dick, now of Phoenix, Arizona. He and Carolyn married 8 years after this photo was taken and still like to reminisce about the fun they had during high school.

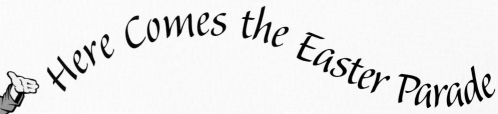
EASTER FINERY. Bernice Prior's family always dressed up for Easter dinner at her grandparents' house in Hoboken, New Jersey, then had family photos taken before a drive in the country. Bernice, now of Wood-Ridge, New Jersey, was front and center for this photo with her cousin, sister and aunts in April 1957. "My aunts are wearing stylish outfits, and I'm showing off my new dress shoes with Cuban heels," Bernice says.

SEW BUSY. Armand D'Amore (above) ran a busy tailor and cleaning shop in Chicago but found time to make these stylish Easter coats for wife Amelia and their daughters in 1956 (left). "We didn't have a lot of money, but thanks to Dad's talent, we were always well-dressed," says Mary D'Amore Dunn of Great Falls, Montana. She's in front, and her sister Dolores is next to Mom. Dad is holding Patricia. "Our sisters Veronica and Andrea came later, and they wore the coats as we grew out of them," Mary remembers.

STYLISH TRIO. Kathy Werner and daughters Pam (left) and Patty donned new dresses, coats, purses and white gloves on Easter Sunday 1955 in Chicago, Illinois. "Those were the days when little girls loved to get dressed up for any occasion," recalls Kathy, now of San Jose, California. "What wonderful memories!" Note the wide sidewalls on the Werners' new car, a hot pink-and-cream Ford Fairlane convertible.

GUYS WORE HATS, TOO. Lonnie Norris (above left) and his brother Tim were dressed to the nines as they left for Sunday school on Easter morning in 1959. Going to church made a lasting impression on her sons, says Jewel Norris of Fort Wayne, Indiana. "Lonnie's been preaching in Russia for the last 8 years," she relates, "and Tim spends a lot of time 'preaching' to his nine children!"

EASTER TOGS. Bill Gaylor's two "Army brat" sons—Mark, 5, and Kevin, 2—posed in their Easter finery in 1955. The family was living at Fort Belvoir, Virginia at the time. Bill now lives in Alexandria.

Girls Wore Jeans—and Curlers!—on Casual Day

THE DRESS CODE was strict for high schoolers in Chicago in 1950. Girls wore long plaid or pleated skirts with sweater sets, rolled bobby socks and blue-and-white saddle shoes. Peter Pan collars graced the blouses, which were buttoned to the neck.

Pageboy haircuts were the rage for girls, and boys' haircuts were "regular"—no ducktails, pompadours or sideburns. It was the era of button-front Levi's jeans, but those were definitely after-school wear.

Then a miracle occurred. After much prodding, the principal allowed seniors to have "casual dress" on Fridays. Now we could wear our beloved Levi's, rolling the cuffs into inches-long turns that showed off our rolled-up athletic socks.

We girls topped the jeans with our dads' starched white long-sleeved shirts. We were even allowed to wear our hair in curlers so we'd look beautiful for our beaus when we went out that night!

The boys wore Levi's jeans, too, and white T-shirts with the sleeves rolled up twice—to show off their muscles, I suppose.

Ours was one of the first high schools to allow such a change. We considered it a privilege and enjoyed the envious looks from students at other schools as we rode the streetcar or walked home on Friday afternoons.
—Jan Joslin
Zephyr Cove, Nevada

FLOUNCY SKIRTS were all the rage for prom dresses in 1958. "My skirt was very full, thanks to several layers of crinoline and hoops," writes Dorothy Saurer of Santee, California. "I loved the way it looked—but I didn't want to drink any punch at the prom, because visiting the rest room would've been a challenge!" For less formal senior pictures, her female classmates favored dark sweaters with white lace collars, and the boys donned jackets and ties. "Spit curls were big for girls, and every other guy had a crewcut," Dorothy says.

Matching Dresses for First Day of School

MY SISTER Elaine, brother Jim and I had new pencil boxes for the first day of school in 1955 (below). Elaine and I often dressed alike, and we always wore dresses. Slacks were never worn, except under our skirts to keep us warm while we walked to public school. We wouldn't have dreamed of wearing sneakers or jeans.
—Louise LaMarca-Gay
Rochester, New Hampshire

EARLY HOME ENTERTAINMENT CENTER? Robert Hofer's nieces, Gayle and Andrea Jensen, ages 10 and 5, were ready to use that little box on top of the TV at Christmas 1957. "This single-play record player was very popular in the 1950s," reports Robert, of St. Paul, Minnesota. "You plugged it into a wall outlet, then ran a cord to your television set. The sounds from the record came through the TV speakers."

Choir Member's Exit Was Watched by Many

I ATTENDED a church on the northwest side of Chicago in the '50s and sang in the choir. This was during the era when the newfangled girdles came out with rubberized bands in the legs to hold up ladies' stockings.

What I wasn't aware of was that you were supposed to wear elasticized thigh-high stockings, not the regular ones.

I had put them on and they held together quite well until after our choir number. It was our practice to file out of the choir loft and sit in the congregation for the rest of the service.

Just as I stepped off the platform, both nylons fell down to my ankles, and I had to walk in front of everyone to quickly find a seat.

That truly was the most embarrassing and hilarious thing that ever happened to me!

—*Margaret Weyer, Merrillville, Indiana*

UNDER COVER. Barbara Reindl of Galion, Ohio has had this veiled hat since 1954. "I was a senior in nurses' training at St. Vincent's Hospital in Toledo, Ohio," she relates. "We were asked to dress up for our senior banquet with hats and gloves, and that's when I bought it. I still wear it when I return for an alumni banquet. It's become quite a conversation piece. I wore it recently at a mother-daughter dinner at my church, which is when this picture was taken."

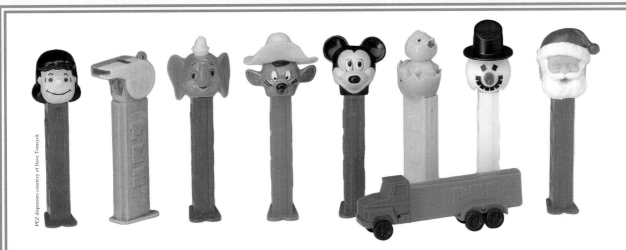

PEZ dispensers courtesy of Dave Tomsyck

Pop a PEZ, But Is It a Candy or a Toy?

PEZ CANDY came to the United States in 1952. While the dispenser wasn't invented until 1948, the candy was created in 1927 in Vienna, Austria as a breath mint. (The German word for peppermint is **p**feffermin**z**.)

The shape of the original dispensers resembled cigarette lighters. The candy was offered as an alternative to smoking or as a breath freshener.

When the dispensers began sporting character heads, the company motto was "A Treat to Eat in a Puppet That's Neat". Over the years, many PEZ character heads have been created, although Santa Claus and Mickey Mouse remain the favorites.

Other series have included U.S. bicentennial figures, circus figures, monsters, trucks and whistles. Comics and cartoon characters have included favorites from the Flintstones, Garfield, MGM (such as Tom and Jerry, and Spike), Smurfs, Snoopy and the Peanuts Gang, Walt Disney (Bambi, Donald Duck, Jiminy Cricket, Mary Poppins, Pluto, Snow White and Tinkerbell) and Warner Bros. (like Bugs Bunny, Daffy Duck, Road Runner, Wile E. Coyote and Foghorn Leghorn).

And don't forget Batman, the Joker, Wonder Woman, Popeye, Bullwinkle, Little Orphan Annie and Casper.

Holiday dispensers have included Christmas, Easter and Halloween seasonal figures.

The candies themselves come in several flavors—assorted fruit, grape, lemon, orange and strawberry as well as sugar-free orange, lemon and strawberry.

Levi Jeans Transformed Self-Conscious 'Beanpole'

By Claudette Mogle, Federal Way, Washington

OUR MOTHER made all the clothes my siblings and I wore, except for a few things we bought through the Sears, Roebuck catalog. I'd never bought anything from a clothing store.

In 1953, though, that was about to change. I was 13 and had saved my money all winter for a special purchase.

Our tiny town of Alberta, Michigan had no stores, so my father drove me to nearby L'Anse. I kept my hard-earned $10 clutched in my hand, imagining myself walking into the store to make my purchase.

Dad parked at the grocery store to do the weekly shopping, and I walked on alone to the clothing store. I had never been inside, although I'd spent many hours peering in the windows to examine the wonders it held. I timidly opened the door, wincing as the bell overhead jangled loudly.

The Real Thing

I glanced around, looking for the item I'd waited so long to buy. There they were, on the rack against the right wall. Real Levi jeans! Not just overalls like in the Sears catalog, but *real* Levi jeans!

The owner walked over and asked if she could help me. I pointed to the stack

DELIGHTFUL IN DENIM. Author (above right) is wearing her new jeans in this 1953 photo taken near her family's home in Alberta, Michigan. Top photo shows Claudette today.

of Levi's and stammered, "Those please, ma'am." She smiled and asked me what size I needed. Horrified, I realized I had no idea.

The woman smiled again, whipped out a tape and began measuring me—another embarrassment. I was tall for my age, and I just knew she wouldn't

"Red-faced, I slipped into the dressing room..."

have a pair of jeans long enough to cover my beanpole legs.

But the woman plucked a hanger from the rack, held the pair of jeans out to me and said, "Try them on, dear."

"Here?" I squeaked. "Oh, no, ma'am, I couldn't."

The smile appeared again, though it seemed a bit strained this time. The woman took me by the arm and led me to a dressing room. I was relieved, but mortified. Now this woman knew that I'd never been in a proper clothing store in my life!

Red-faced, I slipped into the dressing room and pulled the curtain closed behind me. I slipped out of my shoes and skirt and pulled the Levi's up over my legs and almost nonexistent hips.

I zipped, snapped and finally risked a look in the mirror. I looked good! I didn't look skinny anymore, but slender.

The jeans worked a miracle on my thin legs. Now everyone would see that I really did have a shape and wasn't "just bones", as my older brother always said. I admired myself as long as I dared before changing back into my skirt.

Didn't Wait for Change

At the cash register, I handed the woman my much-folded $10 bill. She laid the money on the counter, then placed the jeans in a paper bag, folded the edges precisely and handed the package to me.

I grabbed it, breathed, "Thank you, ma'am" and hurried for the exit. As I ran through the door, I could hear the woman calling after me, "Your change, dear!" But I sped up and raced down the block before she could catch me.

The jeans were on sale for $8, but nothing in the world could have induced me to return for my change. I felt stupid and awkward...but I had my Levi jeans!

Levi's made jeans only for men in those days, so the waist was too low and too big. But in my eyes, the jeans were a perfect fit. I felt special when I wore them. No other piece of clothing ever did for me what that first magical pair of Levi's did.

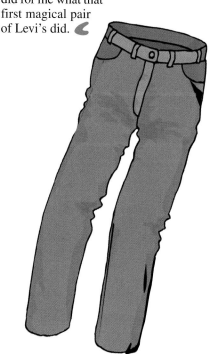

Chapter Two

Entertainment

Entertainment

IN THE late 1930s, television was but a flickering promise, one of those goofy futuristic ideas that ranked right up there with trips to the moon and cars that could be driven without shifting gears.

But soon after World War II, appliance stores proudly displayed television sets in their windows. The pictures were grainy, small and often distorted…but, by golly, they sure were pictures that came through the air. Wow!

By the early '50s, a 12-inch picture was considered immense, most areas got only two or maybe three channels, and most of the time all you got was a test pattern or a sign that said, "Technical Difficulties. Please Stand By."

But when everything was working, you had the whole world in your living room.

Rarely has a new product been so widely and rapidly accepted. It was one of those "See it, gotta have it" items. On top of that, dealers made it irresistible.

Couldn't Live Without It

"Here, try it in your home free of charge for 30 days. We'll bring it out to the house and hook it up this evening," they'd say. I fell for that one, not realizing that after a week, there was no way you could live without it.

What a beguiling devil TV was. Those radio voices you'd listened to—Jack Benny, Fibber McGee and Molly, Ozzie and Harriet—now had faces. And game shows were even more exciting when you could *watch* contestants squirm, then jump with joy if they won.

You could even "attend" a political convention or a presidential inauguration. You could see news as it happened or watch the Bears and Packers play in a snowstorm while you sat by the fire.

Fred Waring and his Pennsylvanians would serenade you on Sunday night, and in the morning you could catch up on events with Dave Garroway and J. Fred Muggs, the chimp.

Electronic Baby-Sitter

An unexpected bonus was that you had not only purchased entertainment but also an electronic baby-sitter. In those early days, there was first-rate entertainment specifically for young kids…shows that amused and educated at the same time in a painless way. The Mouseketeers became a kid cult, and every little tyke could sing the "M-I-C-K-E-Y" theme song.

By the mid-'50s, rooftops everywhere sported spidery TV antennas, an eyesore,

> *"When everything was working, you had the whole world in your living room…"*

but essential in most areas. Early sets took a lot of tinkering and adjusting, sometimes ending with loud requests to "just *leave* it alone".

TV sets were cantankerous, illness-prone critters, so a good TV repairman was vital—especially one who showed up the same day, and before the Milton Berle show came on. The most dreaded words of the era were, "It looks like I'll have to take it back to the shop."

Today's generation can't imagine life without a remote control, much less a world without television and 240 channels. TV is indeed the guest that came to stay. But whatever happened to all those TV repairmen who made house calls?

—Clancy Strock

It's Howdy Doody Time!

Early kids' TV show invited children to yell and cheer with delight.

By J.D. Brookhart, St. Marys, Ohio

IN THE EARLY '50s, I'd rush home from elementary school, change clothes and position myself in front of our little black-and-white TV set to watch *Howdy Doody*.

Buffalo Bob would come on following a TV focus pattern that first appeared on the screen with Howdy's face on it. Then Buffalo Bob would say, "Hey, kids, what time is it?"

And all of us—at home and in the studio audience—would yell, "It's Howdy Doody time!"

The show featured other characters who made regular appearances, including Clarabell the Clown, Princess Summerfall Winterspring and Mr. Bluster. We paid little attention to the fact that some of the characters were puppets.

They were alive to us. And the kids in the audience—the Peanut Gallery—yelled and cheered and clapped, and we followed right along at home.

Howdy Doody may have been a puppet, but he was one of the early pioneers in mass marketing using television. His first sponsors were overwhelmed with the response to sales from his "plugs", often running out of the premiums offered on the show for those who sent in two labels and a nickel.

Can You Name Howdy's Sponsors?

Some of Howdy's advertisers were Royal Pudding, Wonder Bread, Kellogg's Rice Krispies and Poll Parrot Shoes.

Howdy's promoters were masters at advertising and developed a large number of toys and souvenirs for sale in stores or through the mail. They included Howdy Doody clothes, puppets, cups and plates, pocketbooks and coloring books aimed at a new buying public, young TV viewers.

One of my favorite parts of the show was the movie that was shown each day. They were old black-and-white films, some silent, from the 1930s.

Many years later, I got the chance to meet Buffalo Bob Smith and Howdy Doody, and I told Buffalo Bob how much I enjoyed watching his show in the 1950s.

"Well, why didn't you watch it in the '40s? We were on in 1948," he said.

The answer was simple. We didn't have a television until 1951!

HEY, KIDS. When it was Howdy Doody time on TV, it was time for the antics of the residents of Doodyville, including Howdy Doody himself and his pal, Buffalo Bob Smith (right). But it was also a golden opportunity for the show's sponsors to tap into a growing market—children. The program was one of the first to use its characters to promote a sponsor's products (left).

Navy Trainee Captured Movie Stars on Film

Actress Jeff Donnell

IN 1951, I was attending dental technician school at the Great Lakes Naval Training Center in northern Illinois.

While I was stationed there, a Hollywood crew began filming a musical comedy about WAVEs taking their boot training. The stars included Miss Jeff Donnell, Vivian Blaine and renowned swimmer and actress Esther Williams.

One day I happened upon an area where the crew was filming. Luckily, I had my cheap camera with me and took several photos of Miss Donnell (left), who was very friendly. I snapped a few pictures of Vivian Blaine and Esther Williams, too.

The movie was titled *Skirts Ahoy!* and was released in 1952. I did get to see it once and remember it included a lot of swimming. —*Ron Dannheiser Elkhart, Indiana*

Disappearing Dot Was Tot's Bedtime Signal

NIGHT-NIGHT. Mary Rae Collins, age 3, watches an episode of *Santa's Workshop* in '53. When the TV was turned off, the set's disappearing dot signaled it was time for bed for the dot—and Mary Rae.

REMEMBER what used to happen when a television was turned off? The white screen would fade away until it became a tiny dot of light in the center.

To get our 3-year-old to take her naps or go to bed at night in 1953, I'd turn the TV off.

Mary Rae would watch the little light until it disappeared completely, and I'd assure her that "the little star went night-night".

Then she would happily trot off to bed to go night-night, too.

—*Patricia Collins Bend, Oregon*

White-Turbaned "Wrestler" Made Dramatic Entrance

OUR FAMILY got its first TV in 1953—black and white, of course. My older brother Gene and I began to watch professional wrestling on Thursday evenings. One wrestler was called "The Sheik" because he wore a white turban for his entrance to the ring.

One evening Gene stepped out of the bathroom on the second floor of our farmhouse dressed as The Sheik—white T-shirt, white boxer shorts and a bath towel wrapped around his freshly washed head.

Instead of going to his bedroom, Gene proceeded down the open staircase, which was located along the back wall of the living room, in clear view of the front door. About halfway down the steps, he spread his hands, like an umpire signaling a runner is safe, and cried, "The Sheik!"

Imagine his surprise and embarrassment when he looked up and discovered the man standing inside the front door, talking to Mother, was not our dad, but the dry-cleaning deliveryman!

Gene's hurried retreat back up the stairs wasn't nearly as dramatic as his grand entrance had been a few moments before. —*J. Herman Fisler State Line, Pennsylvania*

Boys' Two-Bit Allowance Bought Priceless Memories

IN THE LATE 1940s and early '50s, my brother Jack and I got an allowance of a quarter a week, providing we did our chores and didn't get into too many fights with each other.

On Saturday, we'd go to the matinee at the State and Princess theaters in Rockford, Illinois. We lived just far enough out that we had to take the bus to get there.

For the quarter to last the entire trip, we spent 6¢ on bus fare (3¢ each way), 15¢ for a movie ticket and 4¢ for a chocolate and peanut candy bar across the street at Walgreen's. Candy bars at the theater cost a nickel, which would put us over budget.

What fun we had, seeing all our favorite cowboy stars shoot the bad guys in black hats 20, 30 or 40 times without reloading! The serials were always exciting, and once in a while there were sing-alongs during which we followed the bouncing ball.

Jack and I sat through *The Babe Ruth Story*, starring William Bendix, two times. "The Babe" was our sports hero.

We didn't have much money then, but we consider those days priceless. —*Jim Batchelor, Loyal, Wisconsin*

Drive-Ins Were Dreamy for Girls with Steadies

By Susan Barto, Lebanon, New Jersey

MY FRIENDS and I loved going to the drive-in, especially if we were going steady. Sitting in a warm, cozy car with the boy of your dreams guaranteed an evening of romance while the movie played outside... sometimes without an audience. If a movie really seemed worthwhile, we could always see it at the theater later with a girlfriend.

We also enjoyed going to the drive-in with boys who were just friends. One summer when I was between boyfriends, my friend John and I went to the drive-in each Friday evening and actually *watched* the movies and the raucous snack commercials. One commercial claimed that if we drank Yoo-Hoo, we'd be drinking it along with Yogi Berra, who came to that drive-in often.

IDEAL DATE. Susan and Harry Barto (engaged at the time of this 1959 photo) enjoyed going to the drive-in before and after they were married.

The only problem occurred when a boy we didn't know invited us to the drive-in. You were virtually trapped, possibly for the duration of a double feature, so we needed to know our dates could be trusted. Unless the first date was a double date, we usually demurred and suggested an alternate destination.

Because I was cautious, I never had a bad drive-in date.

But I inadvertently caused trouble for my cousin Christine once.

She was visiting from New York, so I arranged a double date for us with my steady and his brother, a handsome boy who'd always been quiet around me. At the drive-in, however, he turned into quite an octopus. I had to intervene to rescue Christine from his tentacles.

My fiance, Harry, and I went to the drive-in nearly every weekend. In winter we had to drive around for a while to find a working speaker and a working heater for the car, but it was worth it.

We created our own little world there in the front seat, planning our wedding as we watched the movies.

After Harry and I married and became parents, we'd pop Billy into his pajamas on warm summer evenings and return to our old haunt. We'd buy hamburgers and fries from the food stand, then take Billy to the drive-in's playground, where he could slide, swing and climb. Harry and I would sit nearby to watch, holding hands as we waited for darkness to fall.

Drive-ins may have disappeared, but my memories of them remain etched on my heart. ◀

Mario Lanza Made Opera Accessible to Everyone

MARIO LANZA introduced me to the wonderful world of opera—the kind of music I once believed only elite music lovers could enjoy.

Mario never sang at the Met or La Scala, but in his seven films—especially *The Great Caruso*—and his weekly radio show, he sang beautiful operatic arias, semi-classical music and some of the better pop songs.

With his beautiful tenor voice, he fascinated admirers the world over. His many fan clubs have kept alive the memory of his openhearted style, which we still enjoy on videos and CDs.

—Elizabeth Sokolowski
Sioux City, Iowa

Movie Stars Lit Up Parade in Iowa Town

JOHN WAYNE and Forrest Tucker visited Davenport, Iowa on April 26, 1950, when our son was in kindergarten. A parade was scheduled for the stars, so my son donned his new cowboy boots and we went to see it.

What an exciting day! The sun was shining, flags were waving and crowds of people lined the streets. There were prancing horses, cowboys holding Western hats high in the air and dignitaries going past in open cars.

When John Wayne and Forrest Tucker rode by, we could almost touch them. What a thrill! It was wonderful. We have never forgotten the day when our favorite movie stars came to town.

—Rosemary Baker
Le Claire, Iowa

Farm Family Strung a 1-1/2-Mile "Antenna"

DAD TRIED EVERYTHING in the early 1950s to find a decent television signal. Nothing. We had a brand-new Hallicrafters TV set, but it was impossible to get a signal on our isolated hilltop farm west of Corning, New York.

We tried a local dealer, who guaranteed "crystal-clear reception". This city fellow circled the farm in an old military vehicle loaded with a generator, TV set and various antennas. Our hopes diminished when we saw what he considered a "good" signal for our remote area. The picture looked like a polar bear in a snowstorm.

A neighbor lad who'd recently returned from the military thought he could "pipe in" a good signal. All Dad had to do was find the correct wire. We found it—electric fence wire.

It took weeks of brush-cutting, but finally the 1-1/2-mile line was completed. We strung two parallel copper-coated wires through insulators, which were attached at intervals to small trees—a heavy-maintenance system during high winds or snowstorms, we discovered.

After many trips up the hill and some fine-tuning, we settled down to watch a program on our new TV. What a day! What an experience! The first program we saw, on our one station, was *Big Top*. It was a three-ring circus in our own living room.

Dad also got a terrible electrical shock from our first television set.

"I told you to unplug it!" he exclaimed.

"I did," protested my brother Dave, holding up the ends of two unplugged extension cords.

Our TV picture had started "rolling", so Dad had removed the back panel to look for darkened tubes. Dad could fix anything, but TV repair was a new experience for him.

Years later, we learned that a picture tube could hold an electrical charge for hours after the set was unplugged. Get too close, and you got shocked. —*John Mack
Nelson, Pennsylvania*

Kentucky Miner's TV Attracted a Full House

MY HUSBAND, Johnny, had a small mine on Big Creek in Hatfield, Kentucky. In 1952, we'd left Pennsylvania and moved to a three-room cabin there, taking our black-and-white television set with us.

We lived in the hollow between two mountains. When we first hooked up the TV, the reception wasn't good, so Johnny took the antenna up the mountain.

Ours was the only TV in Hatfield, and once word got around, our living room was always full of people. Some worked for my husband, and a few were relatives.

On nights when the reception was bad, Johnny and the neighbors would take carbide lamps and climb to the top of the mountain to clean the lines or turn the antenna. Everyone waited patiently until the picture was clear again. Their favorite programs were wrestling, boxing and *I Love Lucy*. It was a riot to watch them watch TV.

A lot of these folks were leery of outsiders and called us "foreigners". When they came to watch the TV, they never said hello or good-bye. But I was sure they would talk eventually. One day in 1953 as I was washing clothes, I looked down the hollow and saw several of the women coming. What now? They walked up to the porch and announced, "We came to watch the Queen's coronation." I said, "Come on in." After that, they always talked to me.

One hot summer day, we were watching a show from New York and the reception was poor. Johnny was quite a jokester and told everyone it was snowing in New York. Everyone who heard about the "snow" came to see if it was true, because it was incredibly hot in Kentucky that day. Thinking about it still makes me laugh.

Another day, a couple of neighbor girls who helped me with housework came by with their cousins. To my amazement, the cousins backed into the house and kept their backs to the TV. When I asked why, they said they'd been told that television was the work of the devil and they shouldn't look at it. Judging by what's on TV today, I believe they were right. —*Doris Salat, West Finley, Pennsylvania*

Faces Pressed to Windows, They Watched Neighbors' Set

OUR NEXT-DOOR NEIGHBORS bought a television before we were able to afford one. I've often wondered if they knew that we were watching their TV along with them! Their set was in the living room, facing the windows that our dining room windows looked in on.

On Sunday evenings, *The Wilkens Amateur Hour* ran on both KDKA radio and RDKA television simultaneously. We'd turn on our kitchen radio, raise the volume and hurry to the dining room, pressing our faces as close to the glass as possible so we wouldn't miss a second of the show.

It wasn't easy to see, considering the distance between our houses, the small size of the screen and the snowy picture quality of early television, but we thought it was fantastic.

—*Joy Wyant Sander, Hatboro, Pennsylvania*

Daughter's Generosity Left Parents Teary-Eyed

I DECIDED to buy my parents a television set for Christmas in 1954. I'd been working as a book-keeper at a finance office since graduating from high school 3 years earlier.

My employer helped me choose a TV and arrange the financing.

After all the details were completed, I thought I could sit back and relax and wait for Christmas Eve to arrive.

But shortly after I made my purchase, Dad asked me to go shopping with him. He wanted to buy a TV as a family gift! I gave every excuse I could think of to stall him.

Finally he said, "Well, if you're so busy, I'll just shop on my own."

"Dad," I said, "you are going to get a television set for Christmas. Please don't ask any questions." He did ask one question—what make the TV was.

That was all Dad said on the subject until the first week of December. He'd come up with an idea. Since he and

MEMORABLE GIFT. Dewey and Grace Raymond of Pocatello, Idaho were thrilled with this television set, a gift from their daughter, Barbara. The photo was taken on Christmas Eve 1954.

Mom would be celebrating their anniversary Dec. 11, could I have the set delivered then as a combined anniversary-Christmas gift?

His approach was so cute that it made me a little sad to say no. But this was going to be a Christmas gift.

On Christmas Eve, a couple of men came over on the sly to put the antenna on the roof. To cover any noise they made, I turned the radio up as loud as I dared. I think Mom feared I was losing my hearing! Luckily, they worked quickly and quietly, and Mom never heard them.

After Dad came home from work, my two brothers brought the TV over. When they walked in with it, my mom was so surprised and thrilled, she started to cry. I think my dad had a few tears in his eyes, too. All of us could hardly wait to sit down and watch the new television.

Many years have passed since that joyous Christmas Eve, but I've relived those moments many times since. I can truly say that was one of the happiest nights of my life.

—Barbara Henderson, Grangeville, Idaho

"G.E. makes you feel it's real!"

GE BLACK-DAYLITE TELEVISION

"Look, it's LIFELIKE! LIFE-SIZE!"

You can put your confidence in—

GENERAL ELECTRIC

TELEVISION SCREENS began to expand from plate-size to life-size in the early 1950s, as this GE advertisement explains.

Events Made TV History

VERY FEW of my sixth-grade classmates had television sets in their homes in 1953. But two boys did, and their parents graciously invited the rest of us into their homes on two different occasions to see history in the making.

Our parents sent us off with sack lunches, reminding us to sit still during the program and to thank our hosts when we left. Each of these events was a television "first".

On Jan 20, 1953, we watched Dwight Eisenhower take the oath of office as our new President. As he rode in a convertible down the parade route, we thought he looked a lot cheerier than that old sourpuss Harry Truman.

The second event was Queen Elizabeth II's coronation on June 2, 1953, and I remember it vividly. The pictures were in black and white, but the glass coach was like something out of a fairy tale. It's hard to believe that was almost 50 years ago, because the images are still so clear in my mind.

—Janet Lusch, Vandalia, Illinois

Tot Wanted TV Trimmings

MY HUSBAND was in the Air Force during the 1950s, so we moved around a lot. Television wasn't always available during our travels, but our four sons adapted to that.

When we were stationed in California, the boys noticed that all the military families' mobile homes had TV antennas.

One day our 4-year-old asked why we didn't have TV. I told him we probably would soon.

He replied, "Well, could we just put up an antenna so everyone *thinks* we have TV?"

—Dorothy Stowell Goldfield, Nevada

STAR CHIMP. Remember J. Fred Muggs? This chimp co-starred on the *Today* show with Dave Garroway from 1952 to '57. In the late '50s, Helen Milliken of Honey Grove, Pennsylvania bought a J. Fred doll (left) for her son. "After a few years, he was so worn out that I had to sew a new body for him," Helen says. "I made a Santa Claus outfit for him, and he's had a special place under our Christmas tree ever since." At this writing, the real J. Fred Muggs (top) is still alive and well, enjoying the sunshine in Tampa, Florida at age 49, according to Bud Mennella, his owner and a partner in J. Fred Muggs Enterprises. The dolls sell from $350 to $600 at auction, according to Bud.

Antennas Broadened TV Viewing Horizons

OUR FIRST TV was a black-and-white Admiral. It brought in only one channel, from Buffalo, New York. But in the 1950s, that was enough.

The shows I remember most were the Saturday morning Westerns—*The Lone Ranger*, *The Cisco Kid*, *The Roy Rogers Show* and my favorite, *Sky King*. On Saturdays, I'd get up at about 8 a.m. to start watching these Westerns. My mother always had to warn me several times to get my chores done.

Saturday night was Mom's time in front of the TV. She'd sip a cup of coffee while watching her favorite, *Perry Mason*.

Eventually, Dad bought a roof-mounted antenna. To get a good picture, you had to get up on the roof and turn the antenna in different directions until somebody in the house yelled, "There, you got it—no, no, now you lost it! Turn it some more!"

Of course, this went on for what seemed an eternity until the optimal picture was obtained.

Whenever the wind blew the wires off or turned the an-

tenna, it was back to the roof for more adjustments.

With our new antenna, Mom discovered new horizons and fell in love with Lawrence Welk. During her 2 hours of "bubble time", we knew better than to make noise.

—*David Cunningham, Layton, Utah*

Navy Recruits Talked Baseball With the Commissioner

THE DRAFT was in full swing in 1951, the second year of the Korean War. On the morning of Oct. 16, I left for the train station in Lexington, Kentucky with my friends Roger Shellenberger and Paul Fugazzi. All three of us were Navy recruits bound for basic training in Bainbridge, Maryland.

Before we boarded the train, we noticed reporters and photographers gathered around none other than A.B. "Happy" Chandler, our former governor, now commissioner of Major League Baseball. He was bound for Baltimore, too.

Roger, Paul and I walked over and introduced ourselves. We shook hands with Mr. Chandler and told him about our destination (see the photo below).

After the train was under way, Mr. Chandler sent word via the conductor that he'd like the three of us to join him in his private car. He was a most gracious host, and we spent several enjoyable hours with him, talking about politics, baseball and the beautiful state of Kentucky.

We also were treated to a meal that far surpassed anything the Navy would serve us in the next 3 months. It was truly a memorable occasion.

—*Samuel Barber*
Grand Rivers, Kentucky

STRUCK UP A CONVERSATION. In 1951, Navy recruits Roger Shellenberger (left) and Samuel Barber (center) met A.B. "Happy" Chandler, the commissioner of baseball, while waiting for a train. On board, Chandler invited the boys and their buddy Paul Fugazzi (not shown) to his private car.

Spirited TV Characters Were Her Role Models

MY CHILDHOOD role models came from TV shows—two cowgirls, a drum majorette and a jungle queen.

Annie Oakley was played by Gail Davis. I wanted to be just like her, with a horse named "Target". I had an Annie Oakley coloring book, board game and paper dolls, and my friends and I pretended our bikes were horses. I still have my Annie Oakley rifle up in the attic.

Dale Evans was another favorite of mine, although she wasn't quite as daring and heroic as Annie. I also had Roy Rogers and Dale Evans paper dolls, a Dale Evans cowgirl outfit and a Roy Rogers stagecoach and wagon, which included a Dale Evans figure.

I thought Mary Hartline, the drum majorette on *Super Circus*, was the most beautiful woman in the world. I had a baton just like hers and a hand puppet that I sent away for. Last year I bought a Mary Hartline doll at a doll show and was almost as excited as I would have been back in the '50s!

Last but not least was Sheena from *Sheena, Queen of the Jungle*. One year I actually asked Santa for a spear just like Sheena's for Christmas. I didn't get it. I also wanted a pet chimp like Sheena's. I didn't get that, either. But my friends and I still enjoyed playing Sheena in the backyard.

Within the last few years, I've obtained videos from all four of these shows. I've enjoyed watching all my role models in action again, even though I never grew up to be a cowgirl, drum majorette or jungle queen.
—*Alice Schuler*
Floral Park, New York

Rental TV Got Family Hooked

MY FRIEND Joe Stites rented a TV set back in the early 1950s to entertain his children during a bout with chicken pox. When the rental period ended, Joe unplugged the set and prepared to return it.

As he was carrying the TV out the door, Joe heard one of his daughters say tearfully, "Howdy Doody all gone now!"

Very shortly thereafter, the Stites family bought their first TV set.
—*G.D. Nelson, St. Louis, Missouri*

Chiquita Banana Jingle Saturated Radio, Then TV Airwaves

I'm Chiquita banana and I've come to say
Bananas have to ripen in a certain way.
When they are fleck'd with brown and have a golden hue
Bananas taste the best and are best for you.
You can put them in a salad
You can put them in a pie-aye
Any way you want to eat them
It's impossible to beat them.
But bananas like the climate of the very,
*   very tropical equator*
So you should never put bananas in the refrigerator.

MY HUSBAND and I were both born in 1929 and remember many of the catchy advertising jingles of the 1950s. One of the most memorable came from the Chiquita banana commercial.

This jingle (above) made its debut in 1944, when bananas were still an unfamiliar exotic fruit to many of us. It became one of the most successful jingles ever and was played up to 376 times a day on radio stations across the country. No wonder we can't forget it!
—*Margaret Eskridge*
Boca Raton, Florida

Black-and-White TV Left Color to the Imagination

TV WAS NEW in the 1950s, so anything on it was a marvel. Only a few people had a set, so we would go to their house to watch.

At our house in Philadelphia, Pennsylvania, our first TV was a Motorola with a 10-inch screen, black and white, of course.

Dad bought a big bubble magnifying glass to put in front of the screen. You could only see a bigger picture when you were directly in front of it; off to the sides, it looked like a funhouse mirror.

Then came the color wheel, which was supposed to make black and white look like color. It looked like the color wheels that came out at the time of the first artificial aluminum Christmas trees. It sat in front of the TV and revolved, and as you looked at the screen through it, it vaguely resembled color.

There was also a screen that you placed in front of your screen that gave everything the illusion of color, but people were green and grass pink. It didn't really work.

Programming came about gradually, too. At first it was mostly test patterns shown during the day. Horse racing came on about 4 p.m., and wrestling was broadcast on scattered nights. It was a while before there was something to watch every night and during the day.
—*Richard Staley*
Quarryville, Pennsylvania

Young Mom "Discovered" Popular Singing Star

IN THE MID-1950s, television was still very new, and we received programming only part of the day on a few channels.

We lived 60 miles from the station in Fort Worth, Texas, and our reception was often fuzzy. But we thought TV was the greatest invention ever and kept the set on whenever there was programming.

As a young wife and mother, I was a little beyond sock-hop age, but I still enjoyed the music that was popular at the time. I was drawn to an *American Bandstand*-type program broadcast from Fort Worth every Saturday afternoon.

Local teenagers came to dance and listen to recorded music, and the young host himself sang at least once during the program. I thought he was terrific—nice to look at, with a marvelous voice. I watched each week, eagerly waiting for his solo.

I predicted that young man would go far in the music business, and I was right. His name was Pat Boone.

Not long after that, he moved to New York, and the next time I saw him was on a nationally televised show. I've been a fan ever since. After all, I "discovered" him.
—*Barbara Gerriets Topeka, Kansas*

Teen Got VIP Treatment On *Bandstand* Set

IT WAS November 1959, and I was a senior at Fairfax High School in Virginia. Every day after school, my best friend, Carolyn, and I would come home, tune the TV to *American Bandstand* with Dick Clark and dance to the music. We loved to dance and we loved the show.

My aunt and uncle lived in Philadelphia, Pennsylvania, where the show originated. One day Uncle Richard stunned me by asking if I'd like to appear on the show and meet Dick Clark. Uncle Richard knew the show's producer. I was so excited!

I went to Aunt Mildred and Uncle Richard's the day before I was to appear on the show. That day seemed to last forever. The next morning, I woke up with laryngitis and couldn't talk, but that wasn't going to stop me. We were off to the TV studio.

The producer took me backstage before the show to meet Dick Clark. I was numb. Then I was taken to the set by the producer and a policeman. The other kids thought I must be someone famous. Some even asked for my autograph!

I took my seat in the bleachers, and the show began. I don't remember a single song that was played. All I remember is that I was dancing, live, on *American Bandstand*.
—*Diane Morris, Fort Myers, Florida*

Welcoming Neighbors Were No. 1 on Her Hit Parade

WE LIVED atop a steep hill in Monroe County, Ohio and our neighbors were the first on the ridge to get a television. I must have been in the ninth grade, and I was totally in awe.

Like most teenagers, I loved music and listened to all the popular songs on our little portable radio in the kitchen. What a thrill it was when the neighbors extended a standing invitation for me to come to their house and watch *Your Hit Parade* each week.

I'd perch tensely on the edge of the couch, listening to each song leading up to the No. 1 hit of the week, wondering if I'd guessed it correctly. The anticipation was almost more than I could bear.

The experience was no doubt enhanced by the neighbors' insistence that their son escort me home after the show!
—*Shirley Polen, Durand, Michigan*

She Thought Loretta Young Was The Epitome of Elegance

WHEN I THINK back to the 1950s, three of my favorite television shows come to mind—*I Love Lucy*, *Our Miss Brooks* and *The Loretta Young Show*.

To me, Miss Young was the epitome of elegance. She exited each program with a beautiful smile, saying "See you next week" with a hint of a question in her voice.

The only advertising jingle that's stayed in my memory throughout the years is the one promoting Halo shampoo: "Halo everybody, Halo. Halo is the shampoo that glorifies your hair, so Halo, everybody, Halo. Halo shampoo, Halo!"

Once I started singing that jingle, it was difficult to get it out of my mind.   —*Margaret Williams, Kimball, Nebraska*

Toddler Kissed Crooner On TV Every Morning

TENNESSEE Ernie Ford never knew how many sweet kisses he got!

Back in the late 1950s, it became a morning ritual for me to clean jelly—the remnants of our toddler's breakfast—from the TV screen. Marsha loved "Tennie Ernie Ford" and gave him kisses each morning when his program came on.
—*Velma Souers, Warren, Indiana*

Ozzie's Relentless Gaze Unnerved Studio Visitor

By Ron Ballough, Bellingham, Washington

MOST OF OUR entertainment came from the radio in the late 1940s and early 1950s. Money was scarce in our single-parent household, so we grew up on a steady diet of those familiar radio shows.

As television caught on, many of those performers graduated to TV and we had faces to connect with the distinctive voices we were accustomed to hearing.

Being boys, my brother and I also tuned in to action programs on the radio, then followed when they appeared on television.

These shows included *The Lone Ranger, Gangbusters* and *Mr. District Attorney.* I think Mom kind of tuned out those programs while she busied herself in the kitchen.

But we had family favorites, too, that all three of us enjoyed. We loved Jack Benny, George Burns and Gracie Allen, *Our Miss Brooks* and *The Adventures of Ozzie and Harriet.*

There was laughter in our house, even though Mom often worried about how to make ends meet with a couple of growing boys to feed and clothe.

California Bound

Sometime in the 1950s, my mother received a letter from my aunt on my father's side, inviting her to come to Southern California for a visit. That was a big trip for her. She must have saved for months to be able to do it, but it was important to maintain contact with these long-lost relatives.

After Mom's visit, I saved my money so I could travel to Southern California, too. A year or so out of high school, I made the 1,200-mile trip to Burbank, where my aunt and uncle greeted me warmly.

My aunt and uncle were as generous to me as they'd been when Mom visited. They took me to Disneyland, which had recently opened, and Knott's Berry Farm.

Stage Visit Topped Trip

But the highlight of my stay was a VIP tour of a live soundstage at one of the major Hollywood studios. On the day we visited, an episode of *Ozzie and Harriet* was being filmed. To this day, I don't know how my uncle was able to arrange this.

As we were led to the soundstage, my uncle warned, "You must be very quiet." We took our seats and watched as the lights came on and the cameras

> *"My heart skipped a beat, and I'm sure I turned bright red..."*

began to roll. I marveled at being able to see real live actors with the same voices we'd first heard on the radio, and then on TV.

What impressed me most, however, was David's TV girlfriend. As far as I was concerned, she was the most gorgeous actress in Hollywood.

I was taking it all in, soaking up the atmosphere of a Hollywood stage, when I looked up to see Ozzie Nelson staring right at me. Uh-oh. What in the world had I done?

My heart skipped a beat, and I'm sure I turned bright red. Had I done something wrong? What faux pas had I committed? Did I twitch or make some kind of noise? Or was he eyeing me for a part in some future episode?

I'll never know, because the bright lights suddenly dimmed, the stage smiles faded and the actors became real people again, busily going over scripts while the stagehands got ready for the next scene. ◖

Everett Collection

- The *Adventures of Ozzie and Harriet* started on radio in 1944. It became a TV series in 1952 and ran for 14 years—a combined run of 22 years.

- Professional actors played the parts of "David" and "Eric" until 1949, when Ozzie decided his sons, David and Ricky, were old enough to voice the roles themselves. That's the Nelson family pictured above.

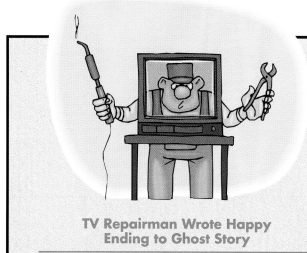

TV Repairman Wrote Happy Ending to Ghost Story

TV SALES and service businesses, such as mine in the Chicago area, thrived in the 1950s. Most dealers had been trained in electronics in the military, so it was a good field for returning veterans.

We didn't know a lot about running a business and handling customers, though, so every day was a learning experience. I divided my time between working the sales floor and making house calls.

Service calls were a challenge. Most of our customers required a rooftop antenna to get good reception on all four Chicago-area channels. The standard 5-foot antenna was usually mounted on the chimney with straps, or to the vent pipe with a bracket.

Once a customer called to complain about "ghosts".

I thought the antenna had turned, picking up a second image reflected from a nearby building or water tank, so I loaded my ladders and made the call.

I checked the reception on all four channels but couldn't see any ghosting. Then the customer explained that the ghosts weren't on the TV.

"The problem is in the bathroom," she said. "It started when you delivered the TV."

Surprised, I followed her to the bathroom. I did hear a sound—a weird, ghostly noise coming from the toilet bowl.

I climbed to the roof and looked around. The antenna vent mount was secure, and the aluminum antenna rods were tight. Then it occurred to me: Perhaps the open rods were vibrating in the wind and carrying the sound down through the stack pipe.

With my pliers, I crimped the ends of each antenna rod. Then I climbed back down and joined the customer in the bathroom for what I hoped would be the end of this unfinished symphony.

Luck was with me, and my simple solution worked. So much for my ghost story.

Customers were always grateful for repairs. When their one TV wasn't working and Uncle Miltie's show was about to start, I was as welcome as Santa Claus. The whole family would watch me work. The look on their faces when the picture was restored was a reward in itself.   —*John Hanson, Morton Grove, Illinois*

Nothing Ever Topped Sunday Night Programs

MY PARENTS bought our first TV, a very large piece of furniture with a small screen, in the early 1950s. Then they told us the rules. There would be no TV on school nights, and we could watch on weekends only after all our chores were done.

My younger siblings were up very early on Saturday mornings, bustling away at chores so they could finish in time to watch *Sky King*, starring Kirby Grant (below left).

I was 16 and had a Saturday clerking job from 8 a.m. until 9 p.m. at the local five-and-dime. Sunday mornings were for church and Sunday school, and the afternoons for hand-washing clothes, polishing shoes and doing homework.

When Sunday evening came at last, I was happy to watch whatever was offered on the screen. No one cared that the pictures were in black and white. Our only concern was that the picture tube might go out and we wouldn't be able to afford to replace it right away.

Today, at 66, I have three TVs wired into a dish system with dozens of choices for watching, and a portable battery-operated TV for power outages. I watch my favorite programs in color on my 30-inch screen.

Yet nothing I watch now gives me as much pleasure as those long-awaited Sunday evening shows in 1950.
—*Aileen Berberich, Wharton, Texas*

Everett Collection

Wait for First TV Seemed Interminable

WE SEEMED to be the last family on our block to enter the television age. I can remember walking my dog very slowly past homes with TVs, peering unashamedly into the windows at the glowing screens.

When we finally got ours in 1951, I was thrilled to invite my boyfriend over to watch the Joe Louis fight on our 7-inch screen. Since his family didn't have a TV yet, he came gladly. (They didn't get one until 3 years later.)

Today, TV can be a source of family separation, with each person watching a different show on a different set. But back then, it brought families together. Before we got ours, we'd drive 10 miles to my mother's cousin's farm to watch Milton Berle host *Texaco Star Theater*.

After I got married, my in-laws positioned their TV set facing the dining room and ate while watching the set. It was similar to the way I'd grown up, eating a meal while listening to Jack Benny, Allen's Alley and the other Sunday evening radio programs.
—*Barbara Suetholz, Racine, Wisconsin*

TV Antennas Popped Up Like Mushrooms

By J.D. Brookhart, St. Marys, Ohio

MY FIRST GLIMPSE of a television show was in Baltimore, Maryland in the late 1940s. I was 8 years old, and we didn't have a television yet at our house. Neither did anyone nearby.

While we were vacationing in Washington, D.C. and the Baltimore area, Dad took us to a bar with a sign in the window reading, "We have TV." We sat quietly in a booth toward the back, ordered Cokes and waited for the show to come on.

The set was high up in a corner, on a little shelf, and the screen was small. I think wrestling was on, but I don't recall clearly. A sailor and his girlfriend were kissing in the booth across from us, and frankly, that show interested me more than my first glance at television.

By the early 1950s, television antennas were popping up all over the neighborhood, like mushrooms on a warm, damp morning. The antennas were like flags telling everyone, "We have TV here."

When the first TV came into the house, it was a special time. Families often gathered around it for a portrait. At our house, even our second television was special enough to warrant a family photo.

SET TO CELEBRATE. For families in the 1950s, the arrival of the first TV was such a special event that it required a family photo. At the author's house, even the second television was special enough for a portrait, complete with a festive ribbon. J.D. is between his mom, Eloise, and brother Peter.

Shortly after we bought our first set, Dad excitedly wrote to his father to tell him our news. Grandpa promptly wrote back, telling Dad he should have spent the money on something we needed, like new spouts and gutters.

In those days, stations didn't broadcast 24 hours a day. Our three stations were beamed from Columbus, Ohio, 32 miles away, but we couldn't get all three clearly.

Before setting the antenna, we had to decide which two stations we wanted to come in the clearest.

After midnight, the stations would sign off and leave a test pattern on. That identified the channel and allowed the viewer to adjust the screen for clarity, brightness and horizontal and vertical "hold".

When TV first came to our house, we'd sit for a long time after sign-off and simply stare at the test pattern. TV was so new and exciting, we didn't care that there was no action. The pattern was enough to make us happy.

By the mid-'50s, few living rooms were without a TV, and few sets were without a black ceramic panther on top, sleek and low and lit up.

There was usually a strip of aluminum foil wrapped around the antenna wire just before it connected to the console. More than likely, a *TV Guide* could be found nearby, too.

Today we have TVs in every room of the house and no time to watch any of them. But in that earlier decade, we did sit in the living room as a family and watch television together. That may have been the most positive thing television did for our lives in the 1950s.

Family's Life Revolved Around 12-Inch Screen

WE GOT OUR first 12-inch television in the early 1950s and were thrilled with it. To pick up one of the two stations we could receive, we had to point the aerial at precisely the right spot.

Mom was always tempted to adjust the reception with the "booster", a little box that sometimes magically cleared away the "snow". She seemed to want to do this at the crucial point of our favorite show, and we'd plead with her to leave the picture alone.

Before long, our whole life seemed to revolve around the little set at the end of the living room.

One day Dad went to turn on the TV, but he got a blank screen and no sound. Deader than a doornail, as Mom used to say.

Dad marched to the phone and called the repairman at the store where we'd bought the TV. "Get up here as soon as you can," Dad pleaded. He sounded like a man whose lifeline had been cut.

The man came up, looked at the TV briefly and plugged it in. Then he turned it on, stepped back and said, "I think it's fixed."
—Audre Foos, Midland, Michigan

the winner

FASHION ACADEMY AWARD

First in quality and value . . . now the recognized FIRST IN FASHION! Motorola TV has been awarded the coveted Fashion Academy Gold Medal "for fine cabinet craftsmanship and beauty of distinctive design."

own a MOTOROLA...
and you know you own the best

20F1...huge 20-in. rectangular tube, FM/AM radio, 3-speed phono

Not just television, but *Motorola* television. The difference is important to you. Motorola gives you **NEW**, BIGGER TV pictures . . . steadier, brighter than ever because of new, improved circuits . . . just 2 simple controls. **NEW** and improved Bilt-in-Antenna. And all yours at **NEW** low prices. Take your choice of 29 "Fashion Award" TV sets . . . from compact 14 inch table model to 20 inch combinations with **NEW** "Multi Play" 3-speed record changer and Golden Voice AM/FM radio.

Model 17K3...16-in. rectangular tube

Model 17T1...16-in. rectangular tube

17F3B...16-in. rectangular tube, FM/AM radio, 3-speed phono

17F2...16-in. rectangular tube, 3-speed phono, FM/AM radio

Motorola TV

See your classified directory for name of your nearest Motorola dealer.
Specifications subject to change without notice

THERE'S A MOTOROLA TO FIT YOUR BUDGET...YOUR HOME...YOUR FAMILY

A SET FOR ANY DECOR. Much like radio, TV entered the home in the early years as another piece of furniture—it was even sold in furniture stores. Early sets were offered in styles to go with any decor. And many held a radio or phonograph as well, becoming early entertainment centers. Whether your home was furnished in Early American or a more contemporary style, there was a set just for you, as this 1950 Motorola ad shows.

MAY I HAVE A GLASS OF AGUA? Author (standing center) taught TV viewers conversational Spanish on one of three early educational TV programs offered by the University of Wisconsin-Extension in Madison. This course was presented on sets that resembled a restaurant (above) and an airport.

Lights! Camera! Teach!

Educational TV was in its infancy in 1954 when "Spanish for Travelers" aired.

By Roma Hoff, Eau Claire, Wisconsin

"SPANISH FOR TRAVELERS" was one of three TV programs offered by the University of Wisconsin Extension Division in 1954 as an experiment.

I was a 28-year-old teaching assistant in the Spanish department and knew nothing about television. These "telecourses" were test programs and among the earliest live educational programs in the country.

The series cost $2 per person per course to cover the cost of the instructional material, including an attractive manual prepared for the course.

We taught Spanish language and culture and worked on sets that resembled, among other places, a restaurant and an airport. The two "TV students" were members of a Spanish class of mine at the university. A fellow grad student opened and closed each program with guitar music.

Learn a Language on TV

Our course was aimed at anyone planning a trip to a Spanish-speaking country, people having daily contact with Spanish-speaking people and those who had a hobby for which a knowledge of Spanish was useful.

The two other televised courses offered were a 10-week study of conversational German and a 24-week course called "Looking at Music". It provided a deeper understanding of classical music, including operas, operettas and chamber music as well as their stories and legends.

The students and I had a practice session every week, usually in a restaurant near campus, and a rehearsal the evening of the program on the sets. We performed the programs in a WHA-TV studio in the old Science Hall on the University of Wisconsin-Madison campus.

Went Off Without a Hitch

Surprisingly, there were no big glitches on the 10 programs after a grammatical error I made in the opening show.

Each program presented Spanish pronunciation and practice of familiar words and began with a dialogue the students repeated following the TV screen.

Technical aspects of the programs were handled by Bill Allen, the producer/director who made actors and staff comfortable with the presentations. We all read his weekly scripts and memorized instructions for the cameramen.

Bill hid microphones behind some of the artifacts I brought from home to help fill the set. The quality of the voices was excellent.

Tapes, or kinescopes, of the programs and the manuals were available for many years through the division.

In 1957, there was some question about whether the TV station would be funded. I like to think our pioneering programs helped. Today WHA-TV remains as a service of the Wisconsin Educational Communications Board and the UW-Extension. ◄

Advent of TV Dinner Solved Many Problems

WHEN THE SWANSON TV DIN-NER appeared in 1954, it was the solution to several different situations.

After Thanksgiving in 1953, Swanson had a surplus of turkeys—520,000 pounds to be exact—and limited warehouse space for the birds, which were being kept in refrigerated railroad cars traveling from coast to coast.

At the time, Gerry Thomas was the company's vice president of marketing. He saw a single-compartment tray being tested by an airline to serve meals on international flights and asked for a sample tray.

Swanson devised a three-compartment aluminum tray and filled the first ones with turkey dinners—turkey and corn bread stuffing, mashed potatoes with gravy and peas.

The resulting "heat and serve" dinner was considered somewhat risky, so only 5,000 were ordered. In 1955, the first year of national distribution, Swanson sold 10 million of the dinners.

The item was a time-saver for millions of women who continued to work outside the home in jobs they'd started during a manpower shortage in World War II. It also allowed families to enjoy a hot meal with minimal preparation while watching television.

Today the concept is such a part of Americana that an original TV dinner package is part of the Smithsonian Institution collection.

Business Boomed When Restaurant Added TV

TED FRANKS hired me in the summer of 1950 to work at his root beer stand in Clinton, Iowa. It was great fun working in a growing business that was well accepted by the community.

It was Mr. Franks' first year in business, and he prospered. Everyone loved the burgers, fries and homemade root beer, which carhops served to hungry people sitting in their cars.

In early fall, Ted's Root Beer Stand experienced a small setback. School had begun, and the autumn chill was in the air. People were not in the mood for root beer.

To survive the winter months, Mr. Franks enclosed the building with aluminum siding, added wide windows and a long counter and turned his root beer stand into a small restaurant. He expanded the menu to serve breakfast, lunch and dinner.

His crowning achievement, however, was installing one of the town's first 13-inch television sets. The television was mounted high on the wall, so the 18 or so people dining at the counter could enjoy the one channel being transmitted from Chicago, 230 miles east of us.

To our surprise, the TV set became very popular. From 6 a.m. to 9 p.m. every day, the restaurant was filled with people eating and watching TV. If the counter was full, people would stand outside and watch through the windows, oblivious to the cold Iowa winter. Some stood out there for hours.

I quickly learned that television was here to stay. People came to Ted's for more than just the food. They didn't want root beer. They wanted TV.

—Gary Happs
San Dimas, California

Asked to "Stand By", Child Did Just That

WHAT FINALLY prompted my father to buy a television in 1950 wasn't Gillette's Friday night fights. It was the *Howdy Doody Show*, which kept me from getting home when dinner was put on the table.

I was always late because the neighbors had a television—a small 13-inch set that all the kids in the neighborhood came to watch. Unfortunately, *Howdy Doody* was on during the dinner hour.

We drove to the next town to pick up our own TV. Boy, was I proud!

The screen was a lot bigger than our neighbors', and all my friends showed up at some point to watch it. We were the talk of the neighborhood.

Mom thought the TV was wonderful. She could put any food at all in front of me while I was watching, and I never even knew what I was eating.

There was one problem, though. At least once a night, the picture would disappear. In its place, we'd see a sign reading, "We Are Having Temporary Difficulties. Please Stand By."

I couldn't read, so I asked my parents what it said. They told me but didn't pay much attention to me afterward.

One night some neighbors were watching TV with us when the picture vanished and the "Please Stand By" sign appeared.

The neighbors couldn't understand why I got up and stood next to the TV. They had a good laugh when Dad told them, "He's learning to read and follow instructions."

—Thomas Stark Jr., Sebring, Florida

Youths Wandered into Role In Cincinnati TV History

By Irvin Goodman, Cincinnati, Ohio

IN 1950, when I was 13, my cousin and I were out exploring the neighborhood and stopped in at WCPO, a local TV studio. The staff kindly showed us around and introduced us to the employees, many of whom we recognized from TV.

Then they told us a new show was about to air. Would we like to appear on live TV? Of course, we would!

The show featured Al Lewis, who also was the station's art director. In the early days of TV, staff members did everything, working behind the scenes as well as on the air.

This particular show featured Al as a "soda jerk", working behind a prop soda fountain while playing the accordion, drawing, doing commercials and ad-libbing. Our role was to sit at the fountain as customers and make small talk with Al, which we proudly did.

We kept wondering whether anyone we knew would see the program. Since it was live, we couldn't see it ourselves. We never dreamed we were part of a historic broadcast, or that Al's show would end up running for more than 30 years.

The program later became a children's show featuring area kids, songs, puppets and characters. Al became "Uncle Al" and his wife, Wanda Lewis, a WCPO artist, appeared as "Captain Windy" (see story below). The *Uncle Al Show* ran so long that many of the children who appeared on it returned years later with their own children.

I'd forgotten about our trip to WCPO until I picked up a book called *Yesterday's Cincinnati*. The book noted that in one early show, to kill time, Al Lewis talked to "a couple of neighborhood kids who wandered into the studio". My cousin and I were those kids!

I was quite surprised to learn about the part we'd played in local TV history. It brought back pleasant memories of growing up in Cincinnati and the early days of TV.

Have Accordion, Will Travel

AL LEWIS thought he got his big break in 1943 when he was filmed in the movie *This Is the Army* while serving as an Army special-services entertainer. Unfortunately his musical comedic sketch ended up on the cutting room floor.

After the war, he attended Cleveland School of the Arts by day and played his accordion in restaurants by night. He also met his future wife, Wanda, at school.

Al became the first art director at WCPO-TV Channel 7 (now Channel 9) in Cincinnati in 1949. He and Wanda were married, and he was asked to fill a late-night hour on the air playing his accordion.

In 1950, he began the *Uncle Al Show* for children. By 1957, with Wanda as Captain Windy (right), the show was broadcast by 130 stations coast to coast.

It went off the air in 1985 and holds the record of the longest-running children's program on commercial television.

How did Wanda become Captain Windy? During the late-night show that preceded the creation of the children's show, Wanda was jokingly called "The Windy One" because she was so quiet, and the name stuck.

Appearance on Dance Show Was Teen Dream Come True

By Donna McGuire Tanner, Ocala, Florida

Author in pre-dancing days

MOST DAYS, I took my time getting home from the school bus stop. But on this warm spring day in Pax, West Virginia, I ran home, threw my books down on the dining room table began racing through the house, looking for my mother.

"Mom!" I hollered. "Jean asked me to go with her and her friends to be on the *Jukebox Dance Party* television show. Can I go? Please?"

Jean lived next door, and she and her friends were several years older. I idolized them. I loved the way they dressed and everything they did. They were teenagers—the thing I most wanted to be.

My mother was familiar with *Jukebox Dance Party*, broadcast from nearby Oak Hill. It was our local version of *American Bandstand*, and I watched it every Saturday afternoon. Each week, the show featured students from a different high school as guest dancers. The minimum age was 13, but I knew that with careful preparation, I could pass.

The biggest hurdle was convincing my parents to let me go. They were the strictest of the strict, and the fact that I wanted to grow up too fast didn't help.

My continual whining finally wore Mom down. She finally agreed—but only if Dad said it was okay. I convinced him by pointing out that they could keep an eye on me by simply watching the program.

As Saturday neared, I grew nervous. Would I be able to dance as well as the real teenagers? I practiced every day, drafting my younger brothers and sister to be my partners. If they managed to elude me, I practiced my rocking and rolling with a chair or bedpost. I just *had* to be ready.

Big Day Finally Arrived

When Saturday came, I spent the whole morning getting dressed. I pulled my long blond hair into a tight ponytail, then donned a blouse, layers and layers of itchy cancan slips, a poodle skirt, white bobby socks and saddle oxfords. The last touches were a neck scarf and a light touch of Mom's lipstick.

At the station, WOAY-TV, I listened breathlessly as someone lectured us about behaving ourselves. We were told to remember that we were representing Pax High School.

A hot light beamed down on us as we assembled on the dance floor. A hush fell over the crowd of teenagers. Suddenly, the familiar theme sound blared all around us. This was it!

Suddenly I was convinced I'd never be able to move. I'd probably be frozen to that spot forever, or at least until someone carried me out.

The red camera light came on. I stared at it. Then I saw my image on the black-and-white studio monitor. That was someone else, not me. Magic filled my soul. The studio was transformed into a land where I was no longer my drab self, but a real 1950s teenager.

No longer self-conscious, I danced to all the hits. The camera seemed to focus on my feet, so I tried to do my fanciest steps.

After the last dance, I felt the deepest sadness I'd ever experienced. It was all over. I must have been exhausted, but I didn't even notice.

As I started toward the door to catch my ride home, the host of the show intercepted me. "We've decided you are welcome to come back any Saturday that you want," he said. "You can fill in some open spaces when we don't have enough students or good dancers."

What a gift! For the next few years, Saturdays found me dancing across the television screen. I always took someone with me so I could share the experience with my friends.

Now when I hear a golden oldie, I'm instantly transported back to that small TV studio, reliving the magic of the Fabulous '50s.

Expectant Mother Got Stuck—Just Like Lucy

I WAS EXPECTING a baby in the early 1950s and was due about the same time Lucille Ball was to have "Little Ricky" on her TV show. Lucy worked her real-life pregnancy into the show's story line.

I Love Lucy aired on the same night my husband participated in a bowling league, so I usually enjoyed the program at home alone.

On one show, a very pregnant Lucy got herself trapped in a low-slung chair and couldn't get up. I was seated in a low-slung chair myself and could identify with Lucy's predicament.

Maybe I identified with it too much, because I laughed so hard that I hurt my back. I couldn't get up until my husband returned and pulled me out of the chair hours later.

I always felt a bond with Lucy after that funny, frantic night.

—*Joan Gessner, Bohemia, New York*

HE LOVED LUCY. Lucille Ball and Desi Arnaz (right) were married in real life and on their popular TV show, *I Love Lucy.*

"SINGING COWBOY" Gene Autry rounded up a few extra cowpokes on this visit to Jackson, Michigan in 1956, recalls Ruth Buckenberger, who now lives in Dearborn, Michigan. "He was a friend of the local newspaper editor and often visited with his buddy Pat Buttram. Gene called our daughter Jean, in the cowboy hat, his Annie Oakley because of her braids. Our daughter Joyce and sons Ronald and Richard are on the right."

 # SADDLE UP!

HEY, COWPOKE, how's your memory of every cowboy and cowgirl's best friend—their horse? See if you can put the right reins in the hands of these TV and movie Western heroes. The answers are upside down below.

1. Bingo	A. Marshall Dillon and Ben Cartwright
2. Buck	B. The Cisco Kid
3. Buttermilk	C. Zorro
4. Champion	D. The Lone Ranger
5. Diablo	E. Annie Oakley
6. El Loaner	F. Roy Rogers
7. Loco	G. Johnny Ringo
8. Midnight	H. Dale Evans
9. Tornado and Phantom	I. Pancho (*The Cisco Kid*)
10. Rafter	J. Gene Autry
11. Scout (also White Feller and Paint)	K. Bret Maverick
12. Silver	L. Palladin (*Have Gun, Will Travel*)
13. Stardust	M. Tonto (*The Lone Ranger*)
14. Target	N. Hopalong Cassidy
15. Topper	O. Bat Masterson
16. Trigger	P. Rowdy Yates (*Rawhide*)

ANSWERS: 1-G, 2-A, 3-H, 4-J, 5-B, 6-K, 7-I, 8-P, 9-C, 10-L, 11-M, 12-D, 13-O, 14-E, 15-N, 16-F.

Alaskans Wed on TV in New York

By Barbara Hassell, Ketchikan, Alaska

I CAME TO Ketchikan, Alaska to visit relatives in early 1951. This small island town, accessible only by steamship or aircraft, had so few young ladies in the workforce that someone actually approached me on the street about a job.

Before long, I was working for the Army Signal Corps' Alaska Communication System, which provided the area's long-distance telephone and telegraph service.

The young Army fellows introduced me to Joe, one of their fishing buddies, and we began dating. We hiked up mountains and over trails, fished for king salmon at every opportunity and hunted for black-tailed deer.

Both of us were in our 20s and very independent—before we met, each of us had said we'd probably never marry. But by the spring of '52, we'd met each other's families and knew we were in love.

Our friends said if we were going to get married anyway, we should try to get on CBS' *Bride and Groom* TV show. We never dreamed we had a chance of being chosen, but we wrote to the show anyway.

When we got word that we'd been selected, we couldn't believe it, but Joe said he wanted to go through with it.

Trek Was Harrowing

On Dec. 19, 1952, we started out for New York in my new car, with Joe's mother as chaperone. We nearly wore out a pair of tire chains just getting through Nevada.

Before we crossed over into Utah, we almost lost Joe's mom at a service station on old Highway 30. We filled up, and Joe bounced into the driver's seat and took off. I asked, "Aren't you going to wait for your mother?"

Joe slammed on the brakes and looked into the backseat, astonished that his mom wasn't there. We went back and called for her at the door of the station's little outhouse. She couldn't get out—the door lock wouldn't budge!

Joe and I tried to open it from the outside, to no avail. The attendant couldn't open it, either. He finally had

THE HAPPY COUPLE. Barbara and Joe Hassell were selected from about 75,000 couples to be married on a national television show on New Year's Eve in 1952.

to get a screwdriver and take the door off at the hinges.

We passed through Iowa on Christmas Day. Very few places were open, but we finally found a small diner where we could get a bite of lunch—and not much more. The owner had scaled back purchases for the holiday lull.

Our ham sandwiches were made with just one slice of bread. When we complained, the owner told us we wouldn't get any more ham with two!

Arriving in New York City, we were astonished by the bright twinkling

"When we got word we'd been selected, we just couldn't believe it..."

lights. It was quite an experience for small-town kids like Joe and me. His mom and I were exclaiming with delight as he drove us through the city.

We stayed at a private home in New Jersey and went back and forth to the *Bride and Groom* set in New York to "practice". Two marriages took place during each half-hour show, before an

audience of about 35. The staff told us they'd received applications from 75,000 couples!

The show was in black and white, but we were surprised that the appliances were yellow, so they wouldn't glare on TV. All of us were adorned with makeup for the same reason. Joe's never gotten over the fact that he had to wear pancake makeup for his wedding!

Our ceremony took place on New Year's Eve. A young fellow from my Alaska office was home in Pennsylvania on leave, so he was Joe's best man. My mother-in-law gave me an old lace veil, a new blue garter and a borrowed diamond pin, so I had something old, new, borrowed and blue.

My beautiful satin wedding gown was provided by the show. Joe's tuxedo never arrived, so he was married in his blue suit. We'd bought our own rings, but the show provided a set for us as well. Joe's was a simple gold band, and mine was set with three Keepsake diamonds.

Honeymoon Was Paid for

After the wedding, the gown was returned to the show, and we left on a 5-day, all-expenses-paid honeymoon to Virginia Beach. We were offered a car but would have had to return it to New York, so we just took our own.

From Virginia Beach, we drove on through Florida, along the Gulf Coast, west to California and then up to Washington and Alaska. It was the trip of a lifetime. We kept a daily diary and still love to read it every few years.

Joe's mom visited family in Massachusetts before returning home. She was able to see herself on TV, when our wedding aired later on the West Coast.

My parents went to Seattle to see it, as TV wasn't available yet in Portland, Oregon. Our brother-in-law took his telephone crew to a TV store in California to watch it. A friend in Denver said she was about to plug in her vacuum cleaner when she heard our names and looked up to see us on TV!

Bride and Groom provided a wonderful send-off for a young couple just getting started.

Chapter Three

Fins to Ragtops

Fins to Ragtops

AFTER A long new car drought, Detroit finally got into full swing again as the '50s dawned. It was high time, because America was starving for new wheels.

Like many veterans, I had other needs for my sparse resources while finishing school and starting a family. I was 25 before I had a car…something my grandchildren cannot comprehend. How could anyone survive that long without a car?

Well, it's easy. You walk a lot. You buy a bicycle and put a very large basket on it or you ride buses.

Our first car was a major event. It was new, and better yet, it was a company car.

Then even better fortune struck. I won a new Hudson automobile—and just in the nick of time, because I'd taken a new job that didn't include a car.

We became suburbanites, and along with the other families out there, we realized we now needed two cars. Like Dagwood Bumstead, I'd carpooled for a few years, but my new job had erratic hours. Carpooling was impossible, and the suburbs lacked public transportation.

A Cheap Commuting Car

The family car was in pretty good shape, but my wife needed it, so I began looking for a cheap, secondhand commuting car.

A neighbor was a used car salesman. On the theory that the "devil you know is preferable to the devil you don't know", I went to him with my requirements: Something cheap and safe that would start in Minnesota's arctic winters. No hurry; I would wait until he got something decent on a trade-in.

Somewhere along the way he mentioned he was a former attorney, disbarred and sent to prison for 3 years for cleaning out two or three trusts in his care. What luck! Working for me was not just a used car peddler, but also a crooked attorney. What more could a person ask?

A few weeks later, he said the perfect car had arrived. It was an enormous olive-green prewar DeSoto that had been the height of luxury. It rode like a pillow, was quiet as a whisper and obviously would win out in any automotive conflict. At $225, it was a steal.

Our "Green Dragon" served us well for several months until numerous geriatric problems arose. It demanded water, oil and gas frequently, rust bloomed

"We became suburbanites and realized we now needed two cars…"

on it like acne on a teenage boy, and the fat balloon tires shed rubber the way a snake sheds its skin.

At trade-in time, I asked the dealer what it was worth. "You're in luck," he said. "It weighs nearly 2 tons, and scrap iron is 4¢ a pound."

So I got nearly as much for the brute as I had paid for it. And I didn't weep a tear as it was towed away.

During the Fabulous '50s, Americans renewed their love affair with automobiles. To the younger bunch, autos represented both freedom and the chance to make a personal statement to the world. All it took was money, time, hard work and a bit of creativity. And to the older crowd, those tail fins and giant chrome bumpers just screamed "Look at me!"

What a great time to be alive!

—Clancy Strock

Dad Was a Cadillac Man

He epitomized the '50s style- and fin-loving car buyer.

By Cookie Curci-Wright, San Jose, California

CADILLAC OWNERS, especially in the 1950s, were interested in the size, shape and style of the tail fins, the scenic windshield, spotlights, chrome and whitewall tires—and how many heads it would turn when they rolled past.

At our house, buying one of these glamorous cars was a family affair. After all, the family car reflected the entire household, making a statement about who we were, our style, taste and credibility. It conveyed esteem to friends, business associates and customers. Above all, it was a hot commodity for status-hungry Americans.

Movie stars, fin-tailed cars and pink poodles set the stage for the explosive 1950s and the popularity of the awesome Cadillac. In a thriving postwar economy, motorists could well afford the gargantuan cars with swaths of chrome along with bigger TVs, Hawaiian cruises and swimming pools.

Late September meant one thing to car-hungry motorists: The new cars had arrived.

Luxurious and Impractical

Chevy, Ford and Lincoln lovers all went to their favorite dealerships. For my dad, a Cadillac man, St. Claire Cadillac was home to the most luxurious cars in San Jose, California.

In the '50s, gas mileage and economy had little to do with car choices. It was a love affair between a man and a magnificent machine.

Dad refused to own anything but a Cadillac. One of his most luxurious, most impractical cars was a 1955 Coupe DeVille. I still remember the night he bought this dream car.

He'd taken us for our usual drive to ogle the new cars on display at the dealership. It didn't take us long to fall head over heels in love with a streamlined baby-blue Cadillac. Bathed in fluorescent light, the car seemed to glow.

It was state of the art. A foot button on the driver's side changed stations on the radio without taking your eyes off the road. A light beam on the dashboard automatically adjusted the car's high and low beams.

A heater, air conditioner, power windows, tinted glass, huge windshield, armrests and an interior cushioned in white leather made the car everything a status-seeking family could desire.

The salesman ushered Dad into that tiny room where deals were made and broken. From our seats in the hall, we watched as the two bartered. Figures flew fast and hard; amounts were scribbled and erased. Dad's head nodded, then shook disapprovingly.

An hour later, Dad and the salesman emerged. Dad was smoking one of his best cigars, a sure sign that he had cemented the deal.

"Just hand me the keys to your old car," the salesman told Dad, "and you can drive your brand-new car off the showroom floor."

Old Car Held Memories

But I could see the look on Dad's face that he wasn't quite ready to say good-bye to our old 1947 Cadillac. He told the salesman he'd bring it around tomorrow, after he cleaned it up a bit.

That blue Coupe DeVille was the most beautiful car we ever owned. And it did make heads turn. But looking back, I can understand Dad's reluctance at parting with the old car.

After all, it was more than just fading paint and metal. It was all the places we'd gone together as a family …the drives to Grandma's house every Friday night…kids in pj's at the El Rancho drive-in…hamburgers and fries at Mel's Palm Bowl…camping trips to Yosemite…and those long, cool summer night drives.

Luxuries didn't come so easily to the next generation. Middle class, as we knew it, would no longer exist— you were either rich or struggling.

Family life would never be the same, but for the time being, we were part of the fast and fabulous, fin-tailed car generation and we were definitely going to enjoy the ride. ✂

PRIDE AND JOY. Author's parents posed with their new baby— baby-blue '55 Cadillac, that is.

Vintage Oldsmobile Is a Family Friend

MY 1953 Oldsmobile Holiday Coupe is one '50s-era item I cannot part with.

Deemed "Old Reliable" with its V-8 Rocket engine and hydraulic power windows that run on brake fluid, it was born before I was and contains a repertoire of childhood memories.

They span my early life and school days and visits to grandparents. With my first pink and white striped hula hoop sitting in the front seat, it took me to stay at Grandma's when my little brother was born.

Dad had begun to teach me to drive that car in 1979, then he suddenly passed away.

My high school drama class put on *Rebel Without a Cause* in 1981, and it was ironic to drive a car from that era.

Lately, I've noticed its emerald green color is back in style, so everything eventually comes around again.

People want to buy it, but it has too many sentimental attachments and a personality of its own. It's now even more cherished since the Oldsmobile is being phased out.

How can anyone let go of an icon, an American automotive innovation? —*Diana Hansen, Denver, Colorado*

IT WASN'T A BOAT. But Victor Bennett of Horicon, Wisconsin says his friends were so taken with the shape of his 1950 Nash Ambassador that they dubbed it the "Inverted Bathtub"! "This car served us well on our first trip from Wisconsin to Rocky Mountain Park in Colorado," Victor says.

MERRY OLDS PICNIC. Diana Hansen (second from right) and her family enjoy an outing with "Old Reliable" in the background.

He Sold Hot Wheels to Buy Cool Rock

MY BOYFRIEND had the coolest car ever—a green 1950 Mercury that he customized himself. It had a chopped top and bubble skirts. He ended up selling that beauty of a car to buy me an engagement ring. —*Angie Youngson Trenton, Michigan*

HEAVY CHEVY. "My husband and I bought this 1951 Chevrolet new in Anchorage, Alaska in February 1951," remembers Luann Cram of San Bernardino, California. "In August, we started a great adventure, driving it down the Alcan Highway to Rochester, Minnesota. A washed-out road at Burwash Landing in the Yukon detained us for 4 days, but we had no car trouble at all."

VW 'Bug' Kept Going and Going and Going

By Ken Yeager, Pleasant Hill, California

THE LITTLE BUG THAT COULD. Sherry and Kim Yeager try a new "front" seat on the 1957 Volkswagen that served as the family car for many years. A vacation trip in the mid-1950s showed the car's worth.

MY VOLKSWAGEN "Bug" story begins in 1956 when we ordered it, then waited 6 months for delivery. It was a '57 model priced at $1,500.

We were happy to take whatever color it came in and that was orange. It had a 36-horsepower engine and a four-speed gearbox. To shift down to low gear, the car had to come to a complete stop.

It had no gas gauge on the panel, just a foot lever for switching to the reserve supply.

We took it on our vacation, towing a small homemade trailer that held most of our luggage. Our two kids, ages 4 and 5, sat in the back, where I had removed the backseat and made a snug-fitting plywood box. It had a hinged section for additional storage, and we covered the box with a thick foam rubber pad.

Because I worked nights and slept days, we left in the late afternoon. We found "no vacancy" signs in Reno, so I continued driving. When I grew tired, I pulled to the side of the road and curled up on the front seats around the gearshift. My wife joined the kids, who were asleep in their nice padded bed.

Bug Was a Workhorse

When daylight came, I started driving while the rest of the family was still asleep. I stopped behind a Pontiac whose driver had signaled me to pull over.

He had car trouble and asked if I would take his wife into the next town to get a tow truck. I told him I'd first like to try to push his car up the hill and see if it would start on the way down. If not, I said, I'd push his car into town.

Well, the Bug did more than its normal job. The Pontiac didn't start and I continued to push it. When we got to the service station, the man and his wife got out of their car to thank us. It was Jack Sprat and his wife! If she had sat in our car, we would have had a squashed Bug!

In 1970, after I had overhauled the engine and increased the horsepower to 40, I gave the car to my son. He did some additional work on it and eventually sold it to a dealer.

The same day he sold it, someone took it for a trial run and never came back. It was eventually found somewhere on the peninsula south of San Francisco.

Somewhere that orange Bug may still be running, like the little pink rabbit, going and going and going.

Dependable Used Cars Sold for Bargain Prices

IN 1950, I spent $75 for a 1927 Model A that had been stored on blocks for 4 years. I drove it for 2 years and never spent a penny on repairs.

In 1953, while in the Air Force, I bought a 1946 Nash in Elgin, Illinois for $400. I drove it back to the base in Idaho and sold it 3 months later for $650.

After my discharge in 1955, I bought a 1953 Ford for $1,250 and drove it for 8 years. A friend bought it for $100 just so he could have the engine, which was still in perfect condition. —*Art Conro Merrillan, Wisconsin*

DOES ANYONE REMEMBER when VW Bugs were customized by their owners? Some humorously added a windup key on the lid above the rear engine compartment as a jibe about how they were powered. Others replaced the front hood with a hood and grille resembling a Rolls Royce, the ultimate in luxury vehicles.

Many were made over as dune buggies with oversize tires, no roof and a roll bar for safety.

The split-window Volkswagen microbus, the Bug's big brother, was a box on wheels, made from 1949 to 1967.

It carried passengers or cargo or a mix of each. Mileage on the microbus and the Bug was good. When combined with a reasonable purchase price, they were very economical transportation.

They Wrestled with a Problem Car

IN 1954, my husband, Dick, and I traveled from Battle Creek, Michigan to Lincoln, Nebraska, where I was to be matron of honor at my sister's wedding.

We had picked up my Aunt Theo in Chicago, and everything was going fine until we reached a small town near Muscatine, Iowa. Our 1954 Ford hardtop stopped and refused to budge.

It was late in the afternoon, and we were worried about getting the car fixed and having enough money to pay for the repairs in a time before credit cards. We found a gas station, where we were told that the car's generator needed to be rewound.

There was only one person in town who could fix it, the attendant said. We asked where we could find him.

"Oh, you can find him, but he won't fix the generator because he's watching wrestling on television," the attendant said. "He won't do anything while wrestling is on."

Apparently the whole town was watching wrestling, because no one else was around. We sat in our car and waited until the wrestling matches were over.

When they were finished, the man came to hand-rewind the generator. It took quite a while, and we were glad Aunt Theo was with us in case we needed to borrow some money for the repairs.

We were pleasantly surprised when the bill was only $20—cheap even for those days!

With the Ford fixed, we soon were on our way again. We arrived in Lincoln late, but with plenty of time for the wedding the next day.
—*Barbara Farley Bannister*
McMinnville, Oregon

***SPLIT DECISION.** Dick and Barbara Bannister knew what was wrong with their car, behind them in a small Iowa town in 1954. Unfortunately they couldn't get it fixed immediately.*

First Car Steered Him to New Lifestyle

I'D ALWAYS LIVED in the big city, with access to public transportation. For years, I didn't own an automobile—or even know how to drive one.

As time went by, though, I found there were many occasions that required personal transportation. I bought my first car, a 1948 Chevrolet sedan with white sidewall tires (below), on June 3, 1953.

What a different lifestyle I began to live! No more waiting for city buses on street corners in all kinds of weather. No more hassles trying to coordinate train and other transportation schedules for vacations.

My social life increased 100%. Before, I'd had to depend on city buses to escort my lady friends to theaters and other attractions.

I spent hours washing, waxing and polishing my car, being very cautious to avoid mud puddles and dusty roadways. I vacuumed the interior so much that cleanliness became an obsession. I felt heartsick whenever a passenger ate something in my car and crumbs fell to the seat cushion or the floor.

Eventually, of course, the newness wore off and I was able to relax a bit—which allowed me to enjoy my car even more.
—*Charles Martin, Bartlesville, Oklahoma*

Kick, Kick, KICK

MY FIRST CAR, which I acquired in 1959, was a 1953 Ford that one of the previous owners had started to customize.

I continued with the work, including removal of all door handles and the key lock from the trunk lid. The doors then were opened with starter solenoids mounted in the doors and activated by buttons hidden under the chrome strips on the sides of the car.

When young ladies asked how to open the doors, I told them they had to kick the front tires. After a good deal of kicking without the doors opening. I could unobtrusively reach the chrome strip and button while kicking the tire at the same time as all eyes were on the tire. There was a good deal of surprise when I explained how it was done.

To add another distinctive touch, I also swung the gearshift lever over to the left side of the steering column. After I married, however, I moved it back to the right side so my wife could more easily drive it.
—*Arnold Peters*
Terrace, British Columbia

Convertible Was Ticket To Freedom for WACs

Their yellow ragtop symbolized a carefree life away from the military.

By Mary Lu Leon, Grass Valley, California

THE GLEAMING YELLOW CAR sat proudly on the lot in Anniston, Alabama in 1955. Despite its broken windows, my friend Marilyn and I, both PFCs in the WAC band at Fort McClellan, fell in love with that 1951 Mercury convertible.

A mechanic who'd agreed to look at the car advised against the purchase.

"It's been in an accident. Don't buy it," he said.

"I'll fix the windows and polish it," the dealer countered. "It's yours for $900."

We bought it! On our pay of $80 a month, we couldn't afford a car separately, but together we qualified for a loan.

The license plate had base tags and read "Heart of Dixie". It represented youth, carefree jaunts and freedom from Army routine. Of course, all the other girls in the WAC band wanted to ride in it.

Attractive young men, spotting the Southern license plate, would wave and yell, "Hi, y'all!"

Once Marilyn drove from Alabama to Georgia in a rainstorm and had a flat tire. She'd barely pulled off the road when another car with a man and woman stopped behind her. He jumped out and quickly changed the tire.

She offered to pay him, but he waved her off, saying, "I was in the service. I know how it is."

PIT STOP. Marilyn Harris Ferraris checked the oil on the car she and author owned in '55.

Another time, she pulled into a service station in North Carolina with just enough gas money to get back to the base. The attendant said she needed oil and *he* paid for it. She sent him a check later and never forgot how kind people were to young women in uniform.

We drove to the Newport Jazz Festival in July 1955 after I had barely passed the driver's test in April. I got caught in a horrendous traffic jam in New York City that cured me forever of being nervous when cars were too close. In Newport, I quickly backed out of a parking lot and a young man jumped nimbly out of the way. "I almost ran over Chet Baker!" I gasped. He was a trumpet player and vocalist at the festival.

The car broke down repeatedly, leaked in rainstorms and had constant engine trouble. The top didn't always lock properly and flew up at inconvenient times. When the windshield wiper stopped working in a thunderstorm, we tied rope to manually swish the blades so we could see the road and get back to the base on time.

Everywhere we went, we ran into guys who assumed we were Southern girls, although we hailed from California. When you're 20 years old and have a shiny yellow convertible, you own the world!

Deluxe Treatment Turned '41 Ford into "Lead Sled"

DURING MY junior year of high school in Arizona, I bought a 1941 Ford Deluxe two-door sedan for the princely sum of $200. That summer, I had a job in Southern California and took my car with me.

After a few nights of cruising, I quickly saw the need for radical changes on my "stocker". Since I was in the chips, earning $1.50 an hour, the cost of customizing was no object.

I dropped the front end 2 inches, then raised the rear end by adding Chrysler 300 rims and large whitewall tires. Smaller tires in front provided the "rake"—the look that was in.

The Ford quickly became a "lead sled" because it was "nosed" (the front hood ornament had been removed) and "decked" (the rear deck handle was removed and the holes filled with lead). Four rows of louvers were punched into the hood, then I hand-sanded the old finish and had the body painted with a baby-blue primer.

The mellow sound from the dual glass-pack mufflers gave the flathead V-8 a great head-turning rumble. When I drove the car back onto my Arizona campus in the fall of 1955, it was a sensation!

At reunions, the guys and gals still talk about my fabulous '41 Ford.　　—Dave Will
Porterville, California

Caddie Became a Regular In Cedar Rapids Parades

MY UNCLE CHUCK bought a brand-new Cadillac Eldorado in 1955. I remember him saying that he had $50 in insurance on the car before it even left the factory.

The exterior color was "Pacific Coral", and the interior was light blue French leather. We lived in Cedar Rapids, Iowa, and orange and blue happened to be our high school's colors. So the Cadillac appeared in many parades, carrying the homecoming queen.

Uncle Chuck loved a parade, but he never allowed anyone else to drive the car in one. My sister and I were permitted to drive the convertible occasionally, but only with Aunt Laura and Uncle Chuck riding along.

My aunt and uncle had no children. Uncle Chuck's cars were his babies, and he took meticulous care of them, always washing and towel-drying them after a ride. During nice weather, you'd see him driving the Caddie almost every night.

After Uncle Chuck passed away, Aunt Laura sold the car to a collector. It's since been sold again, and I believe it's now in Florida.

I've always said that if I ever win the lottery, I'd do my best to get the car back into the family.

—*Judy Owens, Grand Junction, Colorado*

FIT FOR A QUEEN. Laura Kvach and her husband, Chuck, loved tooling around Cedar Rapids, Iowa in their 1955 Cadillac Eldorado convertible. With its coral exterior and blue upholstery, it made a perfect throne for the homecoming queen in parades, because the high school's colors were orange and blue.

"Old Silver" Carried Couple to New Mexico

WE BOUGHT "Old Silver", a 1957 Chevrolet station wagon, in April 1959. After I graduated from Michigan State University Veterinary College, my wife and I moved to Alamogordo, New Mexico, with all we owned packed in that car.

The Chevy was a great car that served us well. It even had a spotlight!

If I had it now, it would be a collector's item, but it's probably rusting away in some junkyard. I'd rather think that it's been restored and that someone proudly drives it once in a while. —*Jim Fox Sr., Wayland, Michigan*

Sturdy Packard Doubled As Construction Vehicle

TWO GREAT USED CARS were our main mode of transportation in the 1950s.

Our first was a mist-blue 1953 Packard Clipper four-door sedan. I bought it from a dealer in 1957 for $1,000, and it was in mint condition. For a Depression kid whose family never owned wheels, it was the cat's meow.

I put many tough miles on this car, though. I was the general contractor on my own house and used the car as a truck to haul construction materials.

By the time the home was completed, the car was rusty, seemed to burn as much oil as gas and its exhaust resembled that of a jet engine. I finally had to part with it, selling it to a used car dealer for $37.50. The hood ornament alone was worth that much. Who would've dreamed that today it would be considered a collector's car?

Our second car, also bought in 1957, was my wife's—a tan and blue 1953 Chevrolet Bel Air sedan. It had been a one-owner car and was in great shape. I got it for $150 from a senior citizen who could no longer drive.

The Chevy had a stick shift and started instantly even in the coldest weather. It was the best-starting car in our whole neighborhood.

I replaced the points every 6 months, whether the car needed them or not. Several years later, with 25,000 miles on it, the car was still in good condition.

I sold it for $65 and had put very little money into maintenance. The depreciation costs were probably less than a penny a mile. —*Michael Lacivita, Youngstown, Ohio*

Remember These Great Cars from the '50s?

EDSELS FOREVER. Well, at least for 3 years, which is how long Ford made Edsels. Joel and Jeanette Mathistad of St. James, Minnesota own this 1959 model (left).

LEE'S "LIMO". This 1957 Ford Skyliner hardtop convertible (above), owned by Mario and Rosemary Maglio of Wickenburg, Arizona, was bought new by well-known entertainer Liberace.

HIGHWAY HAULER. The rear window on Duane Carpenter's 1957 Mercury Turnpike Cruiser (above) went down. Duane, of Evanston, Wyoming, wins awards with the car.

NEW LOOK. Chevy's style was all new in 1955. M.D. Coleman of Clarksdale, Mississippi inherited this blue Bel Air (above) from his grandmother, who bought it new.

VALUABLE 'VETTE. Fred Daras of Vienna, Ohio was 9 years old when he started dreaming of owning a 1959 Corvette (above). His dream come true is a classic.

THE BEST. Eugene Boomer of North Windham, Connecticut thinks his 1957 Studebaker Golden Hawk (left) is one of the better-looking cars ever built.

"Honeymoon Car" Was His Favorite

MY HUSBAND, R.L., had several old cars, including a Model T, but I think his favorite was this 1953 Cadillac (below), which he always called his "honeymoon car".

He bought it new in 1953, and it was his pride and joy. We married in 1957, and indeed it was our honeymoon car. We drove down Florida's west coast to Key West and back up the east coast to our home in Georgia.

I felt so special when the most handsome man in the world would come and pick me up in such a pretty car.

In later years, R.L. told everyone about his "honeymoon car". At his 1991 retirement dinner from Fruehauf Corp., after 39 years of service and right in the middle of dinner, he announced that he bet he had something no one else had. I really didn't know what he would say, but as friends and family paused to listen, he said his "honeymoon car".

And sure enough, none of them did!

When he died in 1998, we had been married 41 years, and he still loved that car.

By the way, I still have the Model T and, of course, the "honeymoon car".

— *Tommie Gosdin*
Red Oak, Georgia

CHEAP GAS. Gasoline prices weren't budget-busters in 1952, as this sign over Edward Eca's head proves. "This picture was taken at the gas station where I worked in Centralia, Illinois," writes Edward, who lives in Waukegan. "At 25 ¢ a gallon, you could do a lot of driving for just a couple of dollars."

Car with Wood Trim Was Too Delicious to Pass Up

AT THE START of my high school senior year in Sunbury, Pennsylvania in 1956, Dad finally relented and allowed me to buy a car. I had to pay for it myself, along with the necessary insurance.

I took three buddies with me, bought a 1948 Chrysler and drove it away. Three miles later, it conked out. My buddies pushed the car back to the dealer.

The dealer told me he was sorry, but the car had no warranty. He offered to let me trade it in, on the spot, for a handsome 1949 Chrysler Town and Country station wagon with luggage racks, shining wood trim, everything.

I agreed to pay the extra cost and drove it away. The Town and Country was quite a car.

Months later, on the day of the junior-senior prom, I was washing the car and noticed some insects flying around. Then a piece of wood near the back of the car dropped off.

I called my dad, who solemnly proclaimed my car had termites. Sure as shootin', there were little holes in the wood trim!

To this day, no one who remembers me back in Sunbury will ever forget "Shaffer's Termitemobile".

— *Terry Shaffer, Indianapolis, Indiana*

Teen Pampered Ford With Polish and Paint

MY DAD gave me his 1949 Ford as my very first car in 1957, when I was 16. I paid $49 for a cherry-red paint job—which faded in 6 months—and spray-painted the interior dashboard and doors myself.

I spent hours polishing the car's chrome and hubcaps. I loved that car like some girls love diamonds and mink!

My girlfriends and I spent many pleasurable hours cruising around our small town of Hawthorne, California in that great little car. Gasoline was about 21¢ a gallon in those days.

—*Camille Saso-Carpenter, West Hills, California*

He Had His Fair Share of the Billions Served

By Bob Raczka, Des Plaines, Illinois

BACK IN 1955, when I was 15 years old, the first McDonald's restaurant owned by Ray Kroc opened in Des Plaines, Illinois, where my oldest brother, Ben, lived.

Four years later, I bought a '58 Plymouth Plaza four-door sedan from my dad. Many visits to Ben's home included stops with that car for meals at McDonald's, where they had walk-up, window and carryout service only.

Hamburgers were 15¢, cheeseburgers 19¢, fries 10¢ and milk shakes 20¢.

In June 1984, I bought a '58 Plymouth Savoy four-door hardtop, I had told one of my sons, Brian, that if he ever found a '58 Plymouth in good shape, I would buy it. A promise is a promise. We worked on the car and have been driving it for fun ever since.

This picture was taken in July 1985 at the same McDonald's, which by then had become a museum.

Who says you can't go home again?

SEASONED WHEELS. Bob Raczka stands next to his 1958 Plymouth outside the McDonald's he frequented when he had his first '58 Plymouth in 1959. The restaurant, the first opened by the McDonald's Corporation, is now a museum.

Kroc's Is a McSuccess Story

SALESMAN Ray Kroc mortgaged his home and invested his life savings to become the exclusive distributor of a five-spindled milk shake maker called the Multimixer.

He heard about a hamburger stand called McDonald's in California that was running eight Multimixers at a time. He went west in 1954 to take a look. When he got there, he convinced Dick and Mac McDonald that he could expand the operation to several more stands.

He did. In 1955, Ray opened his first restaurant in Des Plaines, Illinois and took in $366.12 the first day.

Today, McDonald's is the world's leading food service retailer with more than 28,000 restaurants in 120 countries serving 45 million customers each day. Approximately 80 percent of McDonald's restaurants worldwide are owned and operated by independent local businessmen and women.

Aside from establishing the world's largest food service retailer, Ray encouraged good work habits among his restaurant employees.

"If you've got time to lean, you've got time to clean," he often told them.

The company also is responsible for a well-known clown, Ronald McDonald. In his first television appearance, the clown was portrayed by TV weatherman Willard Scott, but that's a story for another decade.

Wild One?

NO, my father-in-law wasn't wild, although he certainly looked the part!

This picture of Tony Corrado (above) was taken in 1951 in Detroit. Two years later, he was a responsible, loving husband and father. Despite having lost his own father at the age of 10, he shouldered that burden and many others with a philosophical calmness.

I've often marveled at how this young daredevil turned into the steadiest parent you could imagine—without ever losing his edge. Like many men of that era, he's a prince of a man—and my mother-in-law still thinks he's dishy!

—*Laney Corrado, Harper Woods, Michigan*

Coincidences, Chevrolets Brought Couple Together

MY HUSBAND and I met in 1958, when we were both serving in the Marine Corps. At the time, each of us had our own 1956 Chevrolet. His was a Bel Air hardtop, mine was a convertible, and both had Minnesota license plates.

After a mutual friend introduced us, my husband-to-be confessed that he'd planned to introduce himself anyway, based on our similar taste in cars and the coincidence that we were both from Minnesota.

Today on our mantel, we have models of both of those wonderful cars. They'll always be our favorites.

—*Mary Ann Johnson, Central Point, Oregon*

SHORT AND SWEET. Dorothy Gilliland says she got excellent mileage with this "King Midget" in the early 1950s—about 65 miles to the gallon. "The car was made in southern Ohio and had a removable top," writes Dorothy, of Strongsville, Ohio. "But it was no good in Ohio's ice and snow, so after 2 years, I sold it to a cousin in Florida to use all year-round."

Chrysler Imperial Logged Nearly 500,000 Miles

I DROVE my 1957 Chrysler Crown Imperial convertible—white with gray leather upholstery—all over the country and put more than 230,000 miles on it before I sold it.

As a singer, pianist and actor, I spent a lot of time on the road. When I began doing most of my work near my home in Las Vegas, I finally decided to sell the car.

An atomic scientist from the Nevada test site bought it and put another 150,000 miles on it. Then he overhauled the motor and drove it for 100,000 miles more!

What a great car that was! It was truly an American classic.

—*Bill Kane*
Las Vegas, Nevada

ON THE ROAD AGAIN. Bill Kane put 230,000 miles on this 1957 Chrysler Crown Imperial before selling it. The next owner drove it for 250,000 more. The full-width grille and dramatic fins were new features on all five of Chrysler's car lines in 1957.

'55 Chevy to the Rescue!

Bumpy ride in dumpy car may have been just what the doctor ordered.

By Ron Sturga, Edinboro, Pennsylvania

MY FIRST CAR, a dark blue 1950 DeSoto four-door sedan, served me well during college in the 1950s. When I got my first teaching assignment in Edinboro, Pennsylvania in 1959, I went looking for something more reliable, yet affordable.

I found a 1955 Chevy ragtop in the back row of a used car lot. It was an eyesore to everyone but me. The paint was faded, the hubcaps didn't match and the tires were bald, but the engine started and ran.

I traded my DeSoto and $100 for it. Pieces of candy and pizza littered the floor, and the interior smelled. Once I got the car home, I cleaned it out and hung a car freshener from the rearview mirror, which won the battle of odors overnight.

I removed the remaining strips of chrome and insignias, then filled in the holes. I ruined my high school letter jacket with the foul-smelling fiberglass filler, but it did leave a smooth body shell.

One summer weekend while I was working on my Chevy, I drove home to visit my family, including my sister Karen, who was quite pregnant and more than ready to deliver. Karen, my sister Jan, and my mother and grandmother put on their babushkas and we drove through the nearby town where our dad had grown up.

The shocks on the Chevy were not good, and the backroads were bumpy.

Shortly after we got back home, Karen said she was ready to go to the hospital, and my niece Kristen was born hours later.

Ragtop Helped Stork

We always thought that ride in my convertible had a lot to do with it.

I kept working on the Chevy, sanding and priming it before I had it painted. I carefully masked the windows to keep any paint spray off the glass.

The paint job cost $25, and when I first saw the car, I was worried because it looked like a green blob. Once the tape and paper were removed, however, that Neptune Green Metallic '55 Chevy convertible gleamed.

The car that had earlier received "yucks" now received "oohs" and "aahs".

That Chevy was very special. I wish I had it today. ◄

BLACK BEAUTY. "I had just graduated from Eastern High School in Lansing, Michigan in 1958. That summer I spent many evenings cruising downtown Lansing and going to Sulley's drive-in in my black 1956 Oldsmobile," writes George Mellios from Mulliken, Michigan.

Hudson Rambler Was Safe For Camping and Accidents

Fold-down seats provided comfortable accommodations while Unibody construction protected occupants in a crash.

By Murray Edwards, Victoria, British Columbia

OUR 1957 HUDSON RAMBLER was the only car we ever owned that had a personality. Most owners felt this, and whenever you encountered another Rambler, there was a friendly wave and a toot on the horn from its driver.

For travel, the Rambler was ideal. The front seats folded flat, and a custom-made air mattress turned the interior into a very comfortable double bed.

My wife, Morrie, and I bought the car in 1957 when we were stationed with the Canadian Army — the Princess Patricia's Canadian Light Infantry—in Calgary, Alberta.

We took our first real holiday that year—a trip through the Rockies to the West Coast—staying nights in small provincial campsites, where we were the envy of our fellow campers.

We could put down the front seat of our car and inflate the air mattress for a secure and comfortable night's sleep while they struggled to put up their small tents.

Morrie was only scared in retrospect when she later found out there were bears in the vicinity of many of the campsites.

In 1959, we were posted to Camp Borden, Ontario. In the spring of 1961, I drove into Barrie, the nearest town, to purchase some red, white and blue petunias for a patriotic flower bed that summer.

On the way home, I was stopped behind another car when there was an explosive noise and the car behind crashed into me. Luckily, I had left a good space in front of me and avoided hitting the car in front.

A heavy 1952 DeSoto had hit my car, bending their car and throwing the young couple in-side into the backseat. I was unhurt, but the Rambler was bent down 14 inches at the rear.

Its all-welded "Unibody" body had held safe, and I was able to drive away from the accident. ◄

CAR HAD PERSONALITY. Morrie Edwards poses with her and husband Murray's favorite car, a 1957 Hudson Rambler.

GOOD FOR THE HEART. "This 1950 Hudson Pacemaker was the best courting car ever," says Gene Tillis, at a roadside park near Gallipolis, Ohio with future wife Ruth Hineman. They married in 1952 and now are courting on the beaches in Englewood, Florida, where they live.

They Won Disneyland Trip *and* a Hudson

By Harry Sennott, Kissimmee, Florida

A NEW HUDSON HORNET and a trip to the just-opened Disneyland were the prizes my wife, Anita, and I won in 1955—all for the price of a 3-cent stamp!

While living in Rock Hill, Missouri, we visited our near-by hometown of Waterloo, Illinois. I ran into an old friend who owned the Hudson dealership, and he gave me an entry form.

The contest was sponsored by Hudson Motors and Walt Disney Productions. Anita and I filled out the form, in 35 words or less, on which features we liked best on American Motors cars.

Our entry read: "We like Hudson's Triple-Safe Brake System. With present-day emphasis on power and speed, even 100 special features would be useless without a Guardian Angel Brake System."

We found out later that the phrase "guardian angel", which Anita suggested, was what made our entry stand out from the others.

We were notified by letter that we were one of three grand-prize winners. We got the car on August 5 and were in Disneyland on August 9, our daughter Jennie's fifth birthday. We went to Disneyland for 5 days and spent another day on Santa Catalina Island before flying home. We stayed at the Ambassador Hotel and had a wonderful time.

We kept the car for more than 200,000 miles. By that time, Hudson and Nash were no longer made and there were no dealers. When something wore out, I had to go to a junkyard to get replacement parts.

The Hudson was built on a Packard chassis with a Packard engine and was one of the finest automobiles around at that time. The company's motto was, "Ask the Man Who Owns One."

I put an ad in the papers for the car and got no takers, so a friend suggested I place an ad in an antiques publication. I sold the car for parts to a "horseless carriage" collector for $2,000.

After 35 years with U.S. Steel, I retired and we moved to Florida. My wife got a job at Disney World as a sales hostess in the Magic Kingdom, then at a shop in the MGM Studios and later as a courtesy trainer. A little later, I also went to work there. I dressed as a pirate captain and worked in the Pirates of the Caribbean gift shop.

We recently celebrated our 52nd wedding anniversary and have lots of wonderful memories, many relating to our years as owners of that beautiful Hudson Hornet and vacationing at Disneyland—all for a 3-cent stamp.

No Brakes?
No Reverse?
No Problem

By Gardner Kissack, Chicago Heights, Illinois

MY FIRST CAR was the perfect car to learn to drive in because it had no brakes! That forced me to look and plan ahead.

It was a faded maroon 1937 Ford four-door sedan, and the brakes had gone out sometime in the late 1940s. My family acquired it in June 1951 for $40 and retired it to my grandmother's farm near Saugatuck, Michigan, where I learned to depress the clutch, shift gears and steer.

I had to be very careful to drive around the open fields slowly and shift without looking away from whatever was ahead. Accurate steering was critical. Otherwise I risked running into the windmill, the barns, "Buster" (the dog) or Grandma.

Having no brakes to slow or stop the car taught me certain fundamental things about cars in motion. Those unforgettable physics lessons have served me well through decades of driving.

My second car was a very green 1941 Plymouth convertible that my father bought in the mid-'50s, probably to keep me from driving the family Ford.

We got the car at the beginning of my senior year, and it was great. With the black canvas top lowered, the fresh air was exhilarating and the visibility was unlimited.

Backseat Was a Black Seat

When the top was raised, however, the backseat was enclosed in darkness. There were no side windows in back, and with the top up, rear visibility was somewhere between nonexistent and dangerous.

I went all over town that September with my pals Norm, Judy and Sue. We took the car everywhere—to school, after-school jobs and clubs, the photo club picnic. Well, it seemed like everywhere to us, having only recently outgrown our Monarch Silver King and Schwinn bikes.

For a few weeks, the Plymouth ran beautifully. But by October, it required a lot of extra effort to move the gearshift

CONVERTIBLE HAD A FEW QUIRKS. Author's high school car had very limited visibility when the top was up. Then there was the problem with having no reverse gear.

up or down the column. Then one glorious autumn afternoon as we tried to leave an uptown parking space, the reverse gear simply stopped working.

From that day on, whenever reverse was required, Norm, Judy and Sue would scramble out, push the Plymouth back a few feet and jump back in over the doors, just like in an Andy Hardy movie or Archie cartoon. This jumping maneuver was a great time-saver when we were in traffic.

That was fun for a week or two, but became less so when the weather cooled and we couldn't leave the top down. Eventually, it wasn't fun at all. In fact, it was downright inconvenient, not to mention dangerous and probably illegal.

Not long after that, my father traded the very green convertible for a sedate, polite, pea-green 1950 Plymouth club coupe, which I drove the rest of my senior year and all through college. It not only had brakes, but three speeds forward and one for reverse.

The coupe was certainly dependable, but not as memorable as the convertible that wouldn't back up. ◀

Chapter Four

My Most Memorable Job

My Most Memorable Job

HERE IS perhaps my favorite chapter in this entire book. It's filled with readers' memories of the jobs they held back in the '50s.

The reason I like it so much is it proves that no matter how humble, no matter how tough, nor how little future it has, there's no such thing as a job that doesn't serve you well later in life. The pay may be pitifully meager, but the experience you gain is beyond price.

The '50s were in general a good time to be looking for a job. There was lots of work to be had, even if few of the jobs showed promise as lifetime careers.

One of my sons worked for more than a year for a landscape company. He dug holes, raked dirt and toted heavy things like boulders and railroad ties. He got sweaty and dirty and often was too tired to socialize with pals on Saturday night. Now, nearly a half century later, he and his wife have the most beautifully land-scaped home in the neighborhood. That long-ago job is still paying dividends.

One of my daughters worked after school and an entire summer for a florist. Nowadays she can whip up a dazzling centerpiece from dandelions and a few hunks of rusty barbed wire. Or so it seems.

The jobs I had as a kid thoroughly convinced me that I'd better go to college and learn a skill that didn't involve digging ditches or pushing wheelbarrows of wet cement up steep ramps. So what all those jobs taught me was what I did not want to do.

Even so, in 1958, I managed to get fired by the chairman of the board of one of America's 20 largest companies. Never mind that it was a mix-up and I was innocent as a lamb. But there I was in the lobby of the Royal York Hotel in Toronto, father of four young'uns and abruptly unemployed. I didn't even have bus fare home to Minneapolis.

Our group, including the chairman, was scheduled to meet for dinner that

"The pay may be pitifully meager, but the experience you gain is beyond price..."

evening. I decided to show up and see what would happen. No one mentioned me being fired, so I continued going to work for 3 more years. When I resigned, the chairman wrote me a fine letter of recommendation.

It was a useful lesson in why you shouldn't jump out of windows prematurely, and I subsequently had many occasions to draw upon it. That's the thing with jobs: You never can tell what they'll teach you.

Now find out why what follows is my favorite chapter. I'll bet it will even remind you of some experiences of your own years ago.   —*Clancy Strock*

Hair-Raising Ride Recalled

"Tunnel of Horrors" riders got more than they expected from a fill-in operator who knew less than he should.

By Robert Caulkins, Brunswick, Georgia

THE SUMMER OF 1950 was a scorcher in New England. Thousands of people from the Greater Boston area flocked to the beaches, and one of the favorites was Nantasket Beach, about 15 miles south of Boston.

Aside from the beautiful white sandy beach and cooling ocean breakers, people were drawn to Paragon Park, a massive amusement complex containing a midway with many rides and entertainment attractions and the largest roller coaster on the East Coast.

I was 16 years old and had landed a job at the park in the "Kiddie Park" section, which had a carousel, bumper cars, a railroad and a roller coaster scaled down for children under age 12.

I'd been working there about 2 weeks when a man came up to me and said he worked at the "Tunnel of Horrors" and wanted me to take over while he went to lunch. I thought he was some type of boss, so I went with him to the tunnel.

He briefly explained to me how to operate the ride and, pointing to the line of cars, said, "Don't use car 4. We're having trouble with it. Probably a short circuit or something."

Business Was Slow

He left for lunch, saying he'd be back in about an hour.

Because it was the noon hour and the temperature was extremely high, the majority of visitors were either at the beach, in the water or having lunch in a shaded picnic area or restaurant.

Shortly before the regular operator was to return, a man and his son handed me two ride tickets. They went to the first car in line, got in and pulled the metal safety bar toward themselves, snapping it into place.

At the console, I pushed a level, which caused the chain drive mechanism to pull the car forward to the point where

"The father was wide-eyed and obviously very angry..."

the electrical system would take over and run the car through two large swinging doors into the "Tunnel of Horrors".

The car moved forward and the chain drive "handed over" the car to electrical power. Suddenly, large sparks began flying up from the metal safety bar. The father let out a yell as the car plunged through the two doors and began its trip through the tunnel.

As the doors closed, I saw a large numeral "4" on the back of the car. Car 4 was the one with the electrical short circuit!

I thought the operator had meant the fourth car in line!

As the car moved through the tunnel, I could faintly hear the father yelling. Several minutes later, the car came smashing through the two doors at the end of the ride. The father was wide-eyed and obviously very angry; and the safety bar was still sparking.

"There's something wrong with this car!" the man yelled. "We're being shocked."

The car rolled forward, came off electric power (the sparks stopped) and was picked up again by the chain for movement to the unloading point.

I was so petrified by the father's shouting that I neglected to push the brake lever. Now, to my helpless terror, I watched the father and son go right on by me and the unloading point.

The car again picked up electrical power, sparks once more began to fly and the car flew through the two large doors to begin another trip through the tunnel.

The father yelled, "No, no, stop this thing! I'm going to..." The rest was made incoherent as the two doors swung closed.

Knowing that when they came out again, the father would certainly come after me, I was just about to abandon my position when the regular operator appeared. I left, saying nothing about the customers who were sparking their way through the tunnel.

I left Paragon Park, went home and never returned. My father picked up my paycheck.

63 Third Graders?

A class this large was enough to give a new teacher pause.

By Kathleen Voigt, Claysville, Pennsylvania

AS SOON as I graduated from high school in 1955, I started summer classes at college on the "teaching plan". After 2 full summers and 1 regular academic year, which was equivalent to 2 years of college, I began my teaching career at the tender age of 19.

My assignment at St. Jerome School in Charleroi, Pennsylvania was a class of 63 third graders—all day, every day, for all subjects, including music and art.

I was supposed to work separately with three reading groups twice a day. Realistically, I was lucky if I saw each group once. In the meantime, the rest of the class had other assignments to work on independently.

Every Friday there was a spelling test, so I had 63 papers to correct over the weekend. I was dating my future husband, and he usually helped. Sometimes we went to school on weekends and decorated bulletin boards together.

One little boy in my class was definitely hyperactive, although that condition hadn't been identified in the 1950s. One afternoon I took the class down the block for a special activity, and this boy didn't want to go. I had to carry him under my arm with the other 62 children following behind us.

One rainy morning, one of the girls came to school with soaking wet shoes. I lent her an extra pair of my shoes, which seemed to fit her quite well. As I recall, we were about the same height.

Since I was only 19 and looked even younger, the principal decided that I should wear my hair pulled back in a bun. I don't think it really made me look any older, though. In the photo (above), I'm in the back row at far left.

The school was about 10 miles from my home and since I didn't drive, and public transportation wasn't feasible, my mother took me to work each day. The bus ride home took more than an hour because it followed a roundabout route through several small towns and back and forth across the Monongahela River.

The 1956-57 school year was quite an initiation into a teaching career, which I resumed in 1967. It took me 10 years to recover from the first experience, but it made the later years seem easy by comparison. ❮

She Rose Through the Ranks the Hard Way

DURING WORLD WAR II, I wanted to be an Army or Navy nurse. Regrettably, the military frowned on accepting 13-year-olds.

In 1949, I enlisted in a Marine Corps Reserve that included women to see if I liked it before doing anything drastic like enlisting for active duty.

In 1950, after the United States became involved in Korea, I called my reserve platoon captain to see if there was any information about being called to active duty.

"Yes," she said, pausing, "On August 7, you're being sent to the Marine Corps Supply Depot in San Francisco, PFC Lee."

I was elated! I certainly wasn't happy that my going on active duty was precipitated by a war, but I could hardly wait.

I had the best of all the military occupational specialties that Women Marines of that time were allowed to have—administration. While not exciting, it wasn't restrictive; administrative clerks were used at *all* Marine Corps stations.

I was commissioned a second lieutenant in 1957. Later, as a first lieutenant, I received something I had never seen before—orders in French and English to report to a NATO office in London, England!

As a captain, I was the first female Marine officer to receive upper-level officer training—at a *WAC* school. Women Marines didn't attend Marine Corps schools of higher leadership training then. A few years later, after several other women officers attended the WAC schools, we were finally allowed into the Corps' leadership schools. We had arrived!

Although not all of my stations were exciting, I thoroughly enjoyed my 24 years of active duty and wouldn't trade those years for anything. Being at the right place at the right time seems to have been the story of my career.

—*Lt. Col. Bobbie Lee USMC (Ret.), Napa, California*

BREAK TIME. Bobbie Lee (left) was a Marine Corps sergeant in 1954 when this picture was taken. To her left is June "Dobbie" Doberstein, also a Marine sergeant.

How Sweet It Was!

When Mama worked at a Chunky factory in 1951, the paycheck wasn't the only benefit.

By Naomi Plisky, Las Vegas, Nevada

OF COURSE, SHE WAS SMILING. Surrounded by the Chunky bars she wrapped, the author's mother had a dream job. When the new wrapping machines came in, she really had to hustle.

THE YEAR 1951 was memorable for me. It was the year I started school, but it also was the year that Mama started a job that was the envy of all my friends—she began work as a wrapper of Chunky chocolates.

Mama wrapped Chunkys, then called "Little Chunkys", although they were three times larger than they are now, in a factory on the Lower East Side of Manhattan.

She was an expert at it as she reached into the metal vat filled with bare Chunkys and covered them with foil. The more she foiled, the bigger the paycheck.

She earned 3¢ per Chunky. There were 30 Chunkys in a box, which took about an hour to wrap, translating into 90¢ an hour. Big bucks for those days!

The chocolate was mixed in a big tub in a room that was kept very cold so the chocolate wouldn't melt. Mama's knitting skills came in handy as she kept a heavy homemade sweater over her shoulders while she sat on her high stool.

The finished products were stacked in metal tins, much like a pyramid. Mama recalls many battles among her co-workers over who grabbed the candies first, for there were many times when the supply was depleted, leaving no work for some.

I remember unwrapped Chunkys being everywhere around our house, and I renamed them "Chunks" because of their size. I suspect Mama gave back a good portion of what she earned when the owner, Mr. Silverstein, offered discounts every Friday. He was a round, jovial man who I thought was Santa Claus!

Only recently has Mama admitted that Chunkys often served as breakfast for her when she had to get me to school and she had no time to eat before going to her job. (This had been a well-guarded secret. After all, mothers *must* set a good example, right?)

Subsequently, machines were acquired that wrapped the Chunkys, and Mama had to work *fast* to keep up with the machine and catch the wrapped candies before they fell.

She said it was just like the classic episode of *I Love Lucy* where Lucy is working in a candy factory and stuffs the candy in her pockets, blouse, mouth…everywhere just to keep up with the machine.

Chunkys are still Mama's favorite candy, although she thinks they're not deserving of that name anymore since the size has diminished considerably.

THE CHUNKY BAR was introduced in the mid-1930s in New York by Phil Silverstein, who named it after his then-"chunky" baby granddaughter. The Chunky bar was acquired by Nestlé in 1984.

Job in Candy Department Holds Sweet Memories

BACK IN THE early '50s, I went to work for G.C. Murphy's in Princeton, West Virginia.

I was 16 years old and started out in the toy department. I can still hear Johnnie Ray singing *Cry* over the PA system.

Soon I got the job I really wanted—working in the candy department. We wore white starched pinafore uniforms with clean white shiny shoes and really thought we were hot stuff.

G.C. Murphy's is long gone, but my days working there will live on as one of the happiest times of my life. I can still hear the music and smell the Evening in Paris perfume and the old-fashioned candy.

—*Betty French Hughes*
Rogers City, Michigan

PROUD AS A PEACOCK. Author received this commemorative photo when she made a return visit to NBC headquarters in New York. She's in her 1950s guide uniform at left.

NBC Guide Got a Rare View of Early TV World

By Eleanor Michael Henry, St. Petersburg, Florida

IN THE FALL of 1951, I auditioned as a singer for the Talent Development Division of the National Broadcasting Company, which was located in the RCA Building, 30 Rockefeller Plaza, New York City.

As a result, I joined the guide staff in Guest Relations. This was a talented and ambitious group of young people—actors and singers interested in some phase of the entertainment field. They included Bill Dana (José Jiminez), Kate Jackson, Eva Marie Saint, Regis Philbin and others.

In addition to leading tours through the radio and television studios, we received numerous benefits, such as attending workshops, being able to use recording studios and getting tickets to important shows and concerts of that time, including the NBC Symphony with Arturo Toscanini conducting, the Firestone Hour, the Telephone Hour and

The Big Party, which was hosted by Tallulah Bankhead.

When the *Today* show debuted on Jan. 14, 1952, plate-glass windows looking out onto the street gave the audience a full view of the studio. Quite an innovation at that time!

Dave Garroway was the show's first host. Originally he had been supervisor of the guides and guidettes in the tour division. This was the same position I advanced to a few years later.

I stayed with NBC until my marriage in 1955. I returned to visit many times over the years, especially for NBC's 50th anniversary in 1983 and in March 2000, when they gave me a complimentary tour of the radio and TV studios and took my picture.

Truly it was a reminiscing highlight!

'Man in the Hall!'

Working as a janitor in a girls' dorm put him in an enviable situation.

By Jerry Minson, Honolulu, Hawaii

I WAS 17 years old in 1950, a senior at Brigham Young University High School in Provo, Utah. To put myself through school, I worked 6 hours a day at the newly built Campus Hall, the first girls' dormitory built on the BYU campus after World War II.

The dorm had four floors with 20 rooms per floor. Because of a housing shortage then, four girls shared a room for a total of 320 girls. Each room had two sets of bunk beds, a study

A LOT TO GRIN ABOUT. Author put himself through high school working as a janitor at a girls' dormitory on the campus of Brigham Young University.

table, two dressers, two small closets and a sink. There were communal shower and toilet facilities on each floor.

Most of the girls were juniors or seniors. Because they were a few years older than me, I looked upon them as my big sisters.

Early "Maintenance Engineer"

My duties including hosing the dirt off the sidewalks during good weather and shoveling the snow in winter. Cleaning the larger dining room also was my responsibility. I had to get up at 3:30 a.m. each morning to clean it before the girls came to breakfast.

But the best part of my job was working in the area where the girls lived. I was the only boy allowed on the residence floors. Now the job would be called "maintenance engineer", but in those days it was just plain janitor.

I swept, mopped and waxed floors and emptied trash cans from the hall closets. I repaired drapery cords, door and window locks, holes in the walls and other minor things that needed fixing.

I also would lend a strong hand whenever one of the girls needed something taken from or to the storage room in the basement. This was quite often, as they had very little storage space in their rooms.

When I went onto the floors, I was told by the housemother to yell, "Man in the hall!" That was supposed to give the girls time to be properly attired or to close the door to their room. However, I soon found out that yelling "Man in the hall!" brought them out of their rooms to visit or playfully pull me into their room.

Like a Little Brother

I was the little brother who listened to their troubles, gave (but mostly received) advice or helped them get a date with my friends. At times it was difficult to get my work done with all these distractions, but I loved every minute of it.

My starting wage was 25¢ an hour. There were no benefits as most jobs have today. The benefits I did receive went far beyond the monetary compensation. I literally made hundreds of friends in the 3 years I worked there…and I was certainly the envy of the male students.

I am now retired from a very satisfying career in health care, but that job in the girls' dorm in the early '50s is certainly the most memorable of any I have ever had.

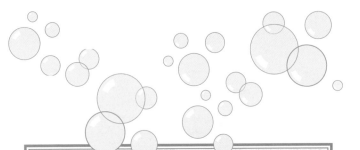

Job Was Fun, But Sneezing Was a No-No

MY MOST MEMORABLE JOB was working in a bubble bath factory in Glendale, California in 1958.

There were 10 or 11 of us, all girls except one guy, from three different high schools in the area. Each of us was assigned to a position, and a different bubble bath fragrance, along the conveyor belt.

The person at the beginning had the bottom of the box. When the belt started, we placed a package of bubble bath in the box. The person at the end of the line put the lid on the box.

We had to pay close attention and not goof around, or the boxes would pile into each other and the bubble bath packages would fly out.

If we so much as sneezed, our supervisor would not keep us because we might be allergic to the powder and fumes.

Still, it was a fun job for high school kids after school. —*Margie Boudinot, Burbank, California*

Nursing School Was Real Work

Classes and hospital shifts went on 11 months a year during intense 3-year program.

By Disca Ann Kovar, Liberty, Missouri

ANGELS OF MERCY. Author (top row, far right) graduated April 1, 1953 as a registered nurse from the Research Hospital School of Nursing in Kansas City, Missouri.

IMPORTANT '50s memories for me include my marriage and the birth of my first daughter, but another has to be my 3 years as a nursing student in Kansas City, Missouri.

Fresh out of high school in 1950, I entered the Research Hospital School of Nursing. Estimated cost of the 3-year program was $245.20. Uniforms during those years were provided by the hospital, but duty shoes and other incidentals were not—those are what added to the cost.

We went to school 11 months a year, working hospital shifts and attending school at the same time. We had clinical rotations in pharmacy as well as emergency, operating room, dietary, psychiatric nursing, pediatrics, surgery and central supply. Smoking was not allowed, engagements were frowned upon and marriage was a definite no-no.

Wasn't Gleeful About Club Choice

We had a mandatory study hour, and room checks were done periodically. We had to participate in an extracurricular activity, but the only one available for me was glee club. I could not and still cannot carry a tune. Fortunately the director recognized this and suggested I just move my mouth when we entertained groups.

At the hospital, narcotics were administered after melt-ing the tablets in water in a spoon over a burner. Some tablets burned dry, and then we had to start over again.

Syringes were glass and cleaned by the central supply department on a mechanical device. Students in central supply usually were assigned to needle sharpening, cleaning and tubing. Surgery packs were prepared individually for each scheduled case. Rubber gloves were washed, dried on racks, powdered, packaged and sterilized.

Hot moist packs, called "stupes", were boiled in an open pan—also boiling dry frequently—then wrung out with two broomstick handles.

Operating rooms were set up early in the morning for the day. Students usually set up the back table and

> *"Engagements were frowned upon and marriage was a definite no-no..."*

handed sterilized items to the scrub nurse, who was at the operating table.

There were no prepared dietary supplements. We mixed tube feeding that included strained baby foods, milk, raw eggs and whatever else was deemed nutritious. Baby formula was mixed in the dietary department, too.

New mothers were flat in bed the first 3 days after delivery. Their head could be elevated the fifth day, and most could be helped to the bathroom on the fourth or fifth day. They usually went home on the seventh day.

Psychiatric nursing was archaic. Our experience was 13 weeks at a state hospital. Treatments included iced wet sheet packs, insulin shock therapy, electric shock therapy and soothing tubs. The use of drugs for treatment was just beginning in 1952 and '53.

We were required to attend six autopsies as students. While not a favorite activity, it did help us learn a lot about anatomy.

Practiced on Themselves

In nursing arts, the actual practice of certain procedures, we practiced on each other. There was no mannequin.

Our isolation experience was at Kansas City General Hospital and consisted primarily of working with polio victims and the many iron lungs in use. It was a terrible disease, and I remember the fear of it spreading during the heat of summer.

Those nursing school years were hard, and treatments and drugs were primitive by today's standards, although patients were treated with dignity and respect.

I went on to work as a nursing supervisor until 1995 and helped open new hospitals in North Kansas City and Liberty, Missouri.

When I graduated in 1953, I worked the 3-to-11 shift and earned about 85¢ an hour. Obviously I didn't enter the nursing profession to get rich.

BE PREPARED. Girl Scouts in Rosemary Baker's troop earned badges by camping (top) and working on pottery (above; the woman at the pottery table is unidentified).

Leading Girl Scout Troop Was a Pleasure, Not a Job

MY MOST MEMORABLE and pleasurable job in the '50s was being a Girl Scout leader for 7 years—2 years in Barstow, Illinois and 5 in Le Claire, Iowa.

I never had a daughter, so the girls quickly became members of the family.

Each one was a joy to work with and we had such fun together. We explored the outdoors with camping trips at Apple River State Park in Illinois and even spent 2 weeks camping in Ontario, Canada. During one camp out, we slept on straw in our tents. We also visited nursing homes, the Dickson Indian Mounds in Illinois and the Lincoln shrines in Springfield.

The troop earned the Curved Bar award, the highest in Girl Scouting. With my husband and his Boy Scout troop, we created a park in Le Claire, named Scout Park in our honor. That project won an award from *Parents* magazine.

I loved my years as a leader and would do it all over again in a minute!
—*Rosemary Baker*
Le Claire, Iowa

He Went to Work Every Day and Took the Heat

DURING THE '50s, I worked for U.S. Steel, now USX Corp., in Ellwood City, Pennsylvania. I endured a lot of unpleasant jobs, but the worst was working in the bar mill.

Ingots of steel were heated to somewhere around 2,000° before they came out of the furnaces. These were rolled down on a steel table and had to be held back with long iron hooks by two men.

The heat was so intense that the men who worked in this part of the mill had to wear long underwear under several layers of clothes to work—even in hot summers.

We also had special protective clothing that was required. We wore leather aprons and vests, full face shields of wire mesh and Plexiglas, plus a hard hat. Our leather shoes had steel toes and a special fiberglass shield over that. We also wore long leather gloves. All these things helped to keep us from burning.

It certainly was not the best job I ever had, but it was the hottest.
—*Al Schuller, Orangevale, California*

Bingo! Amusement Park Had His Number in Summer

IT'S EASY TO REMEMBER my favorite job in the 1950s—it's the only one I had. I worked at Rolling Green Park, a great little amusement park between Sunbury and Selinsgrove, Pennsylvania.

My job was working at Jones' Bingo, starting in April and continuing until late September, when the park closed for winter with a Sadie Hawkins Day celebration. I collected the customers' money, called the numbers and checked the number of players at each counter.

Those were great years. I was paid 80¢ an hour the first year, then 90¢ and finished my third year at $1 an hour. That was a lot of money in those days.

Bingo didn't open until 6 p.m., so we lazed through our afternoons at the park's Crystal Pool. After the bingo games closed, we sometimes crawled over the fence for a midnight dip. What a way to spend summer!
—*Terry Shaffer*
Indianapolis, Indiana

BAKED IN ALASKA. "When I arrived in Alaska in 1952 from Cass Lake, Minnesota with my sister and brother-in-law, my first job was at the Fairbanks Bakery," notes Jeannette Tessore (above) of Anchorage. "I worked the graveyard shift for 3 years, but I have many good memories. We made a considerable amount of baked goods, including beautiful eclairs and jelly rolls. Many of our products were flown to remote villages as well as military bases, restaurants and grocery stores. That's my sister with the doughnut eyes (right)."

Complaints About This Food Sounded Like a Soap Opera

I WAS A WAITRESS at the Boston Cafe in Faribault, Minnesota in the '50s when we had a rash of complaints about our otherwise delicious food.

This particular evening, we were very busy, so the steak sauce and ketchup bottles were left on the tables.

I had served hamburgers, fries and chili to one booth. When I returned, everyone complained about their food, so I took all the orders back to the kitchen and brought out new ones.

Moments later, I was called back to the booth with more complaints about the flavor of the food.

The cook, who was very embarrassed, came out and talked to the customers. One of them asked the cook to try his fries, so he did but found nothing wrong. He noticed, however, that the diners were using ketchup, although he hadn't tasted the fries with ketchup on them.

It didn't take long to realize that their ketchup bottle had been tampered with.

We quickly went around to all the tables and removed the ketchup and steak sauce bottles. Sure enough, others had been tampered with, too. We discovered someone had emptied liquid dish soap into the bottles—apparently from a sample that some company had sent out.

The cook apologized to the customers, and another set of new orders was brought out—along with a new bottle of ketchup. This time, everyone enjoyed their food.

After that, we didn't leave ketchup bottles on the tables for mischief, only bringing them out when requested by customers.
 —*Myrtle Durand, Faribault, Minnesota*

They Called Him "Sugar Daddy Dave"

DURING THE SUMMER of 1955, between my junior and senior years of high school, I happened to travel from my small northern-Arizona town to Southern California for a visit with an aunt.

I met a friend who was meeting his girlfriend and a blind date. The father of one of the girls needed workers at his plant in East Los Angeles.

It turned out that his employer was Welch's Candy Company, maker of the famous Sugar Daddy suckers and other sweet delights.

With a slight fib about our ages, we were hired. I became a candy cutter and my buddy was a box boy. Driving on the freeway each morning in our $35 car, we arrived to the aroma of boiling caramel. That was fantastic.

We spent the evenings at Huntington Beach, meeting girls and enjoying the Southern California drive-ins. I became known as "Sugar Daddy Dave".
 —*Dave Will
Porterville, California*

The Show Biz Bug Bit Her

For a teenager in 1952, the chance to work with stars of the stage and silver screen was heavenly.

By June Spear, Auburn, Maine

FOR ME, the Fabulous '50s was a memorable decade. I lived in Natick, Massachusetts, 20 miles west of Boston. During those years, I graduated from high school and college and embarked upon a career in education.

Those were momentous events to be sure, but the most exciting thing happened in the summer of 1952, when I became an apprentice at The County Playhouse, an affiliate of the Boston Summer Theater, in nearby Framingham.

For a starstruck 17-year-old, this was a dream come true. Producers Al Capp and Lee Falk promised to bring a new group of professional actors to town each weekend to perform a variety of shows.

Each cast was headed by one or two famous actors with other professionals as supporting actors. My job, as apprentice, required long hours, physical stamina and the willingness to do anything that was asked of us.

What an exciting summer it was! I helped build sets and make costumes and props. I went to local businesses to borrow everything from furniture to ice buckets, depending on the requirements of that weekend's show. I helped put up and knock down sets, saw to it that dressing rooms were stocked with whatever the stars requested and made sure props were in place.

Each show was in town only 1 week, so before one show was over, we were beginning preparations for the next one. Our day began before 8 a.m. and ended after the evening

> "Walter Matthau joined us
> for a swim and boat ride..."

performance was over and the stage and backstage area were ready for the next evening's show.

There was no pay, but lots of invaluable experience.

The season opened with Melvyn Douglas in *Season with Ginger*, followed by Edward Everett Horton, Arthur Maxwell, Juliana Larson and a large Broadway cast performing *Kiss Me Kate*.

The incomparable Mae West starred in *Come On Up… Ring Twice*. She arrived in a bulletproof limousine with chauffeur and bodyguards and was rather aloof. However, at the end of the week, she left money as a tip to be divided among the backstage crew. She was the only star to do that.

Veronica Lake appeared in *Gramercy Ghost*, and Dana Andrews and Mary Todd co-starred in *The Glass Menagerie*. The role of the gentleman caller was played by a relative newcomer, Walter Matthau.

He was very friendly and lots of fun. One hot day, we had a short break between the matinee and evening performances. Walter joined another apprentice and me for a swim and boat ride at her home.

Claude Rains arrived next to star in *Jezebel's Husband*, set in Zebulon in 731 B.C. That was the highlight of the summer as I appeared as an Assyrian sightseer. I had no lines and was on stage for less than 5 minutes. But I was paid Equity scale for the week—$41!

The next show, *One Touch of Venus*, starred Carol Bruce. I again had a walk-on part and earned another $41. The season ended after performances of *The Desert Song* and *The Happy Time*.

What a memorable summer for a teenager! To be immersed in the world of show business and meet so many interesting people was a priceless experience. For me, it will always be a fine memory of the Fabulous '50s.

WALT DISNEY and Mickey (above) were on top of the world in 1955. So was the author (below right, then and now) after he first met his hero at the Disney studio in Burbank, California.

This Country Bumpkin Found the Magic Kingdom

By Charles Grizzle, Spokane, Washington

I WAS a 19-year-old country bumpkin in the fall of 1955 when I set out from my home in Indiana in an old Dodge to see the world and find my fortune. I never dreamed that within a few weeks, Walt Disney would be my boss.

I worked my way west. Although I disliked big cities, Los Angeles beckoned, and I wound up applying for jobs there. Walt Disney Studio in Burbank needed another traffic boy and I was hired.

My salary of $45 a week was small potatoes even for that day, but I wanted to see some stars. So I began carrying sacks of mail to movie producers, animators, songwriters and craftsmen of all types.

I discovered that as a traffic boy, I could go anywhere in this magical moviemaking kingdom. I met Roy Disney, Walt's brother, and actors Fess Parker, Jeffrey Hunter and Buddy Ebsen. But I'll never forget the day I met Walt.

On this day, as menial as my task may have been, I felt I was a part of Hollywood.

"Be careful," the head chef implored. "Not only is it valuable, it's late. The producers are having a big party and I promised to get this to them. Watch out for the bumps."

I was hauling a huge bowl of seafood. I pulled a rickety mail cart with my precious cargo down Mickey Avenue and past Dopey Drive. A gardener laughed and scratched his head. Artists opened their windows and called out for samples. I waved but concentrated on my teetering load.

Load Was Precarious

Kitchen workers had heaped one of those fancy serving vessels—smaller at the bottom than at the top—full of shrimp, clams and oysters. They had loaded the bowl above the rim, making it top-heavy.

The chef thought I should carry it in my arms, but I knew I'd never make it to the Studio Penthouse without a cart. Negotiating the double doors at the west ramp to the Animation Building almost resulted in disaster. Bump, bump, bump and the bowl rocked precariously. I began to perspire.

Finally on the elevator, I breathed easier. Then the doors opened and in stepped the major hero of my short life.

My heart began thumping. I had hoped simply to catch a glimpse of Walt Disney sometime, yet here he stood 2 feet away. He looked at me, then smiled at my cargo.

"You new?" he asked.

"Yes, sir."

"That's quite a traffic run."

"Yes, sir."

Pretending he was actually going to do it, he asked, "What do you suppose they would say if I helped myself to a handful of shrimp?"

I laughed nervously.

"Well," I replied, "when they learned it was you, they probably wouldn't say anything."

He exited with a humorous snort. I stood there holding my breath until the doors closed. Then I did my own version of a victory dance, taking care not to bump the bowl.

That was him. Unbelievable! I wonder if I'll ever see him again.

Before leaving work that evening, I had the answer.

Another Brush with Walt

That very afternoon, I delivered a rush memo to Mr. Disney's office. He looked at me with a deadpan expression as I handed the envelope to his secretary.

"No shrimp?" he asked, almost in consternation. My heart jumped again.

"No, sir," I said, backing away, "but I can get some for you." The secretary laughed. Mr. Disney waved me off.

That was the beginning of my career with Walt Disney Productions. I got used to the big city, and during my 12 years with Disney, I became a senior publicist and product development manager.

It was the start of a 25-year association with many incredibly talented people who made Hollywood tick in the '50s, '60s and '70s. ◄

Theater Offered Her First Real Job...and More

By Doreen Scott, Staples, Minnesota

IT WAS 1950 when my uncle put in a good word for me and I was hired to sell tickets at the theater in Staples, Minnesota. Having just turned 16, I was thrilled at the prospect of having a real job instead of relying on sporadic baby-sitting jobs, which only paid 10¢ an hour.

My new haven was the glass-enclosed box office, where I worked from 6 to 10 p.m. 7 days a week and collected a weekly paycheck of $12.50.

Weekends were exceptionally busy because we ran Saturday morning cartoons—kiddies could watch Tom and Jerry or Bugs Bunny for 10¢ while their parents enjoyed a 2-hour break.

The balcony, nicknamed the "passion pit" by the theater staff, opened at 2 p.m. for the matinee. Under the watchful eye of Alvin, the usher, young folks held hands and sometimes stole a kiss while Roy Rogers and "Trigger" solved the problems of the West.

At dusk, the glowing marquee welcomed folks standing in line to purchase a 50-cent ticket to carry them to worlds and adventures far beyond the city limits of our small Midwestern railroad town.

Popcorn Was Hard to Resist

While being ushered to their seats, few patrons could resist the aroma of freshly popped popcorn. It was more of a treat than it is now, and the introduction of hot buttered popcorn was an immediate hit. Extra fluffy white popcorn, topped with two generous squirts of hot golden butter and accompanied by a good supply of napkins, cost 25¢.

Promptly at 7 p.m., Hjalmer, the theater manager, called "Lights!" and immediately the houselights dimmed and silence reigned. "Curtain!" was the next command, and as if by magic, the elegant blue curtain slowly opened to reveal the silver screen.

Patrons were mesmerized for 2 hours while being swept into the worldly adventures, heartaches and humor created by MGM, RKO and Paramount Pictures.

At 9 p.m., Hjalmer appeared out of nowhere and stood at his post in the lobby as the moviegoers exited. His question never changed, "Did you enjoy the feature, folks?"

Their replies, and my ticket sales, told him if the movie was a hit or a miss.

There were no fringe benefits at the Staples Theater in 1950—no 401(k), vacations, overtime, sick days, health coverage, Christmas bonuses or parties. But I received a fringe benefit that lasted a lifetime.

Met Her Mate at the Movies

A tall, handsome man came to the movies at every change of the marquee. He started our relationship by saying "Hi" as he purchased his ticket. After a few months, he offered me a ride home in his dad's shiny 1948 Chevrolet. We were married and spent 39 years together until his death.

The Staples Theater eventually succumbed to the popular drive-in theaters and ever-improving television.

After several decades, an enterprising couple brought family entertainment back to our small town. I found myself once again at the Staples Theater, this time with my granddaughter to see *Titanic*. The refurbished marquee issued a warm welcome, the aroma of freshly popped popcorn filled the lobby and the familiar blue houselights cast a soft glow over the auditorium.

As my granddaughter swooned over Leonardo DiCaprio, my thoughts wandered back to 1950—a simpler time, my first job and my first and only love. ❦

TWO, PLEASE. When the author began selling tickets at the local theater in Staples, Minnesota, there were no sick days or bonuses, but one fringe benefit was a keeper.

He Loved His Jobs as a Jerk and a Caddy

AS A TEENAGER in the early 1950s, I actually had two memorable jobs in my hometown, Pittsburgh, Pennsylvania. The first was when I worked at a drugstore. I ran the soda fountain and drove a canvas-top Jeep, delivering prescriptions and anything else our customers ordered.

My customers included H.J. Heinz and his brother, whose mansions were up on a hill across Fifth Avenue from the drugstore.

Another memorable job was caddying at an exclusive country club. I'd thumb a ride to and from work.

One day, a big green Cadillac pulled up to offer a ride. It was Sam Snead. He had been playing at the club that day. What a nice man. I also got to see Jack Dempsey and Bing Crosby.

The first person I ever caddied for was Don Cherry, who later became a famous singer. At the time I met him, he was working in the clubhouse cleaning clubs. He let me caddy for him so he could teach me what I needed to do to be a good caddy. —*John McKeown Daphne, Alabama*

Her Root Beer Floats Stood Apart

By Janet Packard, Lakewood, Colorado

MY GRANDPARENTS, known as Mom and Pop, moved to the Colorado countryside, north of Denver, in the late 1940s. At Grandma's insistence, my grandpa and stepdad built a roadside stand, called "Mom's Jelly Shack", on the main highway to Boulder. Then my grandma and mother filled it with their homemade pickles, relishes, jellies and jams.

I was the 12-year-old root beer taster. First I'd dip a scoop of creamy Meadow Gold ice cream into my frosty mug. Then I'd pull the spigot on the keg and add some Hires R-J Root Beer, made from roots, bark, herbs and carbonated water. I learned when to stop so the bubbles wouldn't run over.

Because the stand did a brisk business, Mom talked Pop into expanding. They had a restaurant built and called it "Mom's Pantry". Grandma, in her white crinkly nylon dress and Mother Hubbard apron, cooked homemade breakfasts, lunches and dinners.

Pop Waited on Tables

With Pop's wholesale connections, he purchased ingredients. Wearing a white short-sleeved shirt and trousers held up by suspenders, he washed dishes and waited on tables. When Mom and Pop needed help, they rang a buzzer for my mother, who conveniently lived close by.

In the early '50s, my parents, brother and I moved to Southern California. I missed my friends in Colorado, so after a year, Mother sent me back to help in the cafe. It was the summer of 1953, and I was 15.

I preferred socializing and riding around in a convertible

ROOT BEER ROOTS. Author's grandparents (above) ran a successful food stand in the '50s near Denver. When the homemade items at Mom's Jelly Shack were a hit, they opened a restaurant called Mom's Pantry. Root beer floats, the author's specialty, were popular at both places.

to waiting on customers. After the noon rush ended, I'd comfort myself by making a frothy root beer float. From the keg, I'd pour just the right amount of root beer to flavor the ice cream. I'd pay for my 15-cent float with my tip money, but I'm sure I ate more than one scoop of ice cream.

When a turnpike was built, traffic bypassed the restaurant. My grandparents retired to Southern California. Their old neighbors missed Mom's great cooking, and I missed those made-to-order root beer floats.

Years later, as I raised my family, I made a tradition of my favorite comfort food. Today root beer floats are still served at our family gatherings. Of course, the root beer recipe is different and the soda comes in plastic bottles.

Things are never as good as in the good old days.

Chapter Five
Atomic Headlines

Atomic Headlines

IN THE '50s, for the first time in our country's history, there was a very real threat of not just enemy attack, not just devastating destruction, but total obliteration. Huge cities could be flattened and empty of life, just like the pictures we had seen of Hiroshima and Nagasaki.

Sure, there had been a fair amount of concern early in World War II about enemy attacks by air or sea. We had our volunteer coast watchers and air raid wardens on the lookout for enemy raiders.

Some of the concern was justified. The night skies up and down the Atlantic seaboard often were bright with the fires of burning oil tankers sunk by German submarines. But the diligent air raid war-

"The tests were blamed for every patch of unseasonable weather..."

dens craned their heads upward for 4 years without ever spotting a single Zero or Messerschmitt.

But now two big, bad new elements were in the picture. First, Russia possessed hydrogen bombs. And overhead whizzed a Russian satellite capable of heaven only knew what. The idea of bombs bursting over Omaha or Dallas or Walla Walla took some getting used to.

It became a matter of perverse civic pride to claim your town was so important that it would be one of the first to be zapped. "Yes sir, the Rooskies have Happy Hollow right at the top of their target list. They know all about how critical those pitchforks we make would be in an all-out war."

"Duck and Cover"

Worst of all was the terror inflicted on our children. Prudence said we should prepare them to weather a nuclear attack. So even though deep down in our hearts we suspected the futility of it all, kids were drilled on "duck and cover" and other survival tricks. It scared them stiff.

That popular "Now I lay me down to sleep" bedtime prayer had new meaning...especially the part about, "If I should die before I wake."

The government continued its nuclear testing both in the western desert and also in the Pacific Ocean. The tests were blamed for every patch of unseasonable weather as well as grasshopper plagues, two-headed calves, tornadoes and high turnip prices.

On the good side, contractors had a brief period of extra prosperity as they filled the demand for bomb shelters.

The one debate most likely to alienate even your oldest and dearest friends was whether or not you would let those who had no bomb shelter share the safety of yours. And to this day, there are those who still argue whether or not Harry Truman should have employed the A-bomb at all.

For more on the American mood during those worrisome days, read the memories that start on the next page.

—*Clancy Strock*

Atomic Bomb Tests Were in Her Backyard

In the '50s, the light shows were considered entertainment.

By Sally Mooney, Carson City, Nevada

OUT ON OUR RANCH, the "bomb" got blamed for everything from the drought to the hay baler breaking down.

The "bomb" was actually a series of aboveground nuclear bomb tests that began in 1951 just 100 miles, as the crow flies, from our ranch.

For a young teenage girl living on an isolated cattle ranch in eastern Nevada, the whole thing was very exciting. There had been times when my greatest pleasure had been seeing dust from a car 18 miles away, hoping it might stop at our ranch.

Now trucks were pulling into the yard on a regular basis, Many times, good-looking men in flannel shirts and straw hats were in them. The Atomic Energy Commission (AEC) was everywhere those summers, testing water and soil.

They usually showed up right after a bomb had been set off and visited with my father and hired men or any other people who were around the ranch. We wore small badges that they had given us, which measured the amount of radiation we had received.

Collected "Radiation Badges"

Each month, my dad collected all of our badges—his, my mom's, mine, my brothers' and one from each of the hired men. He then placed them in a special envelope and mailed them to the AEC.

Even more exciting, we would hear by way of our big battery-operated radio in the corner of the living room that a bomb would be set off at 4 a.m. a certain morning. We could get radio station KSL from Salt Lake City after dark, and as the testing got into full swing, the AEC began announcing the time of the tests.

Dad would set the alarm and wake us up before making a pot of coffee. We'd get ourselves comfortably seated on porch chairs in the yard to wait for the big event as though it were a Fourth of July fireworks display.

Soon, we would see an enormous flash, and the entire southwest sky would light up. We'd have to look away for a

SPECTACULAR SHOW. Sally Mooney was in her early teens, living on an eastern-Nevada cattle ranch, when she and her family gathered in their yard in the predawn hours to watch nuclear tests.

> *"We'd see a tremendous flash, and the entire southwest sky would light up..."*

few seconds. The smoke and dust rose slowly into a column, *then formed a huge mushroom cloud.*

That sight, just at daybreak, was spectacular. We never missed a bomb if we could help it.

During the early '50s, some of the ranchers questioned the threat of nuclear fallout from the bombs. The men from the AEC who came around were pleasant and willing to answer our questions.

"You are, in a very real sense, active participants in the nation's atomic test program," they told us. "Those tests are contributing greatly to building the defenses of our own country and the rest of the free world."

At times, we were told, some of us had been exposed to potential risk from flash, blast or fallout. But we accepted that risk without fuss, alarm or panic. They tried to keep fallout to the absolute minimum, and we felt the dangers were a small sacrifice when compared to preventing the use of nuclear bombs in war.

The AEC made sure that they would never drop a bomb when the winds were blowing south toward Las Vegas. The wind would blow north and east, so the fallout would pass over sparsely populated areas, including ranches like ours.

Once, as we moved our cattle from the winter range, 25 miles south of the ranch, to the summer range in the mountains north of the ranch, a fallout cloud from an atomic test filled the sky.

My cousin's ranch at Hiko was near the small town of Alamo, just 40 miles from the test site. On occasion, the government sent evacuation vehicles there, in case the wind changed and came directly over them.

It's been 50 years since we watched the first mushroom clouds in the sky. They were entertainment then, but I still think about them today and wonder.

HOOKED ON FLYING. Author (in dark uniform) believes she was the first female Civil Air Patrol cadet in Kansas. This photo from 1951 shows her in her CAP unit in Hutchinson, Kansas, where she learned to fly an airplane, march and forecast weather.

Female Cadet Took Flight from Boredom

Her first CAP flight hooked her in 1950.

By Corrine Oliver Dale, Bay Point, California

I SEEMED TO BE at loose ends in 1950 while my fiance, Bill, was stationed in California in the Air Force. I was 17 and in Hutchinson, Kansas, going to high school and working in a five-and-dime store.

I tagged along with my stepbrother, Frank Raner, and his two buddies just about everywhere they went.

One evening they showed up at my house all excited. They had just joined a newly formed Civil Air Patrol cadet program and wanted me to join, too.

I became the first girl in the unit and, I believe, the first girl in Kansas to join the CAP.

A few weeks later, we attended a meeting in Wichita, and I was invited to fly back in the L4 trainer, newly acquired after being retired from Korea. The problem was my uniform was a skirt, and I wasn't sure how I was going to get in gracefully. All the men agreed to look the other way. What gentlemen!

It was my first flight, and I was hooked. We had weekly classes and learned about basic flying and weather. We all took turns getting in all the flying time we could.

Since I was the girl who had been in the unit the longest, I was appointed drill sergeant. I took the other girls out on the tarmac and we marched our hearts out. We were pretty good, too.

Bill, my stepbrother and our buddies are gone, but I still have good memories that fly me back to those exciting teenage experiences.

"Duck and Cover" Drills Frightened Young Girl

I REMEMBER the "duck and cover" drills we used to practice in school around 1950 in case of an enemy attack. The teachers also used to show us films on A-bomb destruction.

My mother told me our Duluth-Superior area was a prime target because of the shipping, iron mines and grain elevators.

That made me a very nervous child. I begged my parents to build a bomb shelter in the backyard, but, of course, they didn't.

I had a secret plan that if we were under attack, I would run across the street to one of the neighbors who had a basement. I don't know of anyone in the whole Duluth-Superior area who built a bomb shelter.

—*Janice Korpela, Cornucopia, Wisconsin*

They Celebrated Statehood with Horns And Conch Shells

Hawaii's admission to the United States in 1959 was a joyous event.

By Jeanne Price, Naples, Florida

Hawaii's state flag

ON MARCH 12, 1959, our Navy family was stationed in Hawaii. Our home overlooked Pearl Harbor and the entire southern coast of Oahu.

My husband, Walt, was on duty at the submarine base, where he was commander of a division of submarines. Our two children, Winn and John, were attending school.

I was glued to the radio, waiting for word that Congress had passed the bill to give Hawaii the statehood it had so long deserved after being a territory for 59 years.

The statehood bill had been approved by the Senate the night before. Suddenly newscasters shouted that the House of Representatives just approved their bill. Approval of the 50th state by President Eisenhower was assured.

The wail of the civil defense siren swept through the air. Every ship in Pearl Harbor and Honolulu Harbor blew its whistle. Motorists leaned heavily on their horns as church bells chimed.

An Island of Happy and Excited People

I ran out of the house and joined other Navy wives gathered on a hill. We added to the joyous noise by beating on pans, blowing horns and singing.

Fantastic sounds came to us from all sides and reverberated off the mountains. I never experienced such a celebration. There was no use trying to carry on a conversation; we just listened to an island of happy and excited people.

We had been told that when statehood was announced, all the children would be released from school and sent home by bus. The drivers were delighted to get rid of the students because they were yelling and screaming their excitement at being part of this historic day.

That night, there was dancing in marked-off streets and in shopping centers. All the musicians had offered to play free. Everyone was covered with flower leis. People were playing their ukuleles, blowing on conch shells and calling out greetings of "Aloha!" to friends and strangers.

Army planes dropped flares off Waikiki, and Navy ships fired flare ammunition. Fireworks lit up the sky for hours as rockets filled the skies. It was a day to remember!

President Eisenhower signed the statehood bill March 18, and the people of Hawaii had to vote for or against admission to the United States. In July, they voted for delegates to Congress, a state legislature and governor.

Hawaii is the only state in the Union made up entirely of islands and the only state with a royal palace, Iolani Palace, where Hawaiian royalty ruled an independent kingdom for many years.

When the state was formally admitted on August 21, 1959, the celebration began again. And we were there to remember it with a fond aloha.

PARTY TIME. Walt and Jeanne Price (top) celebrated after Hawaii's statehood was announced. Their son Winn (center) shows the banner headline reporting the event. Earlier photo (bottom) shows the Prices with Diamond Head in the background.

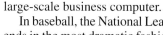

FOND FLASHBACKS...

Our lives went through dramatic changes during the Fabulous '50s. How many of these events do you recall?

1950

The end of World War II didn't bring an end to turmoil in the United States. The spread of Communism is alarming and Americans are concerned about the "Cold War", competition between the world's two superpowers, the Unit-

Everett Collection

PERFECT PAIR. "Lassie" and her master shared many adventures on their '50s TV show.

ed States and the Soviet Union.

Senator Joseph McCarthy creates a stir by claiming that Communists working in the U.S. State Department are shaping the country's foreign policy.

In mid-year, President Truman authorizes the use of American troops to repel the North Korean invasion of South Korea. Later, Communist China enters the "police action" supporting North Korea. Truman declares a national state of emergency, asking all Americans to join in the battle against "Communist imperialism".

In sports, Boston Red Sox star Ted Williams makes news when he signs on for the 1950 season with a record-breaking $125,000 contract. American Florence Chadwick breaks a 24-year-old record when she swims the English

The 1950s

Channel in 13 hours and 20 minutes.

TV's most widely watched hour is *The Milton Berle Show*, although the producers of *Kukla, Fran & Ollie*, a children's puppet show, are receiving 8,000 fan letters a week.

1951

Continued tensions in Korea are on everyone's minds as they worry about the possibility of another world war. After General Douglas MacArthur urges an attack on positions within China itself, President Truman relieves him of his command.

Back at home, mobster Frank Costello allows only his hands to be shown on TV as he testifies before the Senate Crimes Committee, investigating organized crime.

The Public Health Service reports fluoridation of water supplies greatly reduces tooth decay.

The U.S. Census Bureau purchases UNIVAC, the first commercially produced,

Brown Brothers

large-scale business computer.

In baseball, the National League race ends in the most dramatic fashion imaginable. Trailing the Brooklyn Dodgers by 13-1/2 games in August, the New York Giants, led by Willie Mays, rally to catch the Dodgers on the last day of the season.

During the third and final playoff game to determine the league champion, the Giants enter the ninth inning three runs behind. They get one run in and two men on base, then Bobby Thompson hits an electrifying home run to give them the pennant.

Entertainer Milton Berle is given much credit for television's increasing popularity and signs an unprecedented 30-year "seven-figure" contract with NBC, whether he works or not.

1952

As the presidential election approaches and the Cold War continues to intensify, debate focuses on which party can better lead the country. In the November election, Dwight Eisenhower and Richard Nixon, Republican nominees for President and Vice President, win.

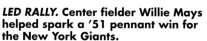

Before the election, Nixon was nearly thrown off the ticket because an $80,000 "slush fund" for him was discovered. He takes his case to the people, telling them he didn't use the money for personal expenses, but will keep a little dog named "Checkers" given to his daughter.

In New York City, new three-colored traffic lights—adding yellow—eliminate the annoying and dangerous 3-second delay between red and green lights.

Reports of unidentified flying ob-

LED RALLY. Center fielder Willie Mays helped spark a '51 pennant win for the New York Giants.

jects, or UFOs, continue to increase.

At the Indianapolis 500 auto race, Troy Ruttman becomes the youngest winner ever at age 22. His average speed of 128.9 mph sets a course record.

The New York Yankees defeat the Brooklyn Dodgers for a fourth consecutive World Series title.

A flop-eared, freckle-faced imp named Alfred E. Neumann makes his appearance in the first issue of *Mad* magazine.

Theatergoers flock to see *Bwana Devil*, the first motion picture in 3-D, and receive special glasses that bring the action up close.

1953

In Korea, a truce is signed at Panmunjom, formally ending the Korean War. The negotiations began in 1951 but were moved to a neutral site, called the Demilitarized Zone, between North and South Korea.

In events involving famous people, Dwight D. "Ike" Eisenhower (below) is inaugurated U.S. President, Elizabeth

II is crowned Queen of England, Dag Hammarskjöld is elected Secretary-General of the United Nations and Soviet leader Joseph Stalin dies.

Sir Edmund Hillary of New Zealand and Tenzing Norgay, a Nepalese Sherpa tribesman, become the first men to reach the summit of Mt. Everest and return. At 29,028 feet, it's the world's highest mountain.

Baseball phenom Mickey Mantle, a 21-year-old from Oklahoma, amazes

the sports world when he hits the longest home run ever—565 feet.

For the first time, the Academy Awards are shown on television.

POLIO FIGHTER. Dr. Jonas Salk found a vaccine that stopped a killer.

1954

Amid a continuing outbreak of childhood polio, massive field trials begin to test the effectiveness of Dr. Jonas Salk's polio vaccine on children. The vaccine works.

A postwar building boom continues and the New York Stock Exchange has its most active year since 1933.

The Navy adds two remarkable vessels to its fleet—the *Nautilus*, the world's first atomic-powered submarine, and the *Forrestal*, the largest warship ever built.

Transistor radios are becoming widely available, although the sound is reported as "tinny". The world's largest shopping mall, Northland Mall, opens in Detroit, Michigan with 100 stores.

A rookie named Hank Aaron breaks into the lineup with the Milwaukee Braves. He hits 13 home runs and bats

.280. In football, Philadelphia Eagles quarterback Adrian Burk establishes an all-time record by throwing for seven touchdowns in one game.

Roughly 29 million U.S. households have television sets. TV's two most popular shows are *I Love Lucy* and *Dragnet*. A three-part series on Davy Crockett

FUR FUN. Davy Crockett's TV appearance started a nationwide craze.

spurs the coonskin cap craze among children. The TV series *Lassie*, about a boy and his collie, debuts as do *People Are Funny* with Art Linkletter and *Father Knows Best*, with Robert Young making the transition from radio to TV.

1955

President Eisenhower suffers a heart attack, fueling speculation about his attempt to seek re-election the next year.

The New York Yankees win the first ↷

TRUE SPORTS CAR. Ford's Thunderbird competed with Chevy's Corvette for fans.

FAMILIAR FACES. TV series about cowboys became popular in the '50s. Chuck Connors (below) starred in *The Rifleman*. Dobie Gillis and his pal Maynard (center) lamented their lot in TV's *The Many Loves of Dobie Gillis*. Elvis Presley (right) took the country by storm with three hits.

Everett Collection

CBS-TV (courtesy Kobal)

SuperStock

two games against the Brooklyn Dodgers in the World Series. The Dodgers win the next three. The Yanks win the sixth game to tie the series, then Johnny Padres pitches a shutout to give the Dodgers their first world championship ever.

An estimated 65 million Americans watch *Peter Pan*, starring Mary Martin, as the show comes to TV fresh from a successful Broadway run.

1956

Congress authorizes the mammoth Federal Aid Highway Act, freeing $33 billion to build a 42,500-mile system of interstate highways.

Two luxury liners collide in dense fog off Nantucket Island in Massachusetts. The *Andrea Doria* sinks. Although 52 passengers die, 1,600 are rescued.

In November, President Eisenhower and Vice President Nixon defeat Democratic presidential and vice-presidential nominees Adlai Stevenson and Estes Kefauver, marking the first time in the

century that a Republican President has been elected to consecutive terms.

The biggest name in the news is a Memphis truck driver turned singer, Elvis Presley, who sells 75,000 records a day. Teens buy more than 10 million copies of his records, including *Don't Be Cruel*, *Heartbreak Hotel* and *Blue Suede Shoes*. Elvis appears on *The Ed Sullivan Show* as an estimated 54 million people—82.6% of the viewing public—watch.

In sports, boxer Rocky Marciano brings his incredible career to a close, retiring from the ring as the only undefeated world heavyweight champion in history.

In baseball, yes, it's the Yankees versus the Dodgers again in the World Series. Yankee pitcher Don Larsen uses a unique no-windup delivery to retire all 27 batters in the first perfect game in a World Series. New York goes on to win in seven games.

On Broadway, Eliza Doolittle of George Bernard Shaw's *Pygmalion* is

reborn as *My Fair Lady* with Julie Andrews in the title role.

Yul Brynner and Deborah Kerr delight movie audiences with their performances in *The King and I*. Robby the Robot and some neat special effects make *The Forbidden Planet* a movie success. Starring Leslie Nielsen, it's an updated version of Shakespeare's *The Tempest*.

Prince Rainier of Monaco and Hollywood star Grace Kelly marry; she becomes Princess Grace.

1957

A powerful and unusually early hurricane rips through Texas and Louisiana with winds of 105 mph and huge tidal waves. About 40,000 homes are destroyed, and because many ignore warnings, 550 people are killed.

Massachusetts Senator John F. Kennedy wins a Pulitzer Prize for his book, *Profiles in Courage*.

The Bridge on the River Kwai wins seven Oscars for its gripping story about British soldiers in a World War II Japanese prisoner camp. Adults and children alike leave the theater misty-eyed after watching *Old Yeller*.

Television viewers are enthralled by Charles Van Doren, a Columbia University professor who wins $129,000 on the TV quiz show *Twenty-One* before losing. Ten Western series premiere on television.

The Russians launch *Sputnik*, the first artificial satellite, then follow that feat by launching a satellite with a dog aboard.

American Motors causes a stir by introducing its Rambler, the first "compact" car.

The two best-selling children's books are by Dr. Seuss, *The Cat in the Hat* and *The Grinch Who Stole Christmas*.

1958

Rock 'n' roll idol Elvis Presley is drafted into the Army, and hula hoops are the latest fad.

In Los Angeles, the transplanted Dodgers open with a record 78,672 fans in attendance.

Movie musical *Gigi* wins nine Academy Awards while Alfred Hitchcock's thriller *Vertigo* and the musical *South Pacific* are box-office favorites.

On TV, the Western tide is beginning to turn. While *The Rifleman*, starring former baseball big leaguer Chuck Connors, is the most popular new series, a crime show, *77 Sunset Strip*, attracts adults and teenagers. The teenage draw is "Kookie", a hipster parking lot attendant with a fixation on his hair.

1959

Communist Fidel Castro assumes power in Cuba.

After months of rigorous physical and mental testing, seven Mercury astronauts are chosen.

Edward Teller, so-called "Father of the H-bomb", suggests that every person in the United States should have a bomb shelter in their backyard.

Frank Lloyd Wright, the most prominent architect in the United States, dies. He popularized the Prairie style of architecture and created the round Guggenheim Museum in New York City and Tokyo's Imperial Hotel.

Hammerin' Hank Aaron, in his sixth season with the Milwaukee Braves, leads the league in hits (223) and batting average (.355).

In radio, "payola" scandals reveal that disc jockeys took cash for playing certain songs on the air. TV viewers are shocked to learn that *Twenty-One* winner Charles Van Doren was coached during his appearances on the show.

The Untouchables debuts on TV but is criticized for its violence. A tamer alternative is *The Many Loves of Dobie Gillis*, an offbeat look at teenage life in the '50s.

Westerns still draw big audiences, as the introduction of *Bonanza* proves; it runs for 14 years. ❦

CSU/Everett Collection

Jim Cornfield/Corbis

NBC-TV (courtesy Kobal)

TV RULES. Charles Van Doren (above right) becomes a TV darling when he wins $129,000 on *Twenty-One*, but things sour when he reveals he was coached. Children (right) and adults find TV Westerns captivating. Members of the Cartwright family (far right) entertain us on *Bonanza* for 14 years.

Christmas Was Delayed, But Not Forgotten

By Cindy Erlandson, Rockford, Illinois

WHEN MY FATHER, Richard Cazel, came home from 14 months' service in Korea in the summer of 1954, there was a surprise for him—a Christmas dinner and celebration that had been put on hold awaiting his return.

Dad (inset photo below) was 22 when he returned from serving as a clerk-typist for the 5th Field Artillery near Chun-Chom. Family members first thought he would be back home in Rockford, Illinois in May, so his aunt and uncle, Loretta and Harold Klaman, saved their tree.

The tree was put on the porch and watered to keep it fresh. When his arrival was delayed, it was taken to the basement, so when he arrived in June, it was in good shape.

The 11 members of the family, including his parents, Iola and Clarence Cazel, and a brother and two sisters, gathered on July 17 for the Christmas homecoming.

My parents were married in 1957 (below), and I was born in 1958. They raised three children and are now enjoying three grandchildren.

SPUTNIKS? Lynn Lane's dad never took a liking to the Moravian star Christmas ornaments bought in '58.

Easygoing Dad Had No Use for "Sputniks"

IN NOVEMBER 1958, when I was 4, our local department store in Clinton, New Jersey had a sale on Christmas decorations. Mom and I found a package of five pretty, shiny ornaments for 29¢. They looked like Moravian stars and came in red, silver, blue, gold and pink.

Mom and I bought the ornaments and hurried home, eager to show them to Dad when he came home from the bank for lunch. My father was an easy man to please and never said a cross word about anything.

Imagine our surprise when he looked at our box of ornaments and muttered, "They look like that ugly *Sputnik*!" Of course, *Sputnik* was the satellite launched by the Soviet Union in 1957.

Mom put the ornaments on the tree anyway, but Dad grumbled every time he walked past them. Over the years, as our ornament collection grew, the "sputniks" were forgotten.

After I was married, I asked my parents if I could have the sputniks. My father happily put them in a box, saying it was his pleasure to get rid of them. Every year, when my parents came to our house at Christmas, Dad would grumble, "I see you have those sputniks on the tree."

As the years went by, I started seeing sputniks in antique stores and flea markets and began adding to my collection—but not at the bargain price of 29¢. I saw a bag of five for $18 at an antique market, and some of the hard-to-find colors go for up to $15 each in online auctions.

My father is deceased now, but the sputniks are still part of our Christmas tradition...and my brother has taken over the job of walking into my house and grumbling about them.

—*Lynn Lane, Flemington, New Jersey*

Fourth Grader Joined Presidential Press Corps

By Luella Landis, Cromwell, Connecticut

IN OCTOBER 1952, we heard President Harry Truman and his daughter, Margaret, were coming to my hometown of Middletown, Connecticut to stump for Democratic presidential candidate Adlai Stevenson. I was in fourth grade and wanted to take my old Brownie camera to the event to photograph the President and his daughter.

When our family, friends and I arrived in front of the town hall, where the President was to speak, an area was roped off for members of the press. Since I had a camera, I figured I could go there, too. So I climbed under the ropes and headed for the presidential platform.

A man asked me what I was doing, and I replied that I wanted to get a picture of President Truman. The man, who turned out to be a Secret Service agent, checked my camera to make sure it didn't contain a bomb.

Daughter Was Delighted

Then the Secret Service man conferred with Margaret Truman, who seemed delighted by the whole thing. He passed the camera to her, and she took a side-view picture of her father. Then the camera was returned to me, and I was allowed to take my own pictures of the President and his daughter.

I didn't talk with the President or his daughter, although she and I nodded and smiled at each other.

The story was picked up by news services and appeared in hundreds of papers across the nation. One paper wrote about me: "Truly her cup runneth over."

On a trip years later to the Truman Library in Independence, Missouri, my husband and I saw this picture, or one similar to it, on display.

SMILE! **Luella Landis (white dress), 9, marched into the press area to get a picture of President Harry Truman. His daughter, Margaret (right of author), smiled at her attempt.**

Truman Was Thrust into Oval Office

VICE PRESIDENT Harry Truman was catapulted into the Presidency in 1945 by the sudden death of President Franklin Delano Roosevelt. He had been Vice President only a few weeks and had had limited contact with Roosevelt and no briefings on the atomic bomb or developing problems with the Russians.

Soon after the Allies won the war in Europe, Truman ordered the dropping of two atomic bombs on Japan to end the War in the Pacific.

After World War II ended, he proposed a domestic program that included expansion of the Social Security program, full employment, fair employment practices and public housing.

In foreign policy, he created the Marshall Plan, named for his secretary of state, to stimulate economic recovery in war-torn Europe and ordered a massive airlift when Russians blockaded the western sectors of Berlin in 1948. He also was instrumental in the formation of the North Atlantic Treaty Organization, or NATO.

When troops from Communist North Korea invaded South Korea, he ordered American military support. After a long struggle involving not only U.S. troops but those of the United Nations, he kept the war limited instead of risking a major conflict with China and Russia.

Satellites Are Man-Made Moons

By Donna McGuire Tanner
Ocala, Florida

"WE'RE CLOSER TO HEAVEN than most people," my older brother, Danny, told me one night as we looked at the clear West Virginia night from an old quilt.

"Why?" I asked.

"Because we live in the mountains," he answered with the authority someone 3 years older has on a little sister.

He pointed out the Milky Way, Big Dipper and Little Dipper constellations, then a shooting star.

"Fast, make a wish!" he said.

I wished I could grow up fast and start school so I could be as smart as Danny.

It wasn't until I was in fourth grade, in 1957, that I realized there was more out there than winking bright stars. Every child in the class was excited about the impending launch of what was to become a race to be first in space.

On October 4, 1957, the Russians launched the first artificial satellite, *Sputnik I*, and began sending signals from 558 miles above the Earth. We were disappointed that the United States was not first, but happy that the Space Age had officially started.

On November 3, 1957, the Russians pulled farther ahead by launching *Sputnik II*. Our class was sad because it carried a dog on board. We celebrated on January 31, 1958, when the U.S. caught up with the Russians by sending up our own satellite, *Explorer I*. It discovered the Van Allen radiation belts.

Our teacher, Mrs. Norton, told us the new satellites were man-made moons and that we could see them if we watched the skies for slow-moving stars.

On warm summer nights, it was my turn to teach my younger sister about the lights in the night sky.

I showed her the North Star and pointed at another light.

"See that slow-moving light?" I said. "That is a man-made moon."

OCTOBER 4, 1957. The Soviet Union won the first leg of the space race by launching *Sputnik I*. The first man-made satellite—183 pounds and slightly bigger than a basketball—crossed the United States seven times a day about 500 miles above the earth.

She Looked Up and Saw a Strange, Frightening Sight

GROWING UP in Akron, Ohio in the early '50s, I recall there was a lot in the news about flying saucers.

I was 8 or 9 at the time and a big Captain Video fan, so I couldn't get enough of this information.

One afternoon my mother called me home from the neighbors. As I stood across the street from our house, I heard a strange noise and looked up.

There, right over my house, was a very strange-looking hovering machine.

All I could do was point and scream. I was sure the Martians inside of this strange craft were going to swallow up my home and family.

My mother, who was on the porch, kept saying, "What's wrong?" All I could do was point and scream.

She crossed the street, looked up and said, "You silly, it's just a helicopter."

I had never heard that term before, much less seen one. My father later explained what a helicopter was.

I'm 58 now and still haven't had a "close encounter", but I'll never forget that spring day when I thought for sure that I had. —*Carol Field, Myrtle Beach, South Carolina*

Floating Object Enthralled Massachusetts Antique Seekers

OCTOBER 5, 1957 began like any other crisp fall day as my father and I set out on an antiquing trip from our home in Townsend, Massachusetts.

As we often did on Saturday mornings, we stood in line at the thrift shop in Worcester, waiting for it to open at 9 a.m. so we could scour the store for treasures.

Someone in the crowd spotted a small object floating across the clear blue sky, and we all stood there mesmerized, watching it the way a child views an errant balloon as it disappears from sight.

On the way home, Dad talked about reporting it to the government but decided nobody would believe us.

Fortunately it wasn't long before we discovered what the object was. When we stopped for lunch, Dad spotted a headline in the local newspaper.

"Russia Launches First Artificial Moon," it said. We had witnessed an orbit of *Sputnik I*. —*Nancy Lovell Benoit Marlborough, Massachusetts*

Teens Cut Classes to Greet Richard Nixon

THE PRESIDENTIAL election campaign of 1952 was in full swing when we heard that Richard Nixon was going to be traveling near our high school in Los Angeles, California. The principal said he couldn't give us permission to leave, and most students were afraid to. Remember, this was almost 50 years ago!

Some of us were eager to take advantage of this once-in-a-lifetime opportunity, but we were still nervous about cutting classes. I called Dad and asked him if I should go.

"Of course, you should go see the vice-presidential candidate," he replied. "And be sure to tell him your father was a streetcar conductor." That puzzled me, but I agreed to tell Mr. Nixon if I got the chance.

We left early in the afternoon for Colorado Boulevard, where Mr. Nixon was expected to pass. Some of the band members took their instruments along.

We waited a long time, wondering if Mr. Nixon was really coming. Maybe the route had changed. To pass the time, we got some butcher paper from a nearby market and made a big banner. Some of the band members climbed a light pole for a better view.

Suddenly someone shouted, "He's coming! There he is!" We ran out into the street with our banner, forcing the candidate's car to stop. Mr. Nixon's security men were angry, but the reporters seemed amused. The band began to play, and we all cheered and applauded.

Mr. Nixon seemed to enjoy the welcome we'd given him. He made a short impromptu speech, then shook hands with us. As he touched my hand, I told him, "Mr. Nixon, my dad met you when you were running for the Assembly. He used to be a streetcar conductor." The candidate looked surprised.

Much later, I learned that his father had been a streetcar conductor, too.   —*Mary Workman, Mountain Home, Idaho*

Tyke Unimpressed with President's Stature

DURING the presidential campaign of November 1952, President Harry Truman stumped for Democrat Adlai Stevenson in his private railroad car. One of his speeches was scheduled for Fargo, North Dakota, where we lived.

I'd never seen a President in person, so I drove to the railway station with my 6-year-old son, Greg. I wanted him to see Truman, too. The President was to speak from the rear platform of his rail car.

There was already a crowd around the train when we arrived, so I climbed up a mound of dirt to see over the throng. Then I boosted Greg on my shoulders for a better view.

Truman wasn't a large man, and he looked even smaller when he stepped out onto the platform, dwarfed by two burly Secret Service men.

"He ain't very big, Dad," Greg observed. I replied that presidents didn't have to be big, just able to do their job.

When Truman started to speak, Greg was even more disappointed.

"I didn't know he was gonna talk," he said. "Let's go home, Dad." And we did.
—*Eugene Bovee*
Lawrence, Kansas

She Walked a Mile To See MacArthur Speak

ONE THING from the 1950s that I'll never part with is my snapshot of General Douglas MacArthur.

We'd read in the paper that the general was coming to our small town of Chicopee Falls, Massachusetts to give a speech near his grandfather's home. Everyone was so excited.

On July 26, 1951, I walked over a mile to get a spot near where the ceremonies were to be held. It was very hot, and there were hundreds of people gathering around the platform.

I was squashed like a sardine, but I didn't mind. When the general stepped onto the platform and started to speak, it was worth all the hassle.
—*Carol Derks, Newaygo, Michigan*

TREASURED PHOTO. Carol Derks cherishes this photo of General Douglas MacArthur, taken when he visited her hometown of Chicopee Falls, Massachusetts in 1951. "This is my favorite memory from the 1950s," Carol says.

No One Impressed Reporter Like Young Kennedy

By William Allan, Pittsburgh, Pennsylvania

SEEKING PRESIDENCY. In 1959, John F. Kennedy was running in a primary campaign in West Virginia's "Bible Belt".

I CALL HIM Jack because that's the first thing he said to us: "Call me Jack."

We were a dozen or so reporters from various news agencies, and he was John F. Kennedy, the young senator running for President. He was vibrant, unassuming, friendly, sincere and a natural leader. He was also a Catholic, and the United States had never had a Catholic President, although several Catholics had run.

I was a young *Pittsburgh Press* reporter covering Jack's primary campaign in West Virginia's "Bible Belt" in late 1959.

At a breakfast in Beckley, Jack made a little speech but said nothing about religion. Was he ducking the issue?

Ted Sorenson, his public relations man, passed out several quotes. "This guy doesn't stick to his speeches," he warned, "but he promised me he'll say these sometime today."

There were no quotes about religion, but a couple of the national reporters grabbed the sheets and ran to the phones anyway.

At the second stop, in Charleston, Jack stood on a temporary platform in front of a closed-down theater and went on the attack. "Don't tell me because I was born and raised a Catholic that I can't be President of the United States," he said. Some heads nodded, there was applause, and we reporters were off and running.

We visited a foundry and other factories, with Jack shaking hands all around. In between, as he walked down the streets, women crossed the street just to touch him.

Late in the afternoon, our caravan was inching down a two-lane blacktop road on the West Virginia University campus when a young man on a motorbike sped up in the opposite lane. The young bike rider spied Jack in the first car and his mouth dropped open. His bike went off the road and hit the curb, and the rider catapulted headfirst into a tree.

Jack stopped his car and ran to his aid. He was already leaning over the young man when I got there.

"Do you know what to do?" Jack asked me, obviously concerned.

"Not really," I replied. "But my Boy Scout first-aid training tells me we shouldn't try to move him. We might do more harm than good. The police will get an ambulance."

Jack looked at me, then looked down at the young man, stuck out his hand, smiled and said, "I'm Jack Kennedy, and I'm running for President of the United States."

The young man smiled weakly and mumbled something incoherent as help arrived.

During my career with the *Pittsburgh Press*, I covered all sorts of politicians, four other Presidents and a wealth of industrialists and sports superstars. But in more than 35 years as a reporter, I never met another person as affable and genuine as Jack Kennedy.

She and Mom Liked Ike —Especially Up Close

DURING MY senior year of high school in 1955, my mother and I went on vacation in New Hampshire. On our way home, we stopped in a small town just north of the Massachusetts border for lunch.

The waitress asked if we planned to stick around for a while. She'd heard President Eisenhower was going to be coming through town on his way to the local airport.

Could this be true? This was such an out-of-the-way place. What possible reason could the President have for being there?

But we followed the woman's directions anyway, driving to a dirt road off the highway. A small airport was at the end of the road, with a plane waiting on the runway.

After about half an hour, a Lincoln convertible turned the corner and came down the road, followed by two or three other vehicles. There he was! President Eisenhower stood up in the convertible, waving to the handful of people standing alongside the road.

We were so elated. We could almost reach out and touch him! There were no security guards, and none of the fanfare that you'd see today.

I even got a picture of Ike in the car, waving to my mom (below). At 91, she still remembers the excitement at the end of our vacation.

—Priscilla Elwell
North Falmouth, Massachusetts

Chapter Six
Recreation & Holidays

Recreation & Holidays

STARTING ON the next page, you will read about how Americans celebrated holidays, enjoyed vacations and found ways to fill their leisure hours with fun in the '50s.

Many of the amusements were ageless and still entertain us today. But there were differences, too.

Consider camping, for example. You still operated an iron pump to get your water and cooled your watermelons and beverages in the lake or river. You split your own firewood after scouring the forest for dry kindling and slept on the ground in a sleeping bag, except for the sissies who brought along air mattresses.

The big change was the expansion of state and national campsites and the development of private campgrounds with

> *"A special delight for young families was a drive-in movie..."*

such nice modern amenities that they were practically resorts.

One of our family camping trips in Wisconsin coincided with a time when our youngest was stubbornly resisting toilet training. The campground had the traditional box toilets, which she had never encountered. For some reason, they held special allure for her and she insisted on a trip to the outhouse every 2 hours or so. Acute dehydration became a concern, but by the time we returned home, toilet training was complete. A camping miracle!

Motoring vacations in the '50s were still a pain in the neck. Two-lane roads were crowded with farm tractors and big semis, and there were no rest stops.

Motels were scarce, and truck stop cafes were about as good as eating got. In small country towns, you looked for the cafe on Main Street that had the most pickups parked out front.

Car Trips Before Interstates

But the promise of a better future was everywhere. Huge yellow earth-moving machines were tearing up the American landscape to create something promoted by Dwight Eisenhower and called an interstate highway system. Until it was a reality, the Lincoln Highway (U.S. 30) and the legendary Route 66 were the best you could hope for on long trips.

Remnants of old U.S. Highway 1 down the East Coast still survive and make you marvel at the determination of those '50s snowbirds on their way to a winter suntan. A tough breed, indeed.

A special delight for young families was a spreading idea called drive-in movies. You gave the little ones their baths, buttoned them into their pj's, popped a grocery bag full of popcorn, threw in a few pillows and blankets and off you went to the movies. Eventually the kids dropped off to sleep, leaving Mom and Dad to enjoy a rare bit of uninterrupted cuddling.

Now jump across the page and learn more about how people had fun in the '50s, even though most of them had to do it on a shoestring. —*Clancy Strock*

'We Dove into a Sandpit Sea Hunt'

TV's Lloyd Bridges had nothing on these underwater adventurers.

By Jud Bock, Honey Creek, Iowa

MY FUTURE brother-in-law, Jerry Willhoft, and I were farming near Central City, Nebraska in 1952. We were next-door neighbors as well as best friends at 17 and 19 and always looking for something different or unusual to do.

After working all day in the heat, we went over to the old swimming hole, an old sandpit converted to a recreation area, to wash off the day's field dirt.

As we hit the water on a 90-degree day and were enjoying the bliss of being cool and free of sweat and dirt, we began to think how much fun it would be to dive to the deepest part of the pit and explore its depths.

We decided to build a diving breather so we'd be able to stay down as long as we wanted.

We acquired Jerry's father's old paint compressor and my granddad's old gasoline-powered washing machine motor, two 100-foot lengths of garden hose and a Y-connector for the hoses. Along with our face masks, we had a diving air machine for two!

Bubblin' Fumes

We connected the hose to our face masks, which proved rather crude and had to be held by hand because the weight of the hoses would pull them off.

We found that we could breathe pretty well, al-

though the air was quite foul and reeked of spray paint. I often wondered why we didn't do permanent damage to our lungs, but we seemed to come out of it with no injuries.

As we swam in the old pit, we discovered a problem: As we took in lungsful of air, we would rise to the surface. We recalled a movie of our time, *Wake of the Red Witch*, with John Wayne as a deep-sea diver, and the heavily weighted suits the divers used.

We scrounged in our folks' farm workshops and found the perfect weight—old sash weights, about a foot long with a hole in one end perfect for belting around our waists.

Equipped for adventure, we returned to the pit, fired up the engine and walked into the deeper part of the pit with our 80 pounds of weights.

It was great! We were walking on the bottom, and it was getting deeper and deeper and becoming hard to see much. In previous dives, we'd seen bass, bluegills and carp, some of them pretty good sized.

Suddenly we spotted something *huge*! It was then we remembered that John Wayne had died in the movie in a battle with a giant octopus!

What *Was* It?

We were down about 40 feet and decided to leave posthaste when the unexpected happened—the gas engine quit and so did our air supply.

We knew from the movies that you were supposed to come up slowly, and we intended to. But, being frightened of whatever we saw, we headed for the surface as fast as we could.

That's when we discovered a flaw in our weight system. We were too heavy to swim, and the weights were holding us down.

With only the air in our lungs and a monster somewhere in the murky water, we finally were able to undo the belts and swim for the surface.

Boy, did that fresh air taste good! After a few breaths, we swam ashore and flopped on the sand to get our wind back.

After some more reasoned discussion, we decided we'd seen a very large and ugly catfish. Only a few inches from us, however, it probably looked larger than it was. We guessed it had to weigh between 40 and 50 pounds, which certainly was not impossible in that old sand pit.

We decided we'd had enough for one day and departed. We dived many times the rest of that summer—without the weights that still lie somewhere on the bottom of that pit.

We never returned to the deep part of the lake and never met the monster again. And I, for one, was thankful.

Take Me (Blink) to Your (Blink) Leader!

This electrified trick-or-treater almost got a blast he wasn't expecting.

By Philip Whitmoyer, Leesport, Pennsylvania

WHEN I WAS a teen in the late 1950s, we lived in the country near my present home. At Halloween, all the costumes were homemade.

We always tried to come up with a costume so we couldn't be identified by the neighbors when we went trick-or-treating. Planning a successful costume began soon after school started.

My first reading book from the library one year had to do with basic electricity, so I decided to incorporate some of the things I learned into my costume.

A mechanical man costume seemed to be the best possibility. It would completely cover me, make me look taller and allow me to play electrician.

I found a slightly used battery—one of the large ones with terminals on one end that used to be popular—and secured it to the bottom of a peach basket. The basket, inverted over a large box for a body, became the head. I used the cutout portion for the mouth and as my window to see.

I had lights with old foil Christmas bulb reflectors for the eyes, plus several other lights for good measure. All were controlled by toggle switches mounted on the body.

Houses in our neighborhood were scattered, and we did quite a bit of walking to make the rounds. I decided to take a shortcut through a neighbor's field to avoid an uninhabited curved portion of the road at one point.

Shortcut Provided Chance for Fun

As luck would have it, the farmer was just going back to his house from feeding his steers, so I thought I would have some fun.

I began blinking my eyes to get his attention. When he stopped to look, I turned them off and walked to one side, then turned them on again briefly. I continued this zigzag course for a while until he turned and went into the house.

I assumed he was bored with my show and began walking straight toward his house. Fortunately for me, I reached the porch just before he came back with his shotgun.

It turned out he was really scared that I was an invader of some sort and was about to protect himself however he could. He was very relieved that it was a trick-or-treater and not someone from outer space.

After that, I avoided shortcuts and kept my lights off until shouting "Trick or Treat!"

PARTY HEARTY. The February 1953 issue of *Teen-Topics* offered tips for girls interested in hosting a "hearty" Valentine's Day party. Guests could hunt for hidden heart cutouts or act out words like "heartbroken" and "heartthrob" in a game of "heart charades". The menu? Heart-shaped hamburgers, heart-shaped cookies and glasses of Cranberry Fizz. *Teen-Topics* was sponsored by Dennison Crepe Paper; subscriptions cost 25¢ a year. Sandra Sowers of Dover, Delaware shared this copy.

ICE MAKES TALL STORY. Bill Schildgen get a close-up look at a glacier when he and his friend David Carlson traveled on the Alaska Highway.

ON JUNE 10, 1959, my friend Bill Schildgen and I left Loomis, Washington for Alaska, where we had part-time summer jobs. It took us 10 days to get there.

At that time, the Alaska Highway was all gravel and very rough. Many of the roads were like washboards. We blew out four 4-ply tires on the trip and replaced them with the sturdier 6-ply variety.

Bill and I traveled in a 1953 Dodge three-quarter-ton pickup truck with a tent on the back. We cooked our meals over a Coleman stove and bathed in rivers or lakes along the way. Gas stations were few and far between, so we carried extra gasoline with us.

We spent the whole summer in Alaska, until Aug. 25. I worked in construction at Eielson Army base, until the union went on strike. Bill spent his summer fighting forest fires.

The only problem we had was the mosquitoes. They were the worst I'd ever seen. But we had a terrific time.

It was a summer I'll never forget.   —*David Carlson
Corona, Arizona*

Busman's Holiday? Almost

*Honeymooners took a household
with them, but it wasn't theirs.*

By Joanne Dart, Batavia, New York

THE 1950s were great years for us, beginning June 25, 1950, when Don and I were married in a large country church wedding. All the girls' gowns were borrowed but beautiful.

After living in an apartment for a while, we were able to buy a small home with a GI loan. He drove a moving van and often was gone for days at a time. I was working for the telephone company in Adrian, Michigan.

We'd been married 2 years and hadn't had a honeymoon. We were apart quite a bit, so when Don was scheduled for a trip to Florida, we thought it would be great if I could go with him. It would be nice to be together, even though it was July, in a big old semitruck.

We made good time getting to Florida. When we arrived on a Saturday afternoon, no one at the Miami terminal wanted to unload furniture. We unhooked the trailer and drove the tractor to a motel a block from the ocean.

We were able to rent a motel apartment for $6 a night, including free orange juice! We went swimming Sunday afternoon and went back to the terminal Monday to unload the trailer.

Heading home, the truck broke down in Mansfield, Ohio. That meant another week on the road for us. I called my supervisor at the telephone company and asked for more time off. She wanted me to take the train home, but there was no way I was going to do that.

She agreed I could miss another week of work.

Since the truck was empty and it was summer, we decided to stay in the trailer at night. We just made a bed in the back with all those furniture pads.

We walked to restaurants during the day and went to movies at night.

When we finally arrived home, we figured we'd had a pretty good trip and a wonderful delayed honeymoon.

Joanne and Don Dart

Coastal Weather Bared Its Teeth That Day

A carefree weekend at the beach turned threatening.

By Grace Hale, Raleigh, North Carolina

HALF A CENTURY AGO, the Outer Banks of North Carolina were still connected by sand roads and ferries, making them a fun destination.

My husband, Bob, and I were newlyweds living in Elizabeth City, North Carolina. Almost every weekend, we loaded our old red Jeep, took off across the Pasquotank River bridge and headed to the coast for a day or two of fishing, beachcombing, sunbathing (in season) and just relaxing.

We'd load the Jeep with a picnic basket of sandwiches, potato salad and an ice chest of drinks; fishing tackle; a change of clothes; makeshift tent, etc.

At Nags Head, we'd turn off the main highway, let most of the air out of the tires and head for Oregon Inlet, Avon and on to Hatteras. We often stopped to help landlubber motorists who were stuck in the sand along the way.

On one rather dismal fall Saturday in 1950, we boarded the ferry for a choppy ride across Oregon Inlet and decided to fish on a sand spit, despite a stiff wind, heavy surf and a wild-looking sky.

I don't remember whether or not the fish were biting. I wandered off farther and farther, totally enchanted with the number of sand dollars I was finding. They were floating up everywhere and in rippling tide pools.

While we were engrossed in our quests, the ocean's crashing surf had combined with the wind's whine to a loud roar. From far away, I seemed to hear Bob's voice—or was it my imagination?—saying, "Hurry, we've got to get out of here now!"

I could hardly stand up. The wind had suddenly gotten so strong and the tide had begun rising around the Jeep. We barely made it across from the spit back to the island, abandoning some of our gear, as the Jeep threatened to stall out before we got back to safety.

We arrived at a Coast Guard station in near darkness, startling the occupants, I'm sure. The ferry had quit for the day after nearly capsizing on the return from the trip that had brought us over.

I'll never forget the thrill of venturing a little way out from the shelter of the Coast Guard station onto the dark beach, watching the sand disappearing beneath the crashing surf and the sea oats bending double.

The wind sounded peculiar, the air was very cold and there was no visible boundary between the sky and the whitecaps.

That was the day I began an infatuation with hurricanes—which is what that storm was, back in the days before they were given names.

Millpond Was the Top Spot for Ice Fishing

WE ENJOYED wonderful winter sports when I was growing up in Dowagiac, Michigan—ice-skating, sledding, and building snowmen and snow forts. Another favorite activity was ice fishing on the millpond at the edge of town.

Some fishermen set up a totally enclosed fish house on the ice. Each house was equipped with a wood- or coal-burning stove for heat.

The houses didn't have windows, though. The light coming through the ice illuminated the interior of the house and clearly showed what was in the water below.

Other fishermen braved the weather without a fish house. With your back to the wind and a gasoline lantern between your knees, you could stay plenty warm.

When we fished in the open, we simply laid our catch out on the ice. It would be frozen before we took it home. I've never eaten fish that tasted better.
    —Lyle Lieber
Oak Ridge, Tennessee

IT'S A START! A fisherman eyes his catch, a lone bluegill, as he crouches on the frozen millpond in Dowagiac, Michigan in 1957. Lyle Lieber took the photo for a contest at the plant where he worked and won first prize.

PADDLING PAIR. The author and younger brother Paul enjoyed summers in Washington's Cascade Mountains when they were growing up (left in 1952). In 2001, they recaptured those poses (above), complete with Pete's oar and partially untucked shirt.

Radio Reception Was Great, While It Lasted

Unfortunately, Uncle Sam had other ideas about the antenna system they rigged in the national forest in the '50s.

By Pete Horish, Poulsbo, Washington

EVERY JUNE, as soon as the school year ended, my family would move from our "winter house" in Cle Elum to our remote cabin in the Wenatchee National Forest, in Washington's Cascade Mountains.

We'd load up our 1939 Plymouth and bounce over 18 miles of single-lane gravel road into an area surrounded by dense virgin forests and snowcapped mountains. It was a trip back through time.

Electricity hadn't been introduced to the backcountry yet. Our cabin, and others nearby, were lit with kerosene lamps and fireplaces. We did have the luxury of indoor plumbing, with water from a nearby spring.

An occasional trip to town provided grocery staples, mail and laundry facilities. A telephone at the general store linked this remote area to the "outside world", but it was for use only in emergencies.

For a young boy, life in this setting was thoroughly enjoyable. There were always other children to play with, and we could swim and fish at a nearby lake. Most weekday evenings were spent with friends around a campfire, toasting marshmallows, singing songs and telling stories.

Saturday evenings I spent with my family, discussing the week's happenings, popping corn in a wire basket in the fireplace, drinking hot cocoa and listening to the radio. Dad had modified an old Philco vacuum-tube radio, the model with the green "tuning eye", to operate on power from an automobile battery.

I remember Dad and Mom sitting by the fireplace, frequently adjusting the knobs to hear the news, a favorite opera selection or Mario Lanza's new hit. When increasing static and decreasing volume made the broadcast inaudible, we had to turn the radio off.

We could replenish the radio's power source by returning the battery to the Plymouth and driving to town, but nothing could remedy the poor reception and static. All the big-city radio transmitters were too far away.

Then my brother and I came up with a solution.

During the hot, dry summers, when the risk of forest fires was greatest, the U.S. Forest Service maintained a guard station near our cabin. This station also served as the main telephone switchboard, connecting a number of mountaintop lookout towers throughout central Washington.

Heard Music Loud and Clear

I don't recall what prompted us to think of this, but one day my brother and I laboriously connected numerous short lengths of blasting-cap wire. We linked them to the telephone lines closest to our cabin and then to our Philco radio.

The results were fantastic! With this much-improved antenna, we were able to tune in radio stations from miles away with static-free reception. Our favorite station quickly became KOBY from San Francisco. I still remember sitting with my family, listening to popular tunes like *The Wayward Wind* by Gogi Grant and *Come On-a My House* by Rosemary Clooney. I was so proud, thinking I'd made a brilliant contribution to our family gatherings.

The Forest Service telephone crew rapidly discovered what had lowered the quality of their connections to the vital lookout towers. My brother and I were told in no uncertain terms to remove our wire and warned never to tamper with government lines again.

Today, my sons' solar-powered radios are tuned to orbiting satellite stations. I can't help but wonder what communications advances the next half century will bring. ❧

'I *Hate* My Skates! I *Love* My Skates!'

New ice skates caused problems...until Dad skated in with an answer.

By Deborah Carron, Elk River, Minnesota

EVEN MOM looked surprised when Dad announced, "Get dressed, kids, we're going skating." After all, during the winter in Minnesota, it turns dark early.

It was a moonlit night in 1957. We had just finished the supper dishes and my brothers, Wayne and Gary, should have been starting their homework. I hoped no one would question Dad, though, because skating in the dark sounded so exciting.

"Mom, where are my skates?" my oldest brother, Wayne, called as he dug through the closet.

I didn't have to look for mine. They hung on a hook in the closet where I could see them every day. They had been there since Christmas. They were brand new and shiny white with big red pom-poms that my grandma had made.

So far, I could only stand on the rug in them.

"Don't walk on the floor with your skates, Debbie," Mom had warned. "You will make scratches on the floor and it could make your blades dull."

"Can we go skating today?" I had pleaded every day.

"We need to wait until your brothers can go," Dad had said. They were in school and I was too young to go to school.

Finally, Dad could wait no longer. We were going even it if was dark. He loaded me and my brothers in the pickup and off we went to the lake. He drove down our driveway, across the cow pasture and right onto the lake. He left

TOBOGGAN TIME. Deborah Carron (left) was just about old enough for ice skates in this winter picture. Her brother Wayne is on the right and the other children are their cousins.

the headlights of the truck on so we could see in the dark.

The ice was smooth and shiny. I watched Gary skate off, yelling to Wayne, "I'll race you."

Dad picked me up and stood me on the ice. I took a step to join my brothers, and my skates went up and I went down.

Dad laughed, but when he saw the tears in my eyes, he said, "Here, take my hand and I'll help you." I held onto him with both hands, but I still fell down.

When my brothers came back, Wayne said, "Hang onto the back of my coat, Debbie." He pulled me around the lake, but I fell again.

We saw Dad skating off toward the darkness beyond the range of the pickup's headlights.

"Wait, Dad, we want to come," my brothers called, and off they went.

I sat on the ice where I had landed, once again, and cried.

"I hate my new skates," I said.

Then, out of the darkness, I saw my dad skating back toward me.

"I have an idea," he said. He went to the back of the truck and took out a milk can. Bringing the can to me, he said, "Here you go. This will be a good partner for you." I held onto the milk can, which was just my size, and took a step. I didn't fall!

I pushed off with one skate after the other. Soon I was gliding across the shimmering ice past my brothers, and I didn't fall once.

I loved my new skates, and I loved my dad! ✒

Horsewoman Competed at Madison Square Garden

SOME OF MY fondest memories of the 1950s are of my Paint horse, "Chico" (far right). I rode him in rodeos and shows and was thrilled to win ribbons for events like pole-bending, bareback riding and racing. Chico was a real prancer, and we rode in several parades.

He was a good barrel racer, too. We won many of the barrel races at the Madison Square Garden rodeo, and I was a semifinalist for Rodeo Queen in 1957 and '58. It was quite an experience driving a horse trailer in Manhattan!

—*Mary Sue Stokesbury, Palm Beach Gardens, Florida*

For Over Half a Century, She's Prized This Porker

A FEW MONTHS before we got married in 1950, Guy and I decided to visit Brooklyn's Coney Island amusement park. In the shooting gallery, the barker dared Guy to try to shoot

down the moving target of toy ducks, tempting him with a prize of my choice if he succeeded.

Guy had served in the Army during World War II and was determined to impress me. He took the dare.

To my amazement, I soon found myself walking on the boardwalk, hugging a ceramic water pitcher in the form of an adorable pig (left). We named it "Pork Chop".

Guy and I celebrated our 50th anniversary in 2000, and Pork Chop has been with us all along, in her honored spot atop our refrigerator. I wouldn't part with my ceramic cutie for all the pigs in China.

—*Rose DeProspo, Massapequa Park, New York*

Mom Made Oyster Stew Every Christmas Eve

MY MOTHER'S FAMILY was accustomed to having oyster stew on Christmas Eve, so my mom continued the tradition for our family in the '50s.

My siblings didn't like oyster stew, so they were fed tomato soup instead. After supper, we'd drive into town for the late-night church service.

We also had one other Christmas tradition. On Christmas morning, we'd come downstairs to see lots of packages under the tree, but we were only allowed to open our stockings at first. My father had a dairy, so milking and breakfast came before opening packages. —*Iris Doksansky, Fremont, Nebraska*

PROM QUEENS. Sandee Gaboury (left) and her sisters Pat and JoAnn decided to have their own prom one day in the early '50s. They chased the chickens out of their uncle's barn and had a great time.

Girls Shooed Chickens From Barn for "Prom"

IN THE EARLY 1950s, when I was 10 or 11, my sisters, cousins, friends and I decided we wanted to have a "prom". My cousin said we could have it in her dad's barn, so we swept out the chicken feathers and decorated it with crepe paper and balloons.

Then we asked some of the neighborhood boys to come. A few agreed, as long as they didn't have to dress up or wear ties.

We girls borrowed our moms' dresses and made corsages out of Kleenex. My sister Pat and cousin Kay didn't have "dates", so they served the Kool-Aid and popcorn and played the 45-rpm records for dancing.

Even though the boys spent most of the time eating popcorn and drinking Kool-Aid, we still had a great time—until the chickens came in to reclaim the barn.

We're all in our late 50s now and still reminisce about our "first prom". —*Sandee Gaboury, Ishpeming, Michigan*

BEACH BOYS. Allan Doody snapped this photo of his high school buddies on Nantasket Beach in Hull, Massachusetts in the early 1950s. "We rented our swimsuits there and wore our locker keys around our necks," recalls Allan, of Canton, Massachusetts. "The beach stopped renting suits a few years later." The beach was a popular destination for young people and families, with amusement park rides and a boardwalk along the shoreline. From left, Allan's friends are Charles Callahan (face obscured), Arthur Bougas, Richard Berardi, Joseph Vliano and Joseph Nardelli.

'Has Anyone Seen My Skate Key?'

It fit in the palm of your hand, but a skate key meant big happiness.

By April Thomas, Conyers, Georgia

AS I RAMBLED through the junk and old items at an antique sale, I came across something that took me back to a carefree time of my childhood—a pair of street skates.

No, these weren't the type of skates used by kids today. Modern skates, called roller blades, are worn with sissy things like knee pads, elbow pads, gloves and helmets.

I realize these supports provide protection, but kids growing up in the '50s didn't have such equipment. I think I wore a Band-Aid on my knees or elbows or both until I reached my teens.

No, our skates were made of metal and clamped directly to our shoes. The shoes had to have a hard sole on them or you couldn't get the skates to stay on.

You couldn't wear sandals for fear of taking off a toe, and you certainly wouldn't wear your Sunday shoes. The clamp was tightened to your shoe with a key.

Now *this* is where I had a problem.

How do kids today keep up with everything when they get ready to roller blade? I mean, they must have eight or 10 items on before leaving the house.

Oh, No! Lost *Again*

Keeping up with a skate key was a challenge in itself. I'm talking about an object about the size of a house key. How can an 8-year-old kid be held responsible for keeping up with a skate key?

My sisters and I would try every way imaginable to keep up with that elusive thing, but every time we started to go out to skate, the key was missing again.

Mom was always hearing one of us barge through the door yelling, "Mom, have you seen my skate key?"

With four kids in the house, you'd think someone would have a skate key.

Once you were outside, you still needed that key from time to time because the skates often lost their grip and you would have to sit on the curb and tighten them again.

We even resorted to tying the thing around our necks in an attempt to keep up with it. And you were certainly leery about loaning the key to one of the neighborhood kids.

Tried to Hide It

Although you could be standing right there with them while they made some minor adjustment, you were afraid the key would make a disappearing act right before your eyes.

You tried to hide it under your shirt, but they could see the string tied around your neck and knew what was hanging on the end of it.

I even tried putting mine under a rock at the edge of our yard—I couldn't find string that day—but I was afraid to get more than a block away for fear of someone finding it.

How could such a small item be of such significance to all us kids? A pair of skates and a skate key went hand in hand. You had to have both items. If you didn't have the key, your skate would eventually dangle from your ankle, and skating would be out of the question.

We sure had a good time, though. The kids in our neighborhood skated for hours up and down our street. Eventually I graduated to indoor skating. Thank goodness no skate key was required for that!

As I was leaving the booth at the antique show, the gentleman who owned the skates asked if he could help me.

"No thanks," I replied. Then I grinned and asked, "I bet you don't have a key to go with these skates, do you?"

He chuckled and didn't answer, but I think he knew exactly what I was talking about. ◖

Mobile Skating Rink Had Town on a Roll

A TENT roller-skating rink came to my hometown of Rock Valley, Iowa in the summer of 1951. It was set up beyond the left-field fence of the town baseball diamond.

The tent rink was very popular that summer. Our town was small—only 1,495 people—and we didn't have a lot of entertainment choices. There was a movie theater, and the town baseball team played at home at least once a week, but that was it.

Most of us didn't know how to roller-skate. We could ice-skate, but this was much different. It was a summer of learning and lots of fun. I've kept up my interest in skating ever since and still enjoy it.

—*Bob Oldenkamp, Hawarden, Iowa*

Novice Driver Logged 2,500 Miles in 8 Days

By John Kofton, Baldwin Park, California

MY WIFE, Lou, and I moved from Seattle, Washington to Long Beach, California in 1950. We hadn't been there long before we realized Lou would have to learn to drive.

A husband and wife don't make the smoothest driving-instruction team, but eventually I taught Lou to drive our 1949 Buick. As it turned out, that was an important decision.

In 1952, I was drafted into the Marines. After boot camp in San Diego, I was shipped to Quantico, Virginia for ordnance training. That summer, I urged Lou to drive there to join me.

Although Lou had little driving experience, she gamely agreed to this 2,500-mile trip. Remember, this was a time when women didn't drive much at all, let alone make cross-country trips alone. The roads weren't in great shape, either—many would be considered terrible by today's standards.

As it turned out, that trip was the most exciting thing Lou ever did on her own. She never got lost, though she did get scared a few times.

Help Was Easy to Find

Whenever she wasn't sure what to do or which way to go, all she had to say was, "I'm driving to meet my husband, who's a Marine stationed at Quantico", and she'd get all the help she needed. Servicemen were highly regarded.

Lou followed Route 66 through Arizona, New Mexico, Texas, Oklahoma, a corner of Kansas and Missouri. In St. Louis, she picked up U.S. Highway 50 and followed it through Illinois, Indiana, Ohio, West Virginia and on to Quantico. The only physical record of the trip was the auto decals (right), then very popular, that Lou bought in each state. She saw lots of curio and jewelry shops run by Native Americans in the Southwest…and endless Burma-Shave signs.

There were unusual attractions along the way—the two-headed cow, the steer with four horns, the reptile village. They sound laughable now but were great drawing cards at the time.

An Optimistic Time

Lou left California with about $200. She spent $70 on gas, $65 on lodging and $40 on food, leaving a whopping $25 to cover any problems that might've come up. What a simpler, optimistic time.

After driving for 8 days, Lou arrived in Quantico about noon on a Sunday. No one was around when she got there. I wasn't expecting her that soon. But our luck was good—we accidentally met each other at the gate. What a great moment! I'll always remember it.

We stayed in Quantico for about 2 months, and Lou worked as a waitress while I finished school. It was hotter than blazes every day that summer, but I recall it with great fondness.

The trip back to California that fall was memorable, too…but that's another story.

Beloved Brother Was Home...
But Only in His Dreams

WHEN I WAS growing up in our small town of Wibaux, Montana, I was very close to my brother David. He was a year older, and we shared the same interests and friends. Both of us were into rock 'n' roll, jukeboxes, hula hoops, fast cars and ducktail haircuts. Life was good.

In spring of 1957, when David was 17, he and three friends enlisted in the Navy. They left for boot camp right after high school graduation. We'd done so many things together—movies, dances, drive-ins—that I couldn't imagine life without him. He was so cool.

I missed him a lot but did okay until December, when we found out he wouldn't be home for Christmas. He'd spend his first Christmas away from home at sea, aboard the *USS Safeguard*.

I helped Mom put up the tree, decorate the house, play Christmas music and bake cookies, but my heart just wasn't in it. As we made up a box of cookies and other goodies to send to David, I realized Mom felt just as bad as I did, but she was determined to make the holidays special for the rest of the family.

Just before Christmas, a package of presents arrived from David. He'd mailed it in San Diego, before he shipped out for Japan. I don't remember what anyone else got, but my gift was Elvis Presley's Christmas 45-rpm EP record, with *Blue Christmas* and *I'll Be Home for Christmas* on it. Although I cried when I played it, I knew that David was with us, "if only in his dreams". I'd been feeling sorry for myself when I should've been thankful to be home with my family, where David would've preferred to be.

Happily, we spent many Christmases together in later years. I still have the album David gave me, and I play it every holiday season. It always reminds me of how much I missed my big brother that Christmas. —*Diane Nelson Wibaux, Montana*

SAILOR WANNABE. Author (right) tried on one of her brother's Navy uniforms during his visit home. Christmas without him was a trying time for the family.

CAMP MATES. Joanne Boycourt McAnally (third from right) shares a happy moment in April 1953 with other campers at Killarney Lake in Ironton, Missouri. The young women enjoyed weekends there while their boyfriends were in the Korean War.

War Years Forged
Lasting Friendships

DURING THE Korean War, most of my girlfriends and I had a boyfriend or fiance serving our country. Yet for those "girls who were left behind", 1950 to '53 provided some of the most precious memories of the decade.

We were all members of the 9-to-5 workforce in St. Louis but spent our evenings and weekends together. Many of those weekends were spent at an all-girls' camp at Killarney Lake in Ironton, Missouri. Coed camps weren't even considered at that time, especially when the camp was church-sponsored like ours.

The girls at the camp tended to split up into groups. We called our group "the Birds" and another "the Bees". The third group we dubbed "the COMs". These were the "Crabby Old Maids"—a whole year or two older than us—who thought our ideas of "fun" were too juvenile.

For us, fun was staying awake long enough to paint the faces of sleeping members of the other two groups, or sew their jean legs and jacket sleeves shut. Fun was walking to the quarry to climb the rocks and trees, swimming in the lake, preparing our meals, tramping the country lanes, playing cards and sharing our problems, thoughts and dreams.

Fun was trusting each other and caring for each other. Most of all, despite the different paths our lives took, fun was that fabulous '50s thing called lasting friendships.

—*Joanne Boycourt McAnally, Clovis, California*

Sunday Picnics Were Highlight of Any Week

The whole family looked forward to delicious food and fun.

By Sharon O'Loughlin, London, Ontario

WHEN I WAS a child in the '50s, going on a Sunday picnic was one of my favorite activities. These were the days before Sunday shopping, cable TV and VCRs, when a picnic was a special event. The whole family would go—grandparents, parents, brothers, sisters, even the dog!

After church, we'd load our well-used wicker picnic basket and heavy old tin cooler into the family sedan and head out for a drive. We would stop for a fill-up at the local gas station, where Grandpa always bought two six-packs of ice-cold assorted soda pop. My siblings and I eagerly awaited the moment when we could snap off the caps to "wet our whistles".

Since we lived close to several large lakes, we often ended up at a local beach, where we children could romp in the warm shallow water. The grown-ups watched from the shade as we spent hours building elaborate sand castles. It was a wonderful family time, with no cares or worries.

Grandma's Meals Were Even Better Outdoors

The best part of any picnic was the food. Grandma was a wonderful cook and prepared delicious meals for us, but somehow her cooking tasted even better on a picnic. We'd sit down at a wooden table covered with a fresh gingham tablecloth weighted with wonderful goodies, which varied from one picnic to the next.

We'd delight to yummy potato salad, coleslaw and fried chicken at one picnic, and thick egg-salad sandwiches with homemade pickles and sliced tomatoes at another.

Sometimes we'd take our portable barbecue, and Dad grilled mouth-watering hamburgers and hot dogs. We devoured them with all the trimmings and often washed everything down with ice-cold lemonade poured from a big thermos into small paper cups.

One of Grandma's famous homemade pies completed the memorable meal. Quite often, we also had a whole juicy watermelon, which would set off a seed-spitting contest.

I fondly recall my father's company picnics, too. Rows of picnic tables were set up, each topped with a colorful tablecloth and filled with bowls of homemade food. For the children, there were organized games like kick-the-shoe, three-

FAMILY PICNIC. Sunday was picnic day when Sharon O'Loughlin (back row, left) was a girl. Next to her are her mother and brother Stephen. Seated are her grandmother and sisters Pam and Alana.

legged races and a peanut-in-the-shell scramble. The adults would line up their chairs and root from the sidelines.

The old-fashioned picnic may be a thing of the past, but my husband, Doug, and I are doing our part to revive it. We own a 1952 Chevrolet named "Miss Daisy", and she is perfect for picnicking.

On the chosen morning, Doug heads out to wash and wax Miss Daisy while I try to re-create some of Grandma's menus—potato salad, creamy coleslaw, crispy fried chicken and a fresh peach pie. For me, part of the fun is packing all those goodies into our antique picnic basket.

When everything's wedged in, I cover it with a freshly ironed tablecloth, grab the old cork-topped thermos filled with lemonade and we're off. We never know where we're heading, but my favorite place is still the beach.

A picnic is a lovely way to remember a simpler time in our lives and stir up fond memories…or build some new ones.

SHINING MOMENT. Author's husband, Doug, polishes "Miss Daisy" before they drive to a picnic, a favorite activity since the 1950s.

Tyke Tricked Santa into 'Twofer'

By Alicia Miller, Berkley, Michigan

IN 1953, we didn't have shopping malls in Milford, Michigan, and few of us had TVs, so there were no commercials telling us what toys we wanted for Christmas. Instead, we spent hours looking through the Sears, Roebuck "wish book", deciding just which toy to ask for.

Notice I said "toy", not "toys". I'd always been told that with all the children in the world, Santa couldn't possibly make more than one toy per child. Who was I to dispute this logic? I was only 7.

I'd never dared to ask Santa for two toys, but that year I wanted the "Silver City" cowboy town and a Roy Rogers ranch set. A cowboy town and a ranch went hand in hand, after all. Maybe Santa would count them as a single gift.

I wrote my letter to Santa and sent it off via my dad. I always wondered why I had to give those letters to Dad and not the postman.

Had Second Thoughts

As Thanksgiving came and went, starting the countdown to Christmas, I began having second thoughts about trying to fool Santa. What if he decided to teach me a lesson and not bring me anything?

By Christmas Eve, I was mighty worried. I went to bed hoping to hear the sounds of Santa's sleigh bells, afraid he'd pass me by.

The next morning, I checked with Mother and Dad before racing downstairs—I didn't want to make matters worse by running into Santa unannounced. There I stood, looking at a Christmas tree surrounded with wrapped presents…but nothing from Santa. He never wrapped his—he just placed them under the tree. I'd called his bluff and lost.

Kept Dad Busy

My parents must have taken pity on me as I stood there looking so dejected. Suddenly Dad walked into the room with two large cardboard boxes. I knew right away from the pictures that Santa had come through for me…but why hadn't he placed the toys under the tree?

It took my poor dad all morning and much of the afternoon to put the town together. "Why didn't Santa assemble them?" I asked. "With his magic, he could've done it in seconds."

But the look Dad gave me told me not to pursue that question any further.

Played Cowboys in Kitchen

By evening, Dad had all the pieces assembled, and his blood pressure had returned to normal. The following day, my mother's kitchen table looked like a scene from a Hopalong Cassidy movie, with buildings, cowboys and horses everywhere.

Today's children miss out on so much, having toys that do everything for them. Where is the imagination, the fun of pretending and make-believe? When I played with my town or ranch, I became one of those cowboys. I could even be Roy Rogers if I wanted.

I still have the town and ranch, although a few of the figures have slowly wandered away. When I retire, I'm going to set them up permanently and return to those days of yesteryear, when life was less complicated. The '50s were definitely the "good old days". ◝

SWEET RELIEF. When Alicia Miller looked under the Christmas tree (left) in 1953, she didn't see the two presents she'd asked Santa to bring. Had two been too many? Today, she still has the cowboy town (below) and the Roy Rogers ranch set.

Chapter Seven
Rockin' Round the Clock

Rockin' Round the Clock

THE '50s were as much a dividing point in popular music as the Mississippi River is a dividing line for the United States. By the end of the decade, the entire music industry had changed, primarily dictated by the tastes of teenagers. That's where the money was to be made. Teens in the '50s accounted for 70% of all record purchases.

The end of the '40s had marked the demise of the Big Band era. Yes, Stan Kenton and a few others carried on, but the Dorseys and Shaw and Goodman and dozens more of the great organizations faded away, mostly for economic reasons.

What dominated the early '50s was a remarkable collection of vocalists. Tony Bennett, Nat "King" Cole, Mel Torme,

> *"From a kid's viewpoint, it was a golden age..."*

Eddie Fisher and sobbing Johnnie Ray were some of the top male singers. Frankie Laine was my dad's favorite "because he really belts 'em out".

And the ladies' lineup was just as strong. Doris Day, Sarah Vaughn, Patti Page, Jo Stafford, Kay Starr and Ed Sullivan's favorite, Teresa Brewer, all had their distinctive styles and were blessed with exceptional tunes, lyrics and arrangements. (There's no better example than Peggy Lee's heart-stopping *Fever*.)

And then, practically in the middle of a Perry Como ballad, along came rock 'n' roll. Personally I'd like to blame the whole thing on Dick Clark, but that would be like blaming the telephone for those telemarketing calls at suppertime.

What put the teenies to rockin' and rollin' were Frankie Avalon, Bobby Darin, Fabian, Ricky Nelson and groups like the Everly Brothers. Remember Bill Haley and the Comets? The Platters? The Driftwoods and the Elegants?

Elvis Burst onto the Scene

But it was pretty tepid stuff until a Southern redneck by the name of Elvis Presley poured a bucket of gasoline on the whole industry, and the new music became the new religion of youth. His 1956 chart-topper, *Don't Be Cruel*, and the great *Heartbreak Hotel* firmly established him as the king of the industry.

From a kid's viewpoint, it was a golden age. Pop music was being produced on affordable little 45-rpm disks, two songs to a record. You bought it for the A side, but often the B side turned out to be an even bigger hit. And you could play them on a $9 record player.

Their parents who had danced and fallen in love to Glenn Miller's syrupy *String of Pearls* were aghast. This was music? You must be joking!

But as the memories that follow attest, people who were youngsters in the '50s fell in love and danced just as readily to (You Ain't Nuthin' But a) *Hound Dog*. Just don't ask me how. —Clancy Strock

Superstar Ritchie Valens Started Out as Richard Valenzuela

He was looking for a saxophone player, but he signed this talented young guitarist on the spot.

By Gil Rocha, Lancaster, California

WHEN I WAS 21, in 1957, I decided to start a band in San Fernando, California. I had learned to play the vibraphone and wanted to play the rhythm and blues and rock 'n' roll that were becoming increasingly popular at the time.

I recruited several musicians, and although I was looking for a saxophone player, I agreed to hear a young guitar player who was a friend of one of the other band members.

A few days later, a teenager appeared at my door, guitar and amp in hand, and introduced himself as Richard Valenzuela. After a few minutes of conversation, he began playing and singing and I was just blown away with his talent. I hired him on the spot and the band was complete. We chose the name "The Silhouettes".

A Big Hit with Teens

Soon, we began playing at house parties and then renting the local American Legion hall and promoting our own dances. Richard became "Little Richie" and was a tremendous hit with the teenagers who attended the dances.

At 16, he was very talented and professional. We noticed he pulled on the strings of his guitar to make that "wah-wah" noise that later became popular, either by using a foot pedal or a bar attached to the guitar.

Once we were playing in the rain. Since he was the only one using an electric instrument and had wet shoes, he was getting little shocks. He kept saying "Ow, ow," but kept on playing like a trooper.

I had ambitions of bigger and better things for the band and myself. When an acquaintance mentioned that he knew Bob Keane, president of Del-Fi Records, I decided to record one of our performances and send the tape to Bob via my acquaintance.

Signed Him Quickly

When Bob heard the tape, he was impressed with the talents of Little Richie, but unimpressed with the band.

He quickly signed Richard to a recording contract, changed his name to Ritchie Valens and the rest is history.

Ritchie quickly had three hit records—*Come On, Let's Go, Donna* and *La Bamba*.

Sadly, his brief career came to an abrupt end on February 3, 1959, when a small chartered plane he was in crashed near Clear Lake, Iowa. Also killed in the crash were fellow performers Buddy Holly and J.P. Richardson (the Big Bopper) and the pilot, Roger Peterson.

Although Ritchie's career lasted 16 months—8 months with our band and 8 months after he left—his music lives on. His life story was the basis for the movie *La Bamba*, and the fatal crash was memorialized in Don McLean's song *American Pie*, also remembered as "The Day the Music Died".

There have been several books written about Ritchie, and in May 1990, he was honored with a star on the Hollywood Walk of Fame. In March 2001, he was posthumously inducted into the Rock and Roll Hall of Fame in Cleveland, Ohio.

As honorary president of the Ritchie Valens Memorial Fan Club, I have continued to keep his name alive.

EARLY ROCK 'N' ROLL. The author (right) signed young guitarist Richard Valenzuela for his first band, The Silhouettes. The guitar Ritchie's playing now has a place in the Rock and Roll Hall of Fame.

Elvis' Pal Opened Door On Show of a Lifetime

IN 1956, just before the start of my senior year of high school, I heard that Elvis Presley was going to appear at the Municipal Auditorium in San Antonio, Texas.

I'd been hearing about this new entertainer for the past year or so. His name was strange—I often wondered if "Elvis" was misspelled—but I sure liked his music. I'd been a rock 'n' roll fan ever since hearing Bill Haley and the Comets' *Rock Around the Clock*.

I wanted to see what all the commotion was about, but I didn't have the $1.50 for a ticket. I'd already spent my allowance on records, including one of Elvis'.

The afternoon of the concert, I contacted a couple of buddies and suggested we go downtown and hang around the stage door. We couldn't see the show but maybe we could catch a glimpse of the star.

When we got to the stage door, however, there was no one around. We thought we'd missed the show and that Elvis was already gone.

As we started to leave, the stage door opened. A man stepped out, looked at us and lit a cigarette. We asked him if he was with the show. "No," he said.

We stared at each other for a few moments. Then the man asked us, "Would you guys like to see the show?" Would we ever!

The man told us to follow him into the auditorium very quietly. We were in the wings. All of a sudden, like a bolt of lightning, Elvis burst onto the stage and started singing. Wow! We watched the whole performance from the wings.

When the show ended and Elvis walked off the stage, he headed right for us. He asked the man who'd let us in, "Who're your friends, Red?" The man introduced us. We all shook Elvis' hand and told him how much we'd enjoyed the show. Elvis was very polite. He thanked each of us, then excused himself, saying he had an interview to do.

I think we were all still in shock on the way home. We not only saw Elvis, but shook his hand and saw him perform for free. The man who'd let us in was Elvis' longtime friend and bodyguard, Red West.

—Michael Forney
San Antonio, Texas

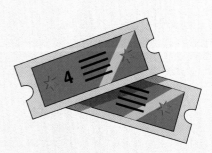

"THE KING". Elvis Presley shows some of the moves that wowed his teenage fans and upset their parents.

Sister's Elvis Getup Bowled Everyone Over

WE ENJOYED The Platters' songs, including *The Great Pretender* and all the others, and anything by Elvis Presley.

My boyfriend especially liked *Hound Dog* and loved to dance to it. We danced "The Chicken"—although it's not the same as today's chicken dance.

My boyfriend dressed like Elvis except for the blue suede shoes—his were plain black and not suede.

One Halloween, my oldest sister borrowed some of his clothes—including black pants with a pink stripe down the sid—styled her hair like Elvis', made and wore some fake sideburns and went to the bowling league Halloween party as "The King". She won first prize!

I wish I had a picture of her—she looked really cool. Her husband couldn't stop laughing. He was "all shook up"!

—Angie Youngson, Trenton, Michigan

ROCKIN' ROUND THE TABLE. When gathering at the malt shop in the 1950s, teenagers enjoyed sipping sodas and shakes and watching the hot rods drive by. Often they could listen to the latest rock 'n' roll hits on the jukebox and select their favorite songs right at the table.

Music of Elvis Touched a Chord

IN TODAY'S WORLD of instant hits and instant forgetting, people listen to music as background noise. In the '50s, you could dance to the music, sing the songs, keep the words in your heart and watch the singers, who were dressed in normal clothes and had a message in their songs.

We could list the big events in our lives by the songs that were playing at the time. I can still sing most of the songs, word for word.

I remember being in a restaurant in 1956, having a Coke with friends, and hearing *Heartbreak Hotel* on the jukebox. All of us girls just went wild!

We had never heard anything so earthy or emotional. After that, of course, "The King" went on to make many more hits and become a trendsetter for the music world

But what I still hold dear is that first youthful feeling I had when I first heard the magic of Elvis Presley.

—*Barbara Lindner*
Wyndmoor, Pennsylvania

His Rockin' Sent Him Rollin' Out the Door

I WORKED at the Chattanooga (Tennessee) Airport in 1956 as a dishwasher and sweeper at their glass-enclosed restaurant for 50¢ an hour.

When I wasn't doing the dishes, I was sweeping the restaurant floor with a push broom. As an Elvis Presley fan, I wore an upturned collar and a ducktail haircut.

One day I was sweeping to his rock 'n' roll song *Heartbreak Hotel* when my boss called me aside and told me I could not dance with my broom in front of the clientele eating there.

"If you do it again, I'll have to let you go," she warned.

I did all right until someone played *Blue Suede Shoes*. Then I was out on the street looking for another job.

Even if I couldn't dance like Elvis, there's one thing I did do like him—I eventually got a job as a truck driver.

I also married, and my wife and and I had nine children and more than 20 grandkids. I retired from my truck-driving career in 1991.

—*Bryant Finlayson, Valley Head, Alabama*

Decade's Music Showed Drastic Changes

IN THE '50s, the music was the best ever. It started with nice dance music from the '40s but ended with rock 'n' roll.

Hit songs included *Slow Poke* in '51, *I Saw Mommy Kissing Santa Claus* in '52, *Shake Rattle and Roll* in '54, *A White Sport Coat and a Pink Carnation* in '57 and *Jailhouse Rock* in 1957.

Patti Page recorded *Old Cape Cod* and it was a hit on *Your Hit Parade* all summer in 1957.

I lived with my grandparents. Even during high school, I wore no makeup, had to be quiet and was in bed by 9 p.m. On Fridays, I often stayed at my girlfriend's house and brought my record player.

It was small and plugged into the wall. It had an adapter for playing 45s but no changer—you had to take one record off and replace it with another.

The old breakable 78-rpm records were going out and being replaced with unbreakable 45s, smaller in size and only 25¢ each.

What an exciting time—low prices and good music.
— *Ruth Davis, Largo, Florida*

FAVORITE PASTIME. "My sister Barbara (left) and I loved listening to our old 78-rpm records in the '50s at home in New Kensington, Pennsylvania," writes Gloria Pomykala of New Kensington. "After high school graduation, we went to Pittsburgh to look for jobs and be on our own. Years later, I believe we could have been called Laverne and Shirley." Note the pull-out record player and fold-out radio behind them.

Words and Music Were Everywhere in the '50s

IN THE '50s, you could buy magazines that featured the words to the most popular songs.

My friends and I would take turns buying the latest issues and then spend hours singing our favorite songs over and over.

I loved those magazines and the weekly TV show *Your Hit Parade*. It was so exciting to have to wait until the end of the show to find out what the No. 1 hit was.

Favorite songs of mine were *The Twelfth of Never* and *Chances Are* by Johnny Mathis. I still get misty-eyed when I hear one of them on the oldies stations.

My mother just about passed out the first time she saw Elvis Presley on television. She thought he was indecent. It was only after he started singing some gospel songs that she thought he was not all bad. And she admitted that he had a good voice.

At local dances, the bunny hop and the stroll were our favorites. They were easy to learn and a lot of fun because they usually got everyone out on the floor.

— *Dorothy Sauer, Santee, California*

Ducktailed Teen Learned To Do Splits at "El Som"

EL SOM (for "sombrero") was a widely known teen dance held after Friday night football and basketball games in Springfield, Ohio. It was introduced at the YWCA in 1945, but for some reason faded away with the Class of '56.

I paid my first 15-cent entry fee, getting the back of my hand smeared with an official El Som stamp, in September 1953. I was a ducktailed 16-year-old decked out in an Eckstine shirt, pegged gray flannel slacks, argyle socks and Bold Looks—polished shoes with extra-thick soles and heels.

Rock 'n' roll had not yet arrived at El Som, but we had no problem jitterbugging to Buddy Morrow's *Night Train* or the cool sounds of Fats Domino, Rusty Bryant and the Clovers. Slow dancing-and-romancing tunes included hits by Joni James, Kitty Kallen and the Four Freshmen. All the music was on 45s, spun by the chaperone. There were no mobile DJs in those days.

I learned how to dance at El Som and eventually got good enough to do the splits. But you really didn't have to know how to dance to attend. It was fun just being there.

— *Dick Hatfield, Springfield, Ohio*

They Rocked Without Saying a Word

Creative teens served noisy rock 'n' roll with a twist.

By Angela Hébert Straight, Savannah, Georgia

MUSIC IS an important part of growing up, and the '50s were no exception.

I remember the day I received my first record player and was allowed to choose three 45s—Dean Martin's *Memories Are Made of This*, Perez Prado's *Cherry Pink and Apple Blossom White* and, of course, Elvis' *Don't Be Cruel*.

One of my favorite memories of the '50s is being a member of the "Junior 199ers", a group of teens named after an American Legion post in our town of Port Wentworth, Georgia. Our pantomime club performed at social events and even at Savannah's Civic Center.

Our opening Big Band number featured all the members of the group pretending to play the recorded music. You can see many of the instruments are really toys (below).

My brother Russell Hebért is standing in the middle, pretending to be the bandleader. The girl on the far right in the back row is now his wife of 36 years.

We also did individual numbers with props and costumes.

TV Landed Her in Jail

When I was 12 and into Elvis and ducktail haircuts, I pantomimed *Jailhouse Rock* on one of our local TV stations—*The Happy Dan Show*. They placed "bars" over the camera lens to make it look like I was in jail. Note my prison uniform, complete with saddle oxfords (right).

Today, whenever I think of the music and being part of this pantomime group, I am so grateful for the adults who gave so much of their time to direct us, build sets, get props and take us around to performances. It was so much fun and such a confidence builder for getting up in front of people.

I began an event at the school where I teach called "Just for the Fun of It". Although they now call it lip-syncing, the result is still the same, and they even allow me to choose the old songs. The students eagerly anticipate this event each year. For me, it's my way of saying thank you once more to those people who took the time for me.

I hope that "my" young people will keep the memories flowing in the future. ◖

QUIET FUN. Author (above) donned prison stripes for a rendition of *Jailhouse Rock* in 1957. The group she was a member of also performed its version of a Big Band number.

Attempts at Bleaching Left Her Hair—and Her Family—Quite Pale

By Jo Sandra Jammerthal, Akron, Iowa

I WAS ALMOST 14, in 1956, when I decided to give myself what I thought would be a nifty new hairstyle.

I was inspired by a popular song of the time, *Seventeen*, that I played over and over. The lyrics included, "Patch of blond peroxide hair, Jukebox baby ain't no square."

I went to Spyherd's Variety Store in my hometown of Akron, Iowa and bought a bottle of hydrogen peroxide. I took it home, went upstairs to the bathroom and dabbed it in my hair.

In several days, I did indeed have a "patch of blond". While most kids in school thought it looked pretty cool, my mom was aghast.

"How could you do such a thing? Your beautiful hair's ruined!" she wailed.

Grandmother Was *Not* Amused

To make matters worse, my very prim and proper grandmother came for a visit the following weekend. She told me in no uncertain terms that I had done a very unladylike thing and I should be ashamed to be seen in public.

I think it was then that I resolved to remedy the situation.

I returned to the store and bought a product called Noreen, a powder form of hair color in little capsules. That evening found me again at the bathroom sink.

The next day, my hair looked almost its original color, perhaps a bit darker. At least the blond patch was covered, or so I thought.

In a day or two, I began to notice a new highlight in my hair. Was it my imagination, or was there a green tinge to it?

Soon there was no doubt. The formerly blond patch was now a sickly, ghoulish green.

My poor mother was at her wit's end with me and my hair. In desperation, she phoned by grandmother and asked if she would make an appointment with Mr. Kenneth, my grandmother's hairdresser in Sioux City.

I can still remember how foolish and uncool I felt as my grandmother, in her hat and gloves, reiterated my misdeeds to Mr. Kenneth.

"Well, young lady, you certainly did a bang-up job of it!" he said.

He went on to explain something about chemical reactions and some other things I didn't understand.

The bottom line was there was nothing to be done for my hair but wait until it grew out. In the meantime, he ad-

NATURAL TRESSES. Author poses with her mother (top) and her grandmother (above) before her bleaching adventure.

vised a short haircut to minimize the damage.

Sypherd's Variety Store and the high school I attended are now gone. I lost my grandmother 25 years ago, but the memories live on. Now my mom laughs with me about the time I tried to be a "jukebox baby". ❮

Live Performance Rocked Her Clock

IN 1956, I was enchanted by *Rock Around the Clock* by Bill Haley and the Comets. Theirs was one of the first records I ever purchased.

My boyfriend took me to hear them at the Coliseum at the University of Nebraska at Lincoln. It was my first exposure to such an event, and I was disappointed because people squealed and screamed so I could not hear the group.

In high school, our group gathered at each other's homes for conversation, food and dancing. Parents were always present. Pizza in our house in Fremont was a do-it-yourself project; it was part of the fun.

—Iris Doksansky
Fremont, Nebraska

45s Recorded Our Clothing Choices

By Tom Morrison, Colorado Springs, Colorado

MANY DRESS STYLES of the Rock 'n' Roll Era were reflected in songs of that time. Some clothing fads were short-lived while others lasted. See how many you recall.

A White Sport Coat and a Pink Carnation, 1957, Marty Robbins
Bermuda Shorts, 1958, The Pledges
Black Denim Trousers and Motorcycle Boots, 1955, The Cheers
Black Slacks, 1957, Joe Bennett/Sparkletones
Blue Suede Shoes, 1955, Carl Perkins
Bobby Sox to Stockings, 1959, Frankie Avalon
Chantilly Lace, 1958, The Big Bopper
Leather Jacket, 1958, Leroy Van Dyke
No Chemise, Please, 1958, Gerry Granahan
Peg Pants, 1956, Bill Beach
Penny Loafers & Bobby Socks, 1957, Joe Bennett/Sparkletones
Pink Pedal Pushers, 1958, Carl Perkins
Pink Petticoats, 1958, The Big Bopper
Pink Shoe Laces, 1959, Dodie Stevens
Pointed Toe Shoes, 1959, Carl Perkins
Pretty Plaid Skirt, 1959, Mel Smith and the Night Riders
Short Shorts, 1957, Royal Teens
Tight Capris, 1958, Jody Reynolds
Tight Skirt & Sweater, 1958, Versatones
Tight Slacks, 1959, Merle Lindsay
White Bucks & Saddle Shoes, 1958, Bobby Pedrick Jr.
White Buckskin Sneakers & Checkerboard Socks, 1959, Bell Notes

WJJD TOP FORTY TUNES - WEEK OF AUGUST 20th. 1956 - SURVEY NO. 11 - VOL. 1

THIS WEEK	TITLE	ARTIST	RECORD NO.	LAST WEEK	WEEKS ON CHART
1.	FLYING SAUCER	BUCHANNAN & GOODMAN	LUN 101	2	3
2.	HOUND DOG	ELVIS PRESLEY	VIC 6604	1	5
3.	BE BOP A LULA	GENE VINCENT	CAP 3450	3	8
4.	MY PRAYER	PLATTERS	MER 70893	4	9
5.	CANADIAN SUNSET	HUGO WINTERHALTER	VIC 6537	7	4
5a.	CANADIAN SUNSET	ANDY WILLIAMS	CAD 1297	7a	3
6.	WHAT EVER WILL BE WILL BE	DORIS DAY	COL 40704	5	8
7.	I WANT YOU NEED YOU LOVE YOU	ELVIS PRESLEY	VIC 6540	6	11
8.	SONG FOR A SUMMER NIGHT	MITCH MILLER	COL 40730	9	4
9.	TONIGHT YOU BELONG TO ME	PATIENCE & PRUDENCE	LIB 55022	18	3
10.	RIP IT UP	LITTLE RICHARD	SP 579	14	8
10a.	RIP IT UP	BILL HALEY	DEC 30028	14a	3
11.	YOU DON'T KNOW ME	JERRY VALE	COL 40710	13	6
12.	ALLEGHENY MOON	PATTI PAGE	MER 70878	8	10
13.	APE CALL	NERVOUS NORVUS	DOT 15485	11	5
14.	I ALMOST LOST MY MIND	PAT BOONE	DOT 15472	12	11
15.	I'M IN LOVE AGAIN	FATS DOMINO	IMP 5386	10	11
16.	MAMA TEACH ME TO DANCE		ABC 9722	21	4

Top Tunes Were a Hit with Her

I GREW UP in the Chicago area in the '50s, graduating from Blue Island (Illinois) Community High School in 1958, and loved listening to the music on the Chicago radio stations.

One of my favorite pastimes was listening to the WJJD Top 40 songs on Saturday. I would walk the 2 miles to the record shop every week just to pick up the weekly copy of "Forty Top Tunes" and maybe a 45-rpm record for 99¢. At 15 or 16, I didn't drive, and I was too old to ride a bike.

I'd use the list to buy the top hits, but at 99¢ each, I didn't buy many. I guess I had about two dozen at one time. I wish I still had them today.

After I bought a new record, my girlfriend and I would go up to my bedroom and play it tons and tons of times. We'd sit on the floor and use my portable record player. We played a lot of 78s, too.

My favorite song? *Oh Julie*, of course!

—*Julie Hoffman, Crete, Illinois*

Car Club Offered Saturday Dances

DURING the late '50s, our local hot rod club, the Road Rebels, held Saturday night dances for all the teenagers and young people in Elwood City, Pennsylvania.

Our car club was sponsored by the Elwood City Elks Lodge, so we were fortunate to have a nice meeting place as well as a controlled environment for the younger generation.

Our club members monitored the behavior at the dances. For us, dressed in our special club jackets, it also was a great place to meet a lot of nice young ladies.

But I believe the end result was that parents were comfortable with the location to send their children on a Saturday night.

—*Al Schuller, Orangevale, California*

Johnnie Ray Concert At Hollywood Bowl Made Teens Feel Grown Up

By David Neuschafer, Vista, California

THE FIRST "real" concert I ever attended was in 1956. My best friend Al, and I got tickets to take our girlfriends to a show at the Hollywood Bowl.

We took extra care getting ready that night so we'd look our best. Both of us were on our best behavior with our dates, opening doors and following everything we'd been taught about proper manners.

We had to climb many, many steps to our seats, which were almost in the last row, but we didn't care. This was a big deal to us. It was a chance for the four of us to show that we weren't just 15- and 16-year-olds, but adults.

As the sun went down, the stage lights got brighter. The orchestra finished its warm-up, and the announcer introduced the man we'd come to see: Johnnie Ray.

Audience Clapped Respectfully

He sang most of his old songs, and we clapped respectfully, following the lead of those around us. We didn't want to behave like those kids who screamed when they saw Elvis Presley. This was a real concert, where the audience clapped quietly.

It was a beautiful night under the stars, and everything was great until Johnnie started to sing *Just Walking in the Rain*. This proved too much for an older lady two rows in front of us. About halfway through the song, she yelled at the top of her lungs, "Oooooh, Johnnieeeee!" Her voice traveled all around the bowl and bounced off the nearby hills.

Everyone looked around for the culprit. The ushers came running up the steps, flashlights in hand. For a moment, the beams focused on us, but the ushers didn't say anything.

Johnnie Ray got through the rest of the song without incident, and the ushers turned off their flashlights. Thankfully, the lady in front of us managed to control herself for the rest of the evening. ✂

Accident May Have Influenced Singer's Style

JOHNNIE RAY was born in Oregon in 1927. His musical talent was recognized early, but a tragic accident when he was 13 may have helped shape his career.

While attending a Boy Scout Jamboree in 1940, he was hurled into the air during a blanket toss. He landed hard, and his left ear was punctured by a stiff straw. He lost the hearing in that ear but didn't tell anyone right away because he thought it would heal.

Several months later, he received the first of many hearing aids he used during his life. The crisp enunciation that became part of his style may have stemmed from over-compensation for that initial hearing loss.

His hits include *Cry*, *The Little White Cloud That Cried*, *Just Walking in the Rain* and *Walking My Baby Back Home*.

Johnnie Ray International Fan Club

Meeting Music Idols Was A Dream Come True

The 1959 Michigan State Fair was the best ever for this determined teen.

By Jane White McCarthy, Livonia, Michigan

THROUGHOUT the 1950s, the end of summer meant the beginning of the Michigan State Fair. Attending the fair was a cherished ritual, and I never missed one.

I'd always enjoyed the animal barns, butter sculptures and merry-go-round, but as I got older, my expectations for the fair changed.

In 1959, the attraction I most wanted to see was the rock 'n' roll show hosted by Dick Clark. I was about to enter high school in Dearborn, a Detroit suburb, and rock 'n' roll ruled my life.

Then I heard about a contest sponsored by *The Detroit Times*, in which teenage readers submitted essays about the lineup of stars. The winners would be honored guests on opening day of the fair and actually get to meet all the stars.

There would be six winners, and I was determined to be one of them. Pen in hand, I assembled my thoughts and added some creative illustrations.

My efforts paid off. I was among the victorious—and the payoff was unreal!

An Unforgettable Day

On opening day, the six of us rode in Corvette convertibles in a parade down Detroit's main thoroughfare. But the best part was getting to meet the stars.

SHE WAS IN HEAVEN. Author could only smile as singer Freddy "Boom Boom" Cannon (center) gazed into her eyes at the Michigan State Fair. She and the other five teenagers were honored guests.

We had photo sessions with Frankie Avalon, Bobby Rydell, Jan and Dean, Santo and Johnny, Freddie Cannon and Dick Clark. We met and got autographs from the Coasters, La Vern Baker, Duane Eddy, Jack Scott, Anita Bryant, Skip and Flip, Dick Caruso and Rusty York. All of these performers were teen idols. I had their 45-rpm hit records at home, stacked next to my hi-fi.

During the show, the winners were seated in a special area and received special programs (right). I must have looked like the cat that swallowed the canary. What would all those screaming girls think if they knew that only 2 hours earlier, I'd been standing on the steps of Frankie Avalon's trailer and was holding the exact same pen with which he'd signed my autograph book? Was I cool or what?

The butter sculptures and merry-go-round charmed me for years. But in the waning days of summer, when it's time for the fair, those aren't the things I remember most.

It's a group of six giddy teenagers, mesmerized by the once-in-a-lifetime event we shared in the summer of 1959.

It was a perfect ending to a remarkable decade. ◄

50¢

Best always Dick Clark

SOUVENIR PROGRAM

Chapter Eight

Family Life

Family Life

BACK IN THE 1950s, every day brought revelations, some good, some bad. How in the world could Eddie Fisher and Debbie Reynolds split up? Or Marilyn Monroe pose in the altogether for a new men's magazine?

Imagine Mickey Spillane and Norman Vincent Peale topping the best-seller book lists, even though the two authors couldn't possibly be more different.

The future of movies was said to be 3-D pictures...until the public had a chance to see one. Next came the Bridey Murphy phenomenon, wherein presumably sane people claimed to have revisited previous lifetimes in faraway places, like Ireland or Mongolia, where they had been queens or knights and never criminals nor serfs.

McCarthy to Mickey

An obscure Wisconsin senator claimed to have proof positive that the federal government teemed with Communists. Joe McCarthy raved and ranted and haphazardly slandered scores of people for 30 days, mesmerizing and at the same time terrifying his national TV audience. He eventually was discredited, but not before setting off a national "Commies under the bed" scare.

Disneyland opened in the Los Angeles area. Who could have guessed that someday the Mouse Kingdom would become the world's largest entertainment empire, spreading even to Europe and the Orient?

During a business trip, I viewed the future and didn't even know it. I was traveling with a man who said, "I've got to show you the darnedest thing you ever saw. It's just down the road in Salisbury, Maryland."

It was an enormous grocery store, big as several football fields. "They call it a supermarket," my friend said. And super it was, with a bakery, delicatessen, flower shop, fish market and even a baby-sitting corral and coffee shop. Good-bye, mom-and-pop groceries.

Quiz shows on television captivated viewers as contestants vied for as much as $100,000. What we didn't know until later was that some shows were "rigged." Good-bye, quiz shows.

An idea called "health insurance" was promoted by Blue Cross. As the father

"I saw the future— they called it a supermarket..."

of four youngsters, I thought the concept held great appeal, but the chances of it ever becoming reality appeared to be between slim and none.

Those of us who were starting new families out there in suburbia reveled in our 1,100-square-foot look-alike tract homes. It took ingenuity, but most months we could make it to the next payday without overdrawing our checking account. Our idea of a fun-filled weekend was to ask the neighbors over for iced tea, popcorn and bridge or canasta, with coffee and pie to wind up the evening.

Fifty years later, most of us look back on those family-building years of the '50s as the very best decade of our lives.
—*Clancy Strock*

Tykes Tried to Help Their Busy Mother

But their "help" caused a lot of work in 1956.

By Marjorie Lee Lori, Anchorage, Alaska

THE HEAT didn't improve the temperament of my 2- and 3-year-old sons, and having the oven on for the cookies I'd promised them didn't help either.

Two little redheads clamored at my skirt, begging to go outside our home in San Francisco, California on this day in 1956. It had been too hot for them to sleep at naptime and they were cross and restless.

"Just keep your shirts on until I get the cookies in the oven, then I'll grease you both and you can go out in the sandbox," I told them.

The telephone rang in the office at the front of the house. I dashed to make sure the screen door was latched to keep the boys inside, then raced the boys for the office door.

I won by a nose and got the door latched behind me before they made it inside. I could hear them fussing on the other side of the door as I picked up the receiver. I switched roles to being my husband's secretary and prepared to take an order as I half-listened to the clamor of the boys in the hall.

The customer was long-winded and apparently felt she had found a sympathetic ear. I longed to check on the boys.

Silence Meant Nothing Good

Suddenly their noise stopped, an ominous thing when dealing with two bundles of energy.

Something crashed in the kitchen and I jumped, but the customer rattled on. Nothing sounded broken and neither of the boys was crying, so I guessed there were no immediate casualties.

I was finally able to hang up, finish writing the order and switch gears back to my mother role.

As I opened the office door, Pat, the younger of the two, let out a squeal and a very vehement "No!"

I raced back down the hall to the kitchen and stopped dead in my tracks at the entrance.

The crash that I'd heard was a 3-pound can of Crisco.

It sat upright, and Mike, the older of the boys, had both hands in it. Pat was crawling rapidly toward me, or at least trying to.

The floor was a veritable skating rink and both boys were covered from head to foot, clothes and all, with

READY FOR ANYTHING. Marjorie Lee Lori's two sons, Mike and Pat, weren't quite so slippery in this 1956 picture...unlike on the day she describes in her story.

Crisco. The legs of the kitchen table and chairs, the stove and refrigerator all were covered with greasy hand marks as high as they could reach.

"What are you doing?" I screamed at Mike as I surveyed the mess.

"Greasing us up so we can go out in the sandbox," he replied matter-of-factly.

I had to laugh in spite of myself. It wasn't safe to step onto the kitchen floor because it was so slippery.

Two Slippery Sons

I called the boys to me, took one under each arm and carried them to the bathtub. I stripped and bathed them. When they were clean, I dressed and greased them—this time with suntan lotion—and put them out in the sandbox so I could clean up the kitchen.

It took 3 hours and three buckets of hot, soapy water and lots of hard scrubbing.

By 5 p.m., the cookies were baked and dinner was ready. The boys were playing quietly on the kitchen floor and I had finally sat down at the kitchen table with the morning paper and a cup of coffee.

My husband, George, came quietly up to the back door, tired after a hard day working in the heat. He looked at the serene family scene through the screen door and said, "This is the kind of day when I wish I could be in your place and take life easy." ❧

WRIGHT DESIGN. Murray and Bobbi Elters spent their wedding night in the Imperial Hotel near Mt. Fuji. Architect Frank Lloyd Wright's floating foundation allowed the building to survive the 1923 earthquake that caused major damage elsewhere.

Air Force Dentist Enjoyed 9-Month Honeymoon in Japan

By Murray Elters Jr., Tinton Falls, New Jersey

WHILE SERVING as a dentist at the Air Force base in Fort Worth, Texas in 1952, I met a young lady who worked at the nearby Bell Helicopter plant. It wasn't long before I fell in love with Bobbi and wanted to get engaged, but the Korean War was under way and I had orders to go overseas.

All I knew was I was going to the Far East, and after my tour there, I'd be discharged. When I told Bobbi this, she just said, "Call me when you get your assignment."

All my professional friends were sent to bases in the Far East where they were not allowed to bring their wives. But I was sent to Yokota Air Force Base, 35 miles west of Tokyo, where wives were permitted. I was soon on the phone with Bobbi, who booked herself on a Norwegian freighter sailing from San Francisco to Yokohama.

At Yokota, the wife of the medical commanding officer organized parties on the last Friday of every month at the Officers' Club. When she learned that Bobbi was arriving and that we were to be married on a Friday night, she said the monthly party could be our wedding reception.

I protested—I couldn't afford 150 dinners! But the CO's wife said that was no problem. Everyone paid their own way for these Friday night parties, and this would be no exception. "Wonderful," I said. "I'll buy the cake and a round of champagne."

At PX prices, the whole thing cost me about $15.

Bobbi and I were married at the ward office in Tokyo—our marriage license is in Japanese—and received a certificate of approval from the American ambassador at the U.S. Embassy.

We spent our wedding night in the Imperial Hotel, which Frank Lloyd Wright had designed in 1915. Our honeymoon was at the base of Mt. Fuji, at the Fujiya Hotel. This was an "R and R hotel" for officers during the Korean War, so all it cost was my housing allowance.

Bobbi and I had a wonderful time in Japan. She was with me for all but 4 of the 13 months I was stationed there. We both considered it a 9-month honeymoon. ◄

Two Cars at Drive-in Doubled the Pleasure

GOING TO the drive-in movies back in the '50s was a perfect place for romantic teenagers and a great family treat, although my husband did not enjoy the "family" part. Every time we'd begrudgingly agree to take the kids along, he'd always come back saying, "That's the last time!"

The three boys would giggle and chat throughout the show at the drive-in near our home in Weymouth, Massachusetts.

We were lucky enough to have two cars—one for Jim to drive to work and one for me to shop and chauffeur the kids around. In 1954, this led to Jim's answer to the drive-in problem—we took both cars! Jim would go in one and I'd follow with the kids in the other. He'd find two spots, side by side, and park. I'd pull in next to him and get in his car, leaving the kids in my car.

The kids had a great time, and we could enjoy the show while keeping an eye on them.

Jim felt very smug when other fathers congratulated him on being so clever.
—*Virginia Fitzgerald*
Quincy, Massachusetts

Stellar Cellar Memories

Their cellar had a special warmth even when the furnace wasn't running.

By Ron Sturga, Edinboro, Pennsylvania

TODAY, people talk about descending to their basement, lower level or utility room. In the '50s, we just went down to the cellar.

The cellar held the all-important furnace in our home in Springdale, Pennsylvania. But it also held much more. It was the center for many daily, weekly or seasonal tasks.

Mom sorted and soaked laundry each Sunday night in the cellar because Monday was always washday. The cellar floor was strewn with piles of sorted clothing, and Mom soaked the clothes overnight in big stationary tubs. The old wringer washer was adjacent to these tubs and right above the floor drain.

Opening the cellar door on Monday mornings, we could smell the boiling Argo starch and Santina awaiting the doilies, aprons, pillowcases and shirt collars. We heard the reassuring chugging of the washing machine.

White clothes were placed in a big copper boiler and became so hot, they had to be removed with a cut-off wooden broomstick. Wet clothes were hung to dry on ropes Dad had strung back and forth near the ceiling. In bad weather, the cellar was filled with the clean scent of damp clothing.

The curtain stretcher, ironing board and mangle were all ready along the wall for Tuesday, ironing day.

"Doctor" Dad Worked Wonders

In one corner, Dad had his workbench, where he repaired everything and anything. He was especially adept when operating on my sisters' dolls. He'd clear the bench to prepare his operating table at "doll hospital".

He'd replace the stuffing and put heads and dangling arms back into their sockets, much to the relief of Karen and Janice. While he worked, they were perched on a stool beside their hero, who could fix things as good as new.

Mom and Dad always worked together on canning and pickling, so we'd have jars of everything stored there. The aromas were great as we'd come home from school and run down the stairs to watch and taste.

All this work was vital, of course. We couldn't afford to hire plumbers, electricians and handymen, so Dad had to do those jobs. Mom washed, ironed and mended so clothes would last. And the canned goods and pickles were unquestionably more affordable than grocery store purchases.

Our cellar also was the place for many family celebrations, birthday parties and anniversaries. Wedding rehearsal dinners for both my sisters and their husbands were held there. There was no need to rent a hall, and catering was out of the question.

Aunts and cousins brought baked and cooked specialties. There were pigs in a blanket, coleslaw, kettles of homemade soup, stuffed peppers and pasta. Sausage and sauerkraut filled

BASE MEANT A LOT. Author's father, Paul Sturga (above), still tinkers at his workbench while his mother, Frances Sturga (below), cans tomatoes. When their kids were growing up, they provided a welcome place for their friends.

plates in a hurry, and there were vegetables from family gardens and fruit from their trees and bushes.

As my sisters and I grew older, our parents made our friends feel welcome in our humble, but loving, home. Our cellar may have been older than many, but it was clean and the gathering place for our friends.

Ducked to Dance

Dad painted a shuffleboard court on the floor, although disks sometimes slid untrue on the rough cement. We brought the record player, pretzels and pop to the cellar to dance. I'd have to duck every time we'd dance near the light bulbs and dangling pull chains since they were only 6 feet from the floor and I'm 6-foot-4.

Whether it was shoveling coal, banking the furnace, washing clothes, patching an inner tube, canning, roller-skating or playing hide-and-seek, our cellar was always a special place. To this day, when we go home to visit our parents, we make it a point to return to that special place just to reminisce.

Bride Was Trusting... Also Penniless

AFTER MY HUSBAND, Alexander, and I were married in Philadelphia, Pennsylvania (right) in October 1953, we had an afternoon reception.

We'd arranged to have dinner, by ourselves, at the Forge Room, where we had gone on our first date. Our honeymoon in the Pocono Mountains was to begin the next day.

Since we had no car, we spent the night at Chancellor Hall, the residence hotel where the restaurant was located. The next morning, we took a taxi to the bus station and checked our bags before walking to Mass at a nearby church.

During Mass, when the collection plate came by, I put my hand on my new husband for some money.

He waited until we were outside the church to ask me why I had no money.

My simple answer was to point out that now he was responsible for me and I had no money!

He was dumbfounded and pointed out that if this was the case, I did not even have a dime to make a phone call if I needed it.

I just smiled at my beloved husband and told him I was very confident, trusting him to take care of me...and he still is doing a great job of it 47 years later!
—Lorrie Siegel
Dover, Delaware

Mom-to-Be Was Flying High—
Until Labor Pains Started

By Zaphra Reskakis, New York, New York

IT WAS MY first flight—17 hours from New York City to Munich. We'd been airborne for some time when suddenly I felt sharp, steady pangs. I pressed the call button.

When the stewardess came over, I whispered, "This is my first baby and I don't know what labor pains feel like. Do you?"

"No," she said, "but I think you'd better start timing them." As she walked toward the cockpit, she called out, "Excuse me, everybody. Is there a doctor or nurse on the plane?"

No one responded.

As the pains kept coming, I struggled to hold back my tears. Why had I fibbed to get on this plane?

I was on a military transport filled with the wives and children of servicemen. It was Oct. 16, 1956, and I was joining my husband, Gus, who'd been stationed in Germany since June.

Ambulance Would Be Waiting

I was 7-1/2 months pregnant, but the Army wouldn't transport wives who were more than 6 months along, and we couldn't afford the airfare on a commercial flight. So I checked with my obstetrician, made sure it was safe for me to fly, then told the Army I was only 6 months pregnant. Now I was somewhere over the Atlantic Ocean, with labor pains 12 minutes apart.

The stewardess returned, patted my arm and said, "Don't worry, honey. We refuel soon in Newfoundland. The pilot radioed them to have an ambulance waiting."

I asked the stewardess where the bathroom was. She helped me up and pointed to the back of the plane.

"Do you need help?" she asked. I shook my head and waddled up the aisle, followed by the sympathetic eyes of the other wives. I felt my hands being patted as I passed. On the walk back to my seat, I heard words of advice and encouragement.

One woman pulled me down, sat me next to her and began chattering. She must have talked for an hour. Suddenly she pointed out the window.

"We're coming in for a landing," she said. "I can see the ambulance outside. When was your last pain?"

I looked at my watch and pressed the call button. As the stewardess approached me, I grinned and said, "My last pain was 25 minutes ago. I guess that was false labor, but it sure felt real enough to me."

The stewardess headed back toward the cockpit, whooping, "It's okay! False alarm!" The plane filled with hurrahs.

Don't Worry, Mom

We landed in Gander, Newfoundland and everyone else deplaned. A doctor boarded, gave me a cursory examination and agreed it had been false labor.

When I got off the plane, I remembered promising to send my mother a postcard from Newfoundland. I was her only child, and we were close. I didn't want her to worry.

I bought a postcard of an iceberg and wrote, "Mama, flying is great. Wonderful trip. So far, no problems."

By the time we reached Munich, I was bloated and very uncomfortable. I grabbed my smelly tote bag, which was filled with feta and provolone cheeses and homemade baklava, and took a rose from my purse. My appearance had changed so much that I'd told Gus I'd stick a rose between my teeth to help him spot me.

We climbed off the plane into pea soup. As I started down the stairs, I panicked. With the fog and everybody in uniform, I couldn't find my husband.

But he saw me, grabbed me and kissed me. We claimed my luggage and quickly walked over to a sea of Mercedes automobiles in the parking lot. Everybody in the Army of Occupation in Germany seemed to have one.

Gus bought our Mercedes, a brand-new black sedan, for $1,000. We called it "Black Beauty". I climbed in and gratefully sank into the soft leather seats.

We took many trips in that car, but the drives to the Army hospital were the most memorable. Our son, George, arrived right on schedule in December, and his sister, Lisa, followed 13 months later. At $7 per delivery, we figured we could afford to have two kids. ◀

EXTRA PASSENGER? Author (right) felt labor pains during a 17-hour flight to Munich, Germany. Baby George is shown with his parents (below) in December 1956.

Their Fifth Anniversary Smooch Was Interrupted

KEN AND I were high school sweethearts and married 2 years after graduation, following his graduation from community college in 1949.

Five years later, we had two small children and not much money, but we wanted to celebrate our anniversary with a nice dinner.

We left the children with my parents and had our special dinner. It was a lovely clear night, so we decided to drive up into the nearby mountains to look at the view of our city and valley with all the bright and beautiful lights.

Of course, we were doing some smooching and hugging while looking down below when suddenly there were red lights behind us.

Oh, no. The police!

An officer walked up to the car with his flashlight on us and growled, "How old's the girl?"

Ken immediately answered, "She's my wife."

The officer's partner then walked up with his flashlight on us and said, "What's the problem?"

"They're married!" the first officer said incredulously.

As they shined their flashlights around in the car, they could see a child's car seat, baby toys, a baby bottle and a blanket.

"Well, take it easy," they said as they walked away.

As we approach our 52nd anniversary, we still laugh about this fifth anniversary intrusion.

—Bee Henisey
Acton, California

TIME FOR WORK! "I was just a tyke in 1953 when I decided to go to work just like my daddy did in Prosperity, Pennsylvania," says Jane Anderson Hannan, who now lives in Middleville, Michigan and shared this picture from her younger days. "I stepped into his overalls, picked up his work coat and lunch pail and walked out the kitchen door, although it couldn't have been very easy. My mother, Bernice Anderson, grabbed a camera and snapped this shot on the porch at just the right moment."

Honeymoon Is Laughable... Today

By Barbara Zimmerman
New Market, Maryland

THE '50s brought new experiences to my husband-to-be and me that we still laugh about today.

We graduated from high school in Frederick, Maryland in June and began to plan our wedding for October. Everyone told us we were too young and it would never work.

On our wedding day, Gene worked all day at his parents' farm, milking and husking corn, but he made it to the church on time. Everything went smoothly up to that point.

We left on our honeymoon about 10:30 p.m. and headed toward Virginia in Gene's 1933 Chevy. Inexperienced as we were, we had no idea about getting reservations and discovered that a big convention in Washington, D.C. had filled all the hotel rooms in the area.

We stopped along the road and tried to catch 40 winks, but tractor-trailers going by rocked our car and kept us awake. We headed on in the fog and went about 25 miles too far down the road.

When we stopped at a gas station and restaurant, the manager told us the bad news and we backtracked, getting to Front Royal, Virginia about daylight.

Gene went in a motel and found the lobby filled with sleeping people. Someone eventually took us to a tourist home, and were we ever glad to see *that* gentleman.

When we got there, Gene was so tired after working all day and driving most of the night that he passed out on me, dropping with a thud.

The folks downstairs came up to see if everything was all right. We told them yes, but it was a little frightening. Today we laugh about it when we retell the story.

The rest of the honeymoon went smoothly. We lived with Gene's parents for nearly 4 years. Our daughter Sherry was born in July 1953. After Edwin Jr. was born in May of 1955, we decided we needed more room, so we moved into the house on his parents' smaller farm and really spread out. Our third child, Julie, was born in 1969.

This year we celebrated our 50th anniversary. For people who said it wouldn't last because we were too young, we sure fooled them. ✄

NOT FOGGED IN. Barbara Zimmerman (above) and husband Gene took this '33 Chevy on their honeymoon in 1951. A lack of sleep and no hotel reservations made the trip memorable.

Cupid's Arrows Detoured Bachelors' Summer Plans

By Richard Mathewson, Norman, Oklahoma

THE SUMMER of 1956, when I was 22, I returned home to Saginaw, Michigan after my first year of dental school. My two best friends from high school, George Hayes and Frank Niedersdadt, had just come home from the service.

George had bought a yellow-and-cream 1956 Dodge Custom Royal convertible with tail fins, a black nylon top and push-button gear selectors. We were ready to roll!

We planned to spend our summer cutting a swath through the class of senior student nurses at Saginaw General Hospital, leaving a path of broken hearts in our wake. Little did we know, we'd be stopped dead in our tracks.

George was dating Willa Hathaway, one of the senior student nurses, and that gave us a foot in the door. Willa called her best friend, Alice Alstott, and told her about this great friend of George's.

Alice was skeptical. She'd been out with some real jerks before. "If this guy is a creep," she told Willa, "I'll never speak to you again."

On June 25, Willa, George, Alice and I set off in George's new convertible to spend the day at the Caseville beach on Lake Huron. It was a beautiful summer Sunday. We swam, walked the beach, talked and watched a beautiful sunset.

Glorious Summer of '56

Not long after that, I arranged a date for Frank with Evon Simon, another senior student nurse. On the way home that night, Frank turned to me and said, "Dick, that is the girl I am going to marry." So the glorious summer of 1956 began.

Since we were all students—George and Frank were returning to college that fall—our dates were often inexpensive. We played euchre and pinochle in the lobby of the nurses' dormitory or went to the movies. Our favorites were *Picnic*, starring William Holden and Kim Novak, *The Seven-Year Itch* with Marilyn Monroe, and *The King and I* with Yul Brynner.

At Frank's home, we rolled back the rugs and danced to the romantic sounds of Jackie Gleason's orchestra playing *The World is Waiting for the Sunrise*, or Doris Day singing with Les Brown and His Band of Renown. Patti Page, Tony Bennett and Kay Starr were other favorites.

It was a great summer—going to the beach for picnics, swimming, dancing, attending concerts in the park, falling in love.

When the nurses graduated in August 1956, we three couples attended the dance honoring their class. Willa and George married later that month, and Frank and Evon got engaged.

At the end of the summer, I gave Alice my fraternity pin and returned to Ann Arbor. Alice took a position at Children's Hospital in Detroit, and we started a long-distance courtship, visiting each other on weekends.

In the spring of 1957, we started planning our wedding. One highlight that spring was seeing our first wide-screen movie, *Around the World in 80 Days*.

Frank and Evon were married in August 1957, and Alice and I followed on September 7. All six of us played roles in each other's weddings.

George, Frank and I are still close friends and have watched our children—and now our grandchildren—grow. And we're still married to the three beautiful student nurses we met in that glorious summer of 1956.

SUMMER ROMANCE. Richard Mathewson and Alice Alstott were married in 1957 (above, second and third from right). The summer before, the couple enjoyed a ride with friend George Hayes (below left) in his convertible.

She Ran Circles Around Them

IN DECEMBER of 1957, when my husband was transferred to Van Nuys, California from Chicago, we packed up the family and went.

We settled in and started getting acquainted with the neighbors. One day I noticed the corner store was having a hula hoop contest.

Our youngest daughter, Linda (above), was all for entering and determined to win. There were a great number of boys and girls entered in the contest, but that didn't bother Linda.

She just kept going and knocked everyone else out of the competition, becoming the first-place winner.

Today, Linda has been married for 30 years and recently became a grandma for the first time.   —*Dorothy Lang*
Carlsbad, California

Misdeed Had a Bittersweet Ending

I WAS a very young bride on June 3, 1950 when I packed a piece of glassware from The Plaza Hotel in New York City, where my husband, Kenneth, and I (right) began our honeymoon.

When Kenneth found it the next night, he was not pleased. In fact, he told me that taking something we didn't pay for on our first day of marriage was hardly the way to start out in life.

I felt awful but told him I would return it on June 3, 2000, our 50th anniversary. I guess my solution did the trick, as he didn't stay angry with me too long.

Sadly, he passed away in 1992, so I wasn't able to keep my promise to him. On Valentine's Day 2000, I sent the glass to The Plaza Hotel manager with a letter explaining my misdeed.

On what would have been our 50th anniversary, I received this letter from Paul Tormey, the hotel manager:

"I received your letter of February 14 with our old Plaza glass. It is always wonderful to read letters from past guests of the hotel who had celebrated spe-

cial events here. Your letter was particularly special and has made the rounds with many of The Plaza's management team.

"It is safe to say that not many were left with a dry eye. I have saved your letter on my desk so that I could write to you on what would have been your 50th wedding anniversary."

These two letters embrace my most fabulous memory—my marriage to Kenneth.   —*Helen Fisher*
Dublin, California

SHOWDOWN. "Our two older sons, Greg (left) and Dana, were hamming it up with their new gun and holster sets in 1959," writes Ray Rowe of Cadiz, Kentucky. "Dana always hoped for a horse for his birthday and at Christmas, but since we lived in the city, he never got one. Now his daughter is bugging him to buy her a horse. Could this be poetic justice?"

Army Sergeant Should Have Been in NASA

IN THE MID-'50s, I was an Army sergeant assigned to the ROTC Department at the University of Scranton in Scranton, Pennsylvania.

At night, I enjoyed being a jazz drummer, swapping shop talk at the music shop, then listening and playing at nightspots in Scranton or neighboring towns.

I had a black-over-yellow 1957 DeSoto with tail fins about as tall as I was. This low-slung beauty looked less like a shark and more like a beached whale as it fishtailed through Pennsylvania snows.

Unsuspecting friends who accepted a ride from me received a rare treat. At one point on the drive back, the road climbed steadily and peaked on Olive Street, where it seemed to take a 45-degree angle down to another part of the city. It was a great view.

However, if I drove my soft-sprung DeSoto at about 35 mph over that crest, it appeared as if we were driving off the end of the earth. This was made more vivid if the driver—me—screamed.

It was years before I could sell the car, probably because of all the fingernail cuts in the vinyl dashboard.

Today many of my friends have forgotten the music and the clubs but still have strong memories of the ride home!
    —*Dave Mitchell, Marietta, Georgia*

Young Family Learned to Expect the Unexpected

By Helen Tullock, Delano, Tennessee

IN THE 1950s, things changed so fast for our family that I often wondered what was coming next.

My husband, John, and I had college degrees and taught at a two-teacher school. John also was pastor of a nearby church. We had two children and a house near our families in Tennessee. I suppose I thought our future was set.

Then John announced that he wanted to attend a seminary in North Carolina. This would change everything, but I didn't object. I'd married him for better or worse, for the expected and the unexpected. Besides, there had to be a church just waiting for him to be its pastor. I'd find a teaching job, and everything would be fine.

We bought a small mobile home big enough for the four of us. Then Mama told us she wasn't going to be left behind. I was her only child, and she did not intend to live that far away.

Just as I'd agreed to the move, John agreed to have Mama live with us. He started building an extra room for our trailer.

Jobs Didn't Come Easy

We left for North Carolina on a Friday, and John already had a preaching job lined up for that Sunday. We were sure he'd become the pastor of that church. But that church didn't hire him. In fact, he had to preach for two more churches before he found one that did.

And the school board didn't want me at all. I didn't have some of the courses required for a teaching certificate in North Carolina, and my Tennessee credentials made no difference. I could work only as a substitute, with no guarantee of how often I'd work or what my income would be.

Our new church built a rather large pastorium, or parsonage, and Mama, the children and I soon moved into it. John and a fellow seminarian stayed in the

BLENDED FAMILY. John and Helen Tullock (above, right front and right back) joined with Helen's mother and the couple's son, Laurens (front left), daughter Beth (center on couch) and foster daughters, Sandra and Thelma Mankin (front row, center) in 1959. Below are the Tullocks (left) and their four children (right).

trailer during the week, and John spent weekends at home.

With no regular teaching job, I was spending more time at home than expected, but our daughter, Beth, came up with an idea to keep me busy.

For years, Beth had wanted a sister. Before our son was born back in Tennessee, she'd announced to all our neighbors, "Mama's going to the hospital to get me a baby sister."

"What if it's a brother?" someone asked.

"Mama won't do me that way," Beth said with assurance. "She'll stay until she can get me a sister."

Boy Baby Was a Surprise

Apparently she convinced us, too. The only name we'd chosen was for a girl. When little brother Laurens was born, we had a hard time convincing Beth he was just what she'd wanted.

But apparently she hadn't forgotten. When Beth heard the North Carolina Baptist Children's Home needed foster

parents, she told me happily, "Now you and Daddy can get me a sister."

Well, why not? We began looking into it. Nine months later, we were approved to become foster parents for Thelma and Sandra.

The girls were wonderful additions to our family and remained in our home until they married. Everything seemed to be a special treat for them.

One day John and I planned a 1-day trip to the ocean for all of us. Everything we did was on a shoestring budget, but with a cooler full of food, all we'd need was gas money. We didn't count on having a blowout.

But that mishap proved we really had become a family. When the kids learned we'd have to scrimp to buy a re-treaded tire, they pulled out every cent of their allowance to help pay for it.

John and I were proud of our blended crew. We were in this new life together, and we'd make it through the '50s...and through many years to come.

Prices Make '50s More Memorable

By Phil Mangum, Athens, Texas

AH, THE PRICES of the '50s! I supported my wife and young son in 1950 on $165 a month, including $35 a month rent for three rooms.

The doctor and hospital bills for our son's birth totaled $180, including 5 days in the hospital.

Later that year, I jumped at a job that would pay $89 a week! I was rich. We moved to the big city, where our rent was $65 a month.

I bought a 1949 Frazier for $1,000, fully equipped with both radio and heater and a windshield visor. Of course, because of the visor, we couldn't see when the traffic light turned green, so we had a prism stuck on the inside of the windshield.

Since power steering didn't exist, I attached a steering knob so my wife would have something to grip while turning the wheel to park.

In 1953, we bought our first house—two bedrooms—for $3,500 and put new furniture throughout for about $650, blond oak, as I recall.

I bought a Packard sedan for our growing family for $650 from a fellow worker at the newspaper while I was making $94 a week.

In 1956, we sold our little house for $3,800 and bought a three-bedroom house for $6,000. I wondered how I was going to make the $75-a-month payments.

In 1957, I sold the Packard and bought a 4-year-old Jaguar Mark VII sedan for $1,200. I was in tall cotton.

The next year, I contracted the only serious illness I have ever had and was in the hospital for 10 days. The hospital charged $1,255 and the doctor $140.

Try those prices today!

He Said the Ceiling Moved, She Said He Was All Wet

MY WIFE, Dora Jean, and I first lived in a military surplus house trailer that her boss loaned us after we were married in 1950.

About 2 months after we moved in, we both came home from work one night following an all-day rain in the Modesto, California area where we lived.

We went to bed and had not yet turned the light off when I happened to look at the ceiling. I mentioned to my wife that the ceiling had moved.

She thought I was letting my imagination get the best of me, but I looked again and, sure enough, it moved again and this time started to leak water.

Dora Jean climbed out of bed and I stood up on it. I started to push the ceiling back up—in my shorts, of course. The ceiling had filled with water all day long, and it was a losing battle. The whole ceiling came down on me and the bed!

Dora Jean was a *great* help—she started laughing and laughing. I had never heard her laugh so hard. If we had not been newlyweds, I would have probably been quite angry.

Then she got me laughing and, from then on, it was a lost cause.

So, I had my second shower of the evening and my wife was stone dry. We slept on the couch for the next few nights.

We've been married now for 50 years, and we and our children and grandchildren still get a good laugh every time I tell this story.
—*Leonard Amos, Modesto, California*

Wedding Cake Came Around

BEING very close to my younger sister, Hannah, I offered to help with the reception after her marriage to Jack Smith in Anderson, Indiana (that's the happy couple below). Not having a lot of money in 1951, we planned a simple gathering with cake, ice cream and punch for a few guests and relatives.

Unfortunately, I forgot to order the wedding cake. After the beautiful ceremony, I was asked, "Where's the cake?"

I quickly excused myself and scurried off to a bakery, but it was closed. I finally found a small country store that had one small 8-inch-diameter round cake. Surprisingly, they had one large cake box.

As I carried the cake in, Jack said, "Martha, you shouldn't have."

I said, "Jack, I didn't."

By the end of the reception, the happy couple and their guests realized that they had just been served the thinnest slices of cake humanly possible.

Recently, we visited Hannah and Jack for their 50th anniversary, and Jack said he had a big surprise for me.

On the table was a large box containing a small 8-inch round cake.

We all laughed and reminisced about the first small cake.

"It took 50 years," Jack said, "but what goes around comes around."
—*Martha Lightfoot*
Brooksville, Florida

Tiny Quarters Caused Trouble in Trailer

By Mary Eileen Trimble, Berryville, Arizona

WHEN AUGIE REETZ and I were newlyweds (above), living in Anchorage, Alaska back in 1950, we didn't have much money.

All we could afford to rent was a small trailer, barely big enough to accommodate a table that folded up against the wall, a two-burner hot plate and a divan that folded down into a hard, sloping narrow bed. We had cold running water that ran into a miniature sink, but no bathroom. An outhouse sat off to the side of the trailer.

One of the first meals I proudly fixed for Augie turned out to be memorable. It was my day off from working as a registered nurse at Providence Hospital, and Augie came home from work for lunch.

I had pulled the table down from the wall and moved the leg that slid to the center and held the table up underneath. Then I heated the chicken noodle soup, poured it into bowls, set out spoons, bread and butter, raw carrots and two glasses of milk. Everything was ready when my new husband walked in the door.

"Hi, honey," he called out. "I'm home."

I gave him a big hug and kiss, and each of us squeezed into the tight space on either side of the table, smiling happily at each other.

Then it happened. Just as Augie started to lift the glass of milk to his lips, my foot caught the leg that held the table in position and down it went. Everything slid to the floor.

I've always been grateful that we both were able to see the funny side of living in that tiny trailer, beset with booby traps.

Augie has since passed away, but we enjoyed some of the best times of our lives when we were young and adventurous and living in Alaska. ✐

Apartment Choices Were All Wet

THE RAINS CAME to Kansas in spring of 1950—and kept on coming. Most of the rivers were hard put to stay within their banks.

Mary, Evelyn and I worked in Salina, Kansas and shared a basement apartment. One non-rainy evening, we went out with friends. When we returned, most of our belongings were wet—and spread out all over the backyard.

Water had backed up through the shower drain to a depth of 18 inches throughout the apartment. Thankfully, our landlords carried out what they could. It took quite a while to get everything dried out and cleaned up.

We didn't want that to happen again, so we moved to a third-floor apartment. Surely we'd be safe on the top floor!

In spring of 1951, the skies opened again. We should've been high and dry—but our roof leaked. We scrounged for anything to catch all the drips from the ceiling.

Rising water continued to cause problems into the summer. Days after my husband and I were married, Neil was to travel to Kansas City for an Air Force assignment. But this was July 13, "Black Friday". Rivers had flooded much of eastern Kansas, and Neil had to travel by car, train and bus to get around the water to Kansas City.

The rest of the decade, Neil and I were busy starting a family and building a new home. Babies arrived in 1952, '54 and '57, and No. 4 came along in 1961. No poodle skirts, sweater sets and bobby socks for me—my closet was full of maternity clothes! —*Donna Arasmith, Phillipsburg, Kansas*

"Sunset Strip" Provided Address for Dream House

WE FINISHED building our dream house in 1957 on a lake in northern New Jersey. I chose the address 77 Lake Drive East, since my favorite TV address was 77 Sunset Strip.

We caught fish off our dock, and our friends gathered around our brick barbecue pit to watch them cook. Our red Studebaker Champion had the most modern design, I thought. Two years later, tail fins were in fashion.

In winter, the lake froze over, and the neighborhood children put on their skates on our dock. We stayed cozy indoors, enjoying our fireplace and watching TV.

On Sundays, Ed Sullivan was the "toast of the town", and on Tuesdays we watched "Uncle Miltie". Thursday evenings belonged to Groucho Marx and *You Bet Your Life*. John Daly was the host of *What's My Line?*

Most of the shows were still in black and white then. Later, the NBC peacock introduced shows "in living color".
—*Elise Brennen, Santa Barbara, California*

Cross-Country Trek Strengthened Marriage

OUR WEDDING was in 1954, but the real beginning of our marriage was in the summer of 1955.

We were living in Santa Barbara, California. I'd just finished college, and Bill had completed his military service and wanted to use his mustering-out pay to visit his family in New Jersey.

I'd never been outside California, so I didn't know what to expect. It turned out to be quite an adventure.

We had little money, so we drove our maroon 1947 Ford woody station wagon (at right) and camped along the way. Bill built a fold-up table on the tailgate, where we cooked on a three-burner camp stove. Folding shelves held our luggage when we slept in the back. Gasoline was about 33¢ a gallon.

We tried to stay in campgrounds or truck stops so we could park safely off the road. Once, when we couldn't find a place, a nice couple we met in a gas station invited us to stay on their farm.

In New Jersey, all the relatives were eager to meet Bill's new wife, which scared me a little. I wanted to make a good impression, but I didn't have much confidence in myself, and that summer was one of the hottest and stickiest in years. I was not used to such heat and humidity and was uncomfortable.

After about a month of visiting and enjoying many hearty German meals, we headed home, with stops in Ohio and Indiana to visit my father's relatives. We were both glad to get back to Santa Barbara.

This trip set the tone for our married life. It taught us how to work together for a common goal, budget our income, get along with each other and plot a course for our lives.
—*Carolyn Weisman Raymond, California*

He Built Their House from the Ground Up

By Helen Govang
Cucamonga, California

ONE MORNING in 1950, my 37-year-old husband of 18 years shocked me into wakefulness by announcing he was going to build a house.

A house? As in doghouse, or playhouse?

"No," Bob said. "This will be a home for the five of us."

Our three daughters were less than enthusiastic, and I was sure he'd gone over the edge.

I thought a good hot cup of coffee and maybe some pancakes would bring him back to reality. It didn't work. I found out Bob and my sister's husband, Harvey, had been planning this for weeks. Their only qualifications: Bob had been a housepainter, and Harvey was in the refrigeration business.

We spent weeks looking at house plans and finally settled on a three-bedroom model pictured in *Better Homes and Gardens*. When we received the blueprints, it looked hopeless to me, but Bob's enthusiasm was never higher.

Big House vs. Little House

Bob bought an 80- by 260-foot defunct orange grove in Ontario, California, 20 miles west. He planned to quit his job and work full-time on the 24- by 24-foot garage we called the "little house", where the five of us would live while he finished the "big house".

Our home in Riverside, California sold quickly, as did our extra furniture. Harvey and Eleanor graciously offered us their spare bedroom in nearby Pomona until the little house was built.

There was a double bed for 5-year-old Ellen and 7-year-old Nancy, a cot for Lynn, 10, and a rollaway for Bob and me. Underclothes were kept in labeled boxes under the bed. Our furniture was in Harvey and Eleanor's garage.

I realized I was going to have to get a job. I started working as a secretary. During the summer of 1950, Bob worked at the lot, I worked in the office, and my dear sister kept a tight rein on

BOB THE BUILDER. Bob Govang (above) worked on the lot where he built a house for his family. At top, the "little house" begins to take shape. That's the finished "big house" below.

my three children and her two.

Bob's first task was clearing orange trees from the lot. He kept the trunks for firewood and hauled away the branches.

A foundation was dug for the big house, and ground was leveled for the little house.

There were no gas or sewer lines in this area. Digging a spot for the septic tank was fairly easy, but the 14-foot-deep area for the cesspool wasn't. Bob dug and filled bucket after bucket with dirt, and Harvey pulled them up and emptied them.

Pomona High School burned down about this time. Bob got enough free bricks for the cesspool and a fireplace and chimney.

A more hectic routine began in September, when school started. Bob dropped me off at work, took the girls to school, then worked at the lot until he picked up the girls at 3. He picked me up at 5, we went to Eleanor's for dinner, then Bob and Harvey worked at the lot until dark.

In June 1951, we were finally able to move into the little house. Half of the house served as our kitchen, living room and master bedroom, and the other held the girls' beds, a chest of drawers and,

wonder of wonders, a 12-foot closet.

In 1952, with finances dwindling, Bob had to go back to work, leaving only evenings and weekends to finish the big house.

The bedrooms and baths were the first rooms we could live in. What luxury—even though we still had to eat and cook in the little house.

Bob reluctantly agreed to let a professional do the plastering, but he did everything else—three coats of varnish on the woodwork, hardwood floors throughout, raised-hearth fireplace and many extras. The outside was beautiful redwood with white trim.

After we'd spent many months cooking and eating in the little house, all the rooms were finished. The beautiful "House That Bob Built" became home at last in 1954.

Bride Had Economical Wedding All Sewn Up

SEWING WAS routinely taught in school when I was a girl, but most of us learned at home. Mother started teaching me at age 7 on her old treadle sewing machine. Sewing at home meant you could have finer clothes for less money, a custom fit and an original design.

By the time I started sewing class in seventh grade, it was a little boring—I'd been making my own dresses for years. In high school, I made full-skirted formal gowns of silk, taffeta, velvet and filmy net.

For my wedding, I made a white taffeta and lace gown from a Butterick pattern. My entire outfit, including the pattern, yard goods, beaded coronet and shoes, cost $31.32.

All the bridesmaids made their dresses, too, or had them made. The yard goods for their dresses cost $20.

Here's what the rest of the wedding cost:

- White Bibles for the bride and bridesmaids to carry, $12.
- Two floral arrangements, daisies on attendants' Bibles, orchid on bride's Bible and carnation boutonnieres for the men in the bridal party, $38.50.
- Wedding cake, $28.50.
- Wedding invitations and napkins, $23.50.
- Wedding reception (cake and punch at church), $100.
- Organist and soloist, $20.
- Janitor, $5.
- Photographer, $44.

The grand total for our 1950 wedding: $322.82.

After we started a family, I continued sewing for our children, my husband and myself.

—*Margie Frank*
Washington, Pennsylvania

PROUD DAUGHTERS. Vickie and Margaret Frank model Easter dresses their mother made for them in 1957.

  ## Friendship Quilt Brought Warm Reminders of Home

MY HUSBAND and I met during World War II, when we were both stationed in Deming, New Mexico. After the war, we married and moved to his hometown of Reading, Pennsylvania. I was a Southern girl and missed my friends and family back in Sardis, Alabama.

Quiltings were popular back then in my hometown. To ease my homesickness, my mother, neighbors and friends surprised me with a friendship quilt for Christmas in 1959. Each woman made a square and embroidered her name on it.

Though I was over 1,000 miles from home, when I looked at that quilt, I could see and feel close to all the people the squares represented.

Reading has been my home since 1945, and I've been blessed with a wonderful husband and children. But that quilt provided warm reminders of Mom and home at a time when I really needed them. I treasured that quilt then…and still do.

—*Elsie Castner*
Reading, Pennsylvania

BLANKETED WITH FRIENDSHIP. Elsie Castner and daughter Melanie, 5, displayed the quilt that Elsie received as a Christmas gift in 1959 from her Southern hometown. The ladies who worked on the quilt stitched their names in the squares.

Mom Wasn't Needled by Lack of Sewing Skills

By Janet Simpson, Albany, Georgia

SEW WHAT? Janet Simpson was pretty as a picture in this taffeta dress, which her mother made for a special event at church. The dress was a triumph for Janet's mom, who had to overcome many obstacles—including nonexistent sewing skills—to finish it.

I WAS SELECTED to carry the Bible at the annual Girls' Auxiliary crowning at the First Baptist Church in Bainbridge, Georgia in 1952.

This was a great honor, and while my parents were pleased, they knew the expense of the dress I'd have to wear was more than our budget would allow. My mother explained this to the ladies at church, and she was told that if she just bought the material, the pattern would be provided and she could make the dress herself.

Luckily, the store selling the required material and notions also gave discounts to families of railroad workers, so Mother was able to save even more. But those were the only breaks she got.

A Major Obstacle

And there was still one big problem: Mother didn't know how to sew. She had never learned the basics beyond replacing buttons.

Our sewing machine had belonged to my grandmother and was very old. Mother had no idea how it worked or even how to thread it. To make matters worse, the pattern, which was cut out of newspaper, arrived with no instructions on it whatsoever.

Then, as if that weren't enough, I came down with the measles. Several ladies had offered to help Mother sew the dress, but now none of them could come to the house. They couldn't risk taking measles home to their own children.

There was a ray of hope, though. Mother moved the sewing machine and my bed into the hallway, where the telephone was, and managed to get instructions over the phone. It was difficult, since we shared a party line with at least six other families.

It took Mother a month, but she did a wonderful job of making my Nile-green taffeta dress. You might think the experience would have dampened her enthusiasm for sewing, but it had just the opposite effect.

Mother enjoyed sewing so much that she kept it up for another 40 years.

Room Mom Did Triple Duty

DURING OUR school years in South Texas, my siblings and I volunteered our mom's services as room mother...for all three of us.

When the high honor of homeroom chairman was bestowed upon her for my seventh-grade class in 1954, Mom wasn't as impressed as I was. She had two other children expecting her to entertain their classes as well, and she had a sick child and a baby at home.

But Mom outdid herself. It was a simpler time, and we were impressed by anything we hadn't previously experienced. At our class Christmas party, Mom engaged a marimba player. She was by far the most glamorous mom there, in a Christmas-tree green dress with gold piping and coordinating earrings.

For our end-of-school party, Mom surveyed us to learn our favorite songs, rented a jukebox and reserved the high school gym for our first "grown-up" dance. She even found the time to make a beautiful yellow and white dotted swiss dress for me.

Our teacher, Mrs. Coleman, was retiring at the end of the school year, so Mom threw a party for her at our home and invited the entire class. Daddy borrowed grills from neighbors to make hot dogs and hamburgers. We had a washtub full of iced drinks, a few side dishes and a freezer full of ice cream.

Mom also contacted all the parents to secretly solicit money to buy Mrs. Coleman a class gift.

Although Mom protested being a room mother initially, she shone in the job and made her children quite happy and proud in the process.

—*Sharon Tallon, Tomball, Texas*

At the Altar, Groom Threw Bride a Curve

PAUL AND I were so poor when we got married in 1950 that all we had between us was $50 and a pair of end tables. My family thought the marriage would never last because he was "so much older"—I was 18, he was 22.

My father had passed away the year before, so there was no one to walk me down the aisle. Paul and I planned to simply meet at the altar.

He and his brother, the best man, barely got there in time. They'd been sitting in the car outside, listening to the Cleveland Indians baseball game.

My bridegroom smiled at me and whispered, "Gee, honey, you look pretty, but did you hear? Al Rosen just hit a grand-slam home run!"

"Well, that's nice," I replied, "but we're kind of in the middle of a wedding here!"

Our big honeymoon was a trip to Cleveland, about an hour away, to see the Indians play.

We raised six children together, and Paul was instrumental in starting Little League programs in our area. He even helped build a ballpark, which was named for him after his death in 1983. I think the Indians would've been proud. I know I was.

—*Joyce Orshoski, Castalia, Ohio*

STYLISH GETAWAY. After their 1950 wedding, Joyce and Paul Orshoski left in a brand-new Plymouth convertible owned by Paul's brother Wayne. "Boy, did we drive away in style!" chuckles Joyce. "The wedding took place at St. Paul's English Lutheran Church in Sandusky, Ohio. And check out my corsage—it was almost bigger than my head!"

BABY BATH...TIMES FOUR. With four toddlers to bathe, including triplets, Joyce Van Liere's mother did the only sensible thing—she put them in a metal washtub and scrubbed them all at once! Ruth, 10 months, is at far left; Joyce is in the back of the tub, between Jerry and Jimmy.

Birth of Triplets Doubled Their Family

MY POOR MOTHER delivered a set of triplets in 1956. This came as quite a shock, as she'd been expecting twins.

When my two brothers and I were born, my parents already had a 10-month-old, a 4-year-old and a 6-year-old. Their family had doubled in a matter of minutes.

Mom bathed the four youngest children together. She would remove two of us to towel us off and dress us. When she'd finished with the first two, she'd remove the other two.

One time, as Mom was dressing the second pair of children, she turned around and discovered the first pair—who were now fully clothed—had climbed back into the tub, shoes and all! I don't know how she did it.

—*Joyce Van Liere, Dell Rapids, South Dakota*

Toddler Eagerly Awaited Dad's Return from Navy

OUR SON John Gregory was almost 2, when his father was recalled to serve in the U.S. Navy in 1951 during the Korean War.

For about 2 weeks, every time Greg heard the sound of a car, he ran to the front window and said, "Maybe that's Daddy now." If one of Greg's toys broke, he said, "Daddy will fix it when he gets home."

Fortunately, Greg had forgotten about the broken toys by the time the conflict was over.

—*Mrs. John Adams New Lexington, Ohio*

"HELLO, DADDY?" John Gregory Adams called his father in 1951 to tell him all about their Christmas tree. His father had been recalled to the Navy a few months earlier to serve in the Korean War.

Children Could Count On Finding Mom at Home

By Gayla Baggett, Hendersonville, Tennessee

MY FATHER was a carpenter who helped build some of the first all-electric homes in the Indianapolis, Indiana area. Mom stayed home and kept house, as most mothers did in those days.

I felt very secure during my childhood, knowing that when all five of us came through the door every afternoon, Mom would be there.

Sometimes she'd be waiting for us with a big plate of fudge or homemade cookies and a pitcher of Kool-Aid, which we drank out of little metal tumblers.

Mom was a soap-opera fan, so we often found her at the ironing board with a big pile of laundry as she watched *The Edge of Night* or *As the World Turns*. We usually took over the TV so we could watch our favorite, *The Mickey Mouse Club*. Television was so new then that just about everything was fun and interesting to watch.

Christmas Was a Special Time

The very best times were at Christmas. My parents would bundle us up, put us in the car and drive downtown to see the Christmas decorations. All the stores around Monument Circle sparkled with lights and music. We stood at the store windows, mesmerized by the mechanical animals that moved and played before us.

At school, we girls wore long red ribbons in our hair with jingle bells tied to the ends. There sure was a whole lot of jingling going on!

At home, we were taught the real meaning of Christmas and realized early on that it was a celebration of Jesus' birth, not just tinsel and lights.

We didn't have a star for our tree, so our mother made one from cardboard and aluminum foil. The star lasted for many years and will forever remain a special memory.

All my memories of the '50s are a treat. I was a member of the Camp Fire Girls, went to sock hops and my brother's baseball games, rode around in my father's shiny black 1956 Chevy, walked to school in the snow with my dress tucked down in my woolen leggings, stopped at the penny candy store to buy Kits and Slow-Pokes, and discovered *American Bandstand*.

Our family did lots of things together, and even though we didn't have much money, we had each other. My parents took us to church, where we were taught to love and care for others as well as ourselves.

For me, those definitely were the happiest of days.

HAPPY HOME. Author's mother (top left) made home a welcome place. Three of the author's siblings—Judy, Charlie with "Petey" the parakeet and Kathy—enjoy TV after school (above).

Baby Fell Short of Her Brother's Expectations

OUR DAUGHTER Marjorie joined our family on Groundhog Day in 1950. When we brought her home, husband Jack and I put her in bed and suggested to our 4-year-old, Terry, that he go see his new little sister. Terry was very excited and ran off to hunt for her.

After a very long time, he came back to us, convinced he'd been tricked. He was expecting someone the age of his preschool friends, and there was no one like that in the house. He turned pale with alarm when he realized that the *baby* was his sister!

Jack and I shared the work of caring for an infant day and night. We boiled bottles, sterilized diapers and hung them outside, made formula, and gave Marjorie five drops each of orange juice and cod-liver oil a day.

—*Alma Laney, San Diego, California*

Kind Neighbor Brought Meals After Blizzard

GROWING UP in the ranching communities of northern New Mexico was a privilege I'll never forget. The 1950s brought some difficulties, but it was also a time of sharing and caring.

The winter of 1958, when I was 5, was particularly difficult for our family. Dad had just brought Mother home from the hospital after surgery, and my 11-year-old sister and I both had the mumps.

The next morning, we woke to find several feet of snow on the ground.

Blizzards were equally hard on cows and cowboy. Since the cattle couldn't get to the grass, Dad would have to drive through the snow from pasture to pasture, throwing out hay.

Before he left that morning, Dad moved our beds into the large kitchen, making it easier for the three of us to stay warm and take care of each other. Then he headed out to tend to the cows.

One of the neighbor women soon arrived with food she'd cooked for us. Melba didn't want to catch the mumps, so she stood at the window next to Mother's bed and talked to her from outside, then left a box of food inside our enclosed porch.

It was almost noon, so I figured she'd brought us our dinner. Much to our surprise, we found enough food for several meals. All we had to do was warm it up.

Each day for almost a week, Melba brought all our meals in a big box. When we saw her coming down the road, my sister and I would put her cleaned pots and pans from the previous day out on the porch. Melba would replace it with another box of goodies and visit through the window for a few minutes.

Thanks to Melba, Dad came home from a hard, cold day's work to a hot meal every night. And it really made things easier on Mother and two girls with the mumps.

Mother didn't stay down for long, but we surely owed a debt of gratitude to Melba for all her help and thoughtfulness.
—Jeane White
Alamosa, Colorado

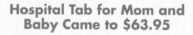

Hospital Tab for Mom and Baby Came to $63.95

I REMEMBER very well what we paid when our daughter Judy was born at the new Osteopathic Hospital in Traverse City, Michigan. She was born July 5, 1950, and the baby and I came home July 9.

We were charged $30 for room and board, $15 for the delivery, $2 for X-rays, $5 in lab fees, $7.45 for medications, 50¢ for dressings and $4 for the nursery. Our grand total, for 5 days in the hospital, was $63.95.
—Dorothy Reed
Interlochen, Michigan

New Mom's 5-Day Stay In Hospital Cost $125

WHEN MY HUSBAND and I married in 1949, I was making $40 a week as an X-ray and lab technician, and Ken made $75 a month driving a truck. The rent for our tiny garage apartment was $40 a month.

Our place was so small that we couldn't have more than two visitors at a time. If they stayed for dinner, we had to put a little table in the doorway between the living room and kitchen. Our guests sat on the living room side while we sat in the kitchen.

When our first child was born in November 1950, our total hospital bill was $125. And remember, in those days, new mothers stayed in the hospital for at least 5 days.

My doctor waived his $100 delivery fee because I'd worked for him for 2 years. When our son was born in June 1953, the doctor's bill was $150. Compare those fees with today's delivery charges!

Our first "real" house cost $9,500. We bought our second house in 1957 for $19,500 and sold it 42 years later for $187,000.
—Bee Henisey, Acton, California

Wedding Was Priceless Yet Inexpensive

IT'S ENTERTAINING to look back at prices from the 1950s. Here are some prices from our wedding on Sept. 23, 1950.

Wedding cake for more than 200 guests, $10.50; wedding gown, $50.95; guest book, $1; flowers for bride, three bridesmaids, five male attendants, two mothers, two flower girls and a ring bearer, $40.25: personalized napkins, $4.75; and decorations, including candles and holders, bells and crepe paper, $5.60.

Major costs of our 1,829-mile honeymoon were $198, including average nightly motel rooms at $4.50 and gas at 28¢ a gallon. *—Marjorie Nordstrom, Melrose, Wisconsin*

JACK DEMPSEY'S
RESTAURANT

Prices Were a Knockout

MY WIFE AND I were high school sweethearts in Lebanon, New Hampshire and married in 1952. For our honeymoon, we drove my trusty 1949 Ford Custom to Burlington, Vermont, crossed Lake Champlain on the ferry to New York, then drove on to New York City.

We had lunch at Jack Dempsey's Restaurant, owned by the famed boxer. We were so impressed that we asked for a menu so we could show the folks back home where we'd eaten in the big city. They were more than happy to oblige, and I've kept it all these years. —*Bob Sharkey*
Lebanon, New Hampshire

COCKTAILS

Dempsey's Special	70
Manhattan	.60
Bronx	.60
Martini	.60
Perfect	.60
Jack Rose	.60
Orange Bloss...	

TAKE HOME A SOUVENIR JACK DEMPSEY ASH TRAY 25c.
— ASK YOUR WAITER

LUNCHEON SPECIALS A LA CARTE

★

SPRING CHICKEN en Casserole Saute Chasseur ..1.95
with New Peas and Saute Potato
BROILED FRESH SWORDFISH STEAK 1.50
Lemon Butter Sauce, French Fried Potatoes
FRIED DEEP SEA SCALLOPS 1.75
Cole Slaw, French Fried Potatoes
BROILED KENNEBEC SALMON STEAK 1.50
Parsley Potato
BROILED SPRING CHICKEN (HALF), TOAST 1.85
Hashed Browned Potatoes
BROILED PRIME CLUB STEAK 3.25
with Onions, French Fried Potatoes
BROILED PRIME CHOPPED
TENDERLOIN STEAK 1.75
Smothered Onions Lyonnaise Potatoes
GENUINE CALF'S LIVER 1.95
Sauted in Sweet Butter, Crisp Onions, Lyonnaise Potatoes
BREADED MILK FED VEAL CUTLET 1.95
French Fried Potatoes
FRIED FRESH JERSEY PORK CHOPS 1.95
Apple Sauce, Lyonnaise Potatoes
VEGETABLE PLATE (All Fresh Vegetables)
WITH EGG 1.25

(SUBSTITUTE FOR POTATOES)

COLD SPECIALS

... CREAM with Creamed Cottage Cheese
... WITH CHICKEN, Lettuce and Tomato, Sliced Egg 95
... 1.65 WITH CRAB MEAT ..1.45
... SEAFOOD PLATTER: Half Maine Lobster, Shrimps, Lettuce, Tomato, Cole Slaw, Potato Salad ..1.85
... SALAD with Julienne of Ham, ...ch Dressing ..1.90
... PLATTER Consisting of:
...f, Turkey and Potato Salad ..1.65
...ato Salad, Cole Slaw, Russian Dressing ..1.75
... Imported Anchovy Filets, ... Salad ..1.35
... 1.25

SANDWICHES

... 65	American Cheese	
... 75	Ham and Swiss Cheese	.55
... 35	Corned Beef	.90
	Chicken	.90
	Melted Cheese and Bacon	1.00
	Turkey and Swiss Cheese	.75
		1.25

...al Property Unless Checked

APPETIZERS A LA CARTE

Soup du Jour	.25
(cup)	.40
Terrine	
Cherrystone Clams	55
Shrimp Cocktail	.85
Chopped Chicken Liver	.50
Crabmeat Cocktail	85
Fresh Fruit Cup	.35
Tomato Juice	.25
(Large)	.40
Grapefruit Juice	.25
Marinated Filet of Herring in Cream Sauce	55
Iced Honey Dew Melon	.40

Grilled Canadian Bacon and Eggs, Lyonnaise Potatoes 1.50
Sugar Cured Ham and Eggs, Country Style .1.35
with Lyonnaise Potatoes
Grilled Ham Steak, Fried Eggs, Lyonnaise Potatoes 2.25
Scrambled Eggs with Chicken Livers, .1.50
French Fried Potatoes
Omelette au Confiture, French Fried Potatoes .1.50

Floragold Grapefruit Juice 20	Cherrystone Clam Cocktail 45
Chopped Chicken Livers Garni 40	
Fresh Fruit Cup 35	Marinated Filet Herring in Cream Sauce 45
Shrimp Cocktail 85	Crabmeat Cocktail 85
	Iced Tomato Juice 20
Iced: Indian River Grapefruit Maraschino 25	

Chicken Gumbo Creole, Fresh Okra (Cup) 20
Consomme, Egg Noodles (Cup) 20
Jellied Tomato Bouillon Madrilene (Cup) 20

COMPLETE LUNCHEONS
(Served From 11 A. M. to 4 P. M.)

ENTREE INCLUDES DESSERT, COFFEE OR TEA

1	CHOPPED VIRGINIA HAM SANDWICH ON TOAST, Cole Slaw, Pickle	.75
2	BAKED ASSORTED FRESH SEA FOOD BONNE FEMME, Boiled Potato	.95
3	BROILED FRESH GULF STREAM SWORDFISH STEAK, Maitre d'Hotel, Whipped Potato	1 35
4	SCRAMBLED EGGS WITH FRESH CHICKEN LIVERS, Lyonnaise Potatoes	1 25
5	FRESH MARYLAND CRAB MEAT AU GRATIN, New Garden Peas	1 35 1.45 1.75
6	MILK FED VEAL RAGOUT, VIENNA STYLE, Home Made Noodles	1 45
7	BREADED JERSEY PORK CUTLET, Tomato Sauce, Garden Peas, Saute Potatoes	1 55
8	ROAST BABY LAMB, OWN JUICE, Mint Jelly, Baby Lima Beans Fines Herbes, Home Fried Potatoes	1 65
9	SOUTHERN FRIED SPRING CHICKEN, Supreme Sauce, New Sweet Corn on the Cob, Candied Sweet Potato	1 65
10	COLD IMPORTED DANISH HAM AND OX TONGUE, Pickled Beets, Potato Salad	1 65

- Choice of -

Danish Butter Nut Strip	Fresh Fruit Jell-o, Whipped Cream
Fresh Apple Pie	Chocolate Pudding, Whipped Cream
Fresh Raspberry Sherbet	Rice Pudding
Stewed Prunes	Vanilla or Strawberry Ice Cream
Coffee or Tea	Individual Bottle of Milk (10¢ Additional)

Iced Chocolate with Whipped Cream (20¢ Additional)
Iced Coffee or Iced Tea (10¢ Additional)

DESSERTS A LA CARTE

Vanilla and Strawberry Ice Cream	.40
Fresh Home Made Peach Cake	.50
Fresh Apple Pie	.40
Frozen Ice Cream Cake with Chocolate Sauce	.45
Chilled Honey Dew Melon	.40
Chilled Persian Melon	.40
Danish Butter Nut Strip	.35
	.15
Coffee	.15
Tea	.15
Milk	.25
Iced Tea	.25
Iced Coffee	.20

(A Charge of 10c. For Bread and Butter with A La Carte Orders)
Please report **any** discourtesy on part of employees to management. Thank you for your cooperation and patronage.

All prices are our O. P. S. ceiling prices or lower. A list showing our ceiling price for each item is available for your inspection.

Dirt Didn't Stand a Chance!

Young bride learned a lesson about cleaning power in 1952.

By Marcia Massey, Collinsville, Illinois

AS A young bride in about 1952, I had no modern conveniences, such as an automatic washer, dryer or even a wringer washer. Clothes were washed on a rub board, then hung to dry outside our home in East St. Louis, Illinois.

And the old song "Monday washday, is everybody happy?" sure didn't apply to me. Every day was washday.

On Monday, I'd start a big kettle of water heating as I ate breakfast, then I'd strip the bed and wash the sheets. Tuesday I washed towels; Wednesday, my husband's underwear; Thursday, colored clothes; Friday, overalls; Saturday, delicates; and every day, diapers and baby clothes.

I took pride in my wash. I would rub until my knuckles blistered and bled and the bleach fumes made my eyes smart, but not one stain or spot remained when I hung the clothes to dry.

here. I want you to see something."

He kicked off his shoes and pulled up his pant legs. I couldn't believe my eyes. His pretty white socks were nothing but shreds. All that was intact were the elastic bands!

He dropped his pants and about all that was left of his shorts was the elastic band. The rest was as shredded as his socks. I couldn't believe it.

Then he took off his shirt and turned around so I could see his undershirt. It was full of big holes.

"How did this happen?" I asked, expecting him to give me an explanation.

"You tell me!" he said. "When I went to the locker room this morning to change into my uniform, they definitely weren't like this.

"After work, when I went to the locker room to change back into my street clothes, this is what I was wearing. I was wondering why I felt drafty all day," he added.

One week my husband, Claude, had worked on his car while wearing his good white T-shirt, so I decided it was time to whiten all his underclothes a little more. In with the bleach, I mixed a cup of Borax and let the underwear soak overnight before washing them the next day.

When I took them off the line, after they'd hung in the bright sun all day, they were sparkling as white as new. I was so proud of my wash!

I thought that Claude looked so nice as he left for work the following day. But when he came home that night, he wasn't so happy.

Setting his lunch pail on the counter, he said, "Come

During the week, the rest of his underwear also disintegrated. Somehow, on his $27.50 take-home pay, we had to make room in our budget for a new supply of white T-shirts, shorts and socks.

The embarrassing part, though, was that all his co-workers had seen him standing in tattered clothes. He was the laugh of the plant for weeks!

It wasn't until sometime later that I realized it was my laundering that had caused his clothes to disintegrate.

Even after all these years, I'm still trying to live that one down!

Chapter Nine

Growing Up

Growing Up

THE DECADE of the '50s was so much more than the calendar midpoint of the 20th century. It also turned out to be a sharp dividing line between two worlds—the America of our ancestors and a new world of profound changes in our manners, morals, dress, home lives and even our music.

As the '50s opened, proper ladies still dressed up for shopping trips "downtown"—hose, heels, gloves, hats, the works. Men with office jobs wore three-piece suits, felt fedoras and shoes with laces, not slip-ons, and most certainly not sneakers.

Home life at the beginning of the '50s hadn't changed much from grandmother's day. Scrub boards were still part of washday, and you boiled great tubs of

"Sure, they cost extra... but look at the time they saved!"

water for the wringer washers. Clothes were hung outdoors even in freezing weather. By the end of the '50s, most homes had refrigerators instead of iceboxes, washers and dryers just like Betty Furness demonstrated on television, and—glory be!—something called no-iron clothes.

The days when even families of moderate means could afford a live-in "hired girl" were long gone, so homemakers welcomed something the food industry called "built-in maid service".

Although putting up hundreds of cans of fruits, vegetables, jams and jellies still wasn't all that rare, frozen vegetables and macaroni and cheese in a box became popular in a hurry. Sure, they cost a little extra, but look at all the time they saved!

No more tedious starting from scratch when you made a cake. Open a box, pour the contents into a bowl, add milk or a couple of eggs and pop it into the oven. You could even buy the icing in a can.

Miracle Drugs

Yet another revolution appeared during the '50s—miracle drugs. When our infant daughter was desperately ill, the doctor gave me a prescription for a drug with a funny name. Not so funny was the fact that 20 pills cost $20. I went into deep shock, but our daughter was healthy and happy in less than a week. And that's why they were dubbed "miracle drugs".

By the end of the decade, doctors had a whole arsenal of pharmaceuticals that controlled and even cured ailments like pneumonia that had been sure killers just a few years earlier.

The memories that follow also remind us there was a sweet innocence in America that got lost somewhere in the midst of all the excitement. The gentle, folksy world Norman Rockwell portrayed so beautifully in his *Saturday Evening Post* covers was disappearing almost unnoticed. Alas, by the end of the '50s, the stage had been set for the tumultuous, confusing, frightening '60s.

But that's another story. And perhaps another book. —*Clancy Strock*

Mommy's Magic!

Those words had different meanings for cousins with too much time on their hands.

By Donna McGuire Tanner, Ocala, Florida

IN 1955, my cousin Linda was everything I wanted to be but was not. She was pretty, talented, a year older (which made her wiser) and an only child.

Being knee-deep in siblings, I would gladly have traded a year of my life—or, better yet, one of my brothers—to be Linda for just 1 day.

The next best thing was spending a week with her and her parents in their Richwood, West Virginia home.

Both her parents worked, so Linda and I did anything we pleased. For an 8- and 9-year-old, that was an invitation to mischief.

My parents gave me $1 spending money for the visit. After 10-cent ice cream cones for breakfast, we had money left for a trip to the roller rink for my first skating lessons, then a movie and a shared 10-cent bag of popcorn.

Thrilled to Be in Town

Being a country girl, I was quite thrilled with the adventures of town living.

Toward the end of the week, Linda and I had almost run out of things to do and definitely run out of money. It was then that she threatened to tickle me, and I couldn't have that. I ran through the house, chased by my giggling cousin.

I took sanctuary in a bathroom and locked the door. She promised not to tickle me if I came out, and I believed her. As I exited, she leaped at me and I banged against the open door.

Suddenly, Linda shouted, "*Mommy's Magic!*"

Thinking we'd switched to a new game, I was delighted to know the secret about my aunt and said, "She is? What can she do?"

"No, no! My mommy's Magic bleach. We've broken it!"

The Truth Began to Sink in

I felt the wet liquid soaking my feet and the sharp odor of bleach burned my nose. "Magic Bleach" came in brown glass gallon jugs. When I jumped back against the door, I unknowingly slammed into the shelf holding my aunt's household cleaners, and the jug broke.

Aunt Olive was and is the world's best housekeeper. Her linoleum floors shined brightly from many coats of floor wax. The bleach ran across the kitchen floor and took aim at the living room. We grabbed the mop and towels and tried to stave off further damage.

We tried to repair the damage by cleaning the floors, but the strings of the mop head had been eaten away by the pure bleach. All we could do was wait for my aunt to come home.

Before she saw the damage, Aunt Olive smelled it. I wondered what our punishment would be as she surveyed the floors and the mop.

She didn't say a word, only making a loud sighing sound as she reached into her purse for money. She told us to go buy a new mop.

As we walked down the street, I felt relief and guilt, but mostly I felt disappointment that my Aunt Olive wasn't really magic after all. ✎

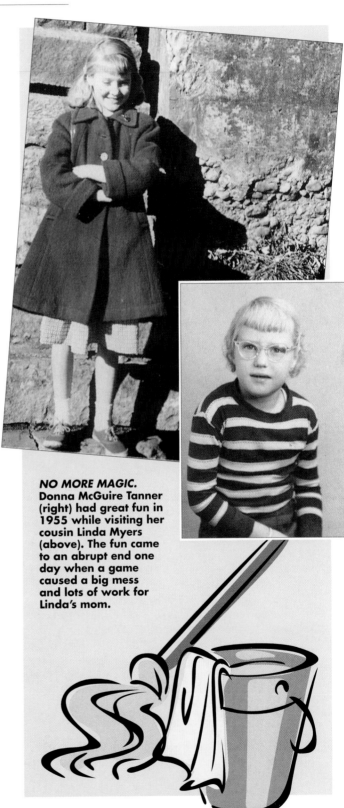

NO MORE MAGIC. Donna McGuire Tanner (right) had great fun in 1955 while visiting her cousin Linda Myers (above). The fun came to an abrupt end one day when a game caused a big mess and lots of work for Linda's mom.

Tough Teacher Ruled Class with Iron Hand

By Bob Hill, Elma, Washington

WHEN MY SIXTH-GRADE class assignment was posted in 1959, it might as well have been a death sentence. No matter how many times I read the list, my name remained beneath Mildred Leisy's.

To me, she was the most feared teacher in all of Portsmouth Elementary School in Portland, Oregon. Being in her class was even worse than getting held back, which suddenly sounded pretty good.

I stared numbly as fellow students gathered to learn their fate. Most didn't know who Mrs. Leisy was. The handful who did felt close to tears or staggered slightly backward, looking for a sympathetic eye. They knew.

Mom had been in Mrs. Leisy's class herself 2 decades ago and had cautioned me about her for years. Now it was my turn to suffer.

"But you'll learn a lot," Mom conceded. "You'll also be a better student and person after what you go through."

On the first day of school, I arrived early and went straight to Room 27. There was no Mrs. Leisy. I sat, quiet and anxious, as fellow classmates arrived, mingling and laughing. The few who knew better took seats in the corners, sizing up the distance and sight lines from the empty teacher's desk.

We heard her before we saw her. At 9 o'clock sharp, a locker slammed violently in the hallway outside. The class held its collective breath. The silence was broken by the ranting of a madwoman.

"If I ever see you do that again, you'll find yourself in the principal's office! Is that clear?" Someone managed a terrified "yes" between choking sobs.

Could've Heard a Pin Drop

Suddenly Mrs. Leisy filled the doorway, with a weeping boy in tow. She was near 60, with silver-rimmed glasses and curly orange hair. If she had an ounce of gentleness in her, you couldn't see it in her face.

The sobbing boy darted to a seat next to me. Thirty-one pairs of eyes lowered as Mrs. Leisy marched across the room. A dropped pin would've sounded like a wrecking ball.

"Good morning, students. My name is Mrs. Leisy—not 'teacher', not 'ma'am'." She wrote her name on the blackboard, the chalk snapping as she dotted the "i".

"I'll be your teacher this year. Hopefully, within the next few weeks I will know all your names."

Somehow that didn't seem like a good thing.

As she passed out name tags for us to fill out, I turned to the kid next to me.

"Hey," I whispered when Mrs. Leisy wasn't looking. "What did you do in the hall?"

"I spit my gum on the floor," he whispered back.

I stared in disbelief. "I thought you got caught slamming your locker shut," I said.

"No," he said, "she lifted me up and shoved me against the locker door."

Mrs. Leisy paced the room majestically, explaining her teaching methods. She was resolved to educate us in more than just academics. Under her tutelage, we would learn discipline, courtesy and good hygiene. She had a long list of dos, don'ts and nevers—never skip stairs, chew gum, loiter in the halls or talk back. If you did, I guessed, you risked getting slammed into a locker.

Mrs. Leisy also monitored our health. She demanded we consume well-balanced meals, which we recorded on daily menu logs. Every morning, she inspected us for brushed teeth, combed hair, clean nails, lice and adequate sleep. We had to get precisely 9-1/2 hours, and she could tell when we hadn't. Many students broke down during her hypnotic eye probes and confessed.

Some Didn't Have Star Power

Each student who passed the health exam got a star next to his or her name on a prominently displayed chart. The student with the best record would be rewarded with a fishing trip in spring. I figured anyone who survived until spring deserved it.

For those of us who bathed only once a week, the chart became an embarrassment, a constant reminder that we'd never catch up. By Christmas, we were buying our own stars at the five-and-dime and sticking them on the chart when Mrs. Leisy wasn't looking.

Like all childhood traumas, sixth grade eventually ended. I missed the last 2 weeks of school with German measles and returned on the last day of class. It was a joy to open my report card and read, "Assigned to the seventh grade"— and know that Mrs. Leisy would continue teaching sixth.

Looking back, I realize Mrs. Leisy was the best teacher I ever had. Although her methods wouldn't be tolerated today, I'm eternally grateful for everything she taught me.

Sometimes I wish the students of today had more teachers like her. She cared.

Bus Stop Encounter Changed Their Lives

SINCE I WAS born in 1939, my entire teenage life occurred during the most sublime of decades. It was during the 1950s that I had my first crush, first date, first kiss, first car and first job. I also joined the Army and got married.

But one of the most memorable events was a brief one in the spring of 1957.

Dad had borrowed my car, a bottle-green 1940 Plymouth ragtop, so I was taking the bus to school in Denver, Colorado. I was so cool as I approached the bus stop in my black leather jacket and white driving scarf, hair combed just so, with a little curl in front like Elvis'.

At the stop, I noticed a tall, skinny girl I hadn't seen before. She looked like she was probably a sophomore. I was a senior, and since I was cool, I didn't say anything to her. But as we waited for the bus, I noticed her sneakily watching me out of the corner of her eye as I slyly watched her out of the corner of mine.

As the bus pulled up, I dropped my token. I only had one more in my pocket, and I needed that one for the ride home, so I hurriedly began searching the ground.

The girl picked it up and handed it to me, startling me with a bold soliloquy: "Here."

Undaunted, I countered with an oration of my own: "Thanks."

We were married 2 years later, on May 8, 1959. We were blessed with seven children and now have 18 grandchildren.

From that spring day in 1957 until now, Diane and I have shared many things and had many great adventures, all of them deserving of a story. But as I look back on my life, it seems that those few precious moments turned out to be the 5 seconds that mattered. —*Greg Hug*
Denver, Colorado

TOKEN ENCOUNTER. Greg Hug (top) wasn't driving his Plymouth convertible on the day he happened to meet Diane Carlson (above) in 1957. Their brief conversation resulted in their marriage.

Boy Couldn't Outrun His Fate on Sadie Hawkins Day

I'LL ALWAYS REMEMBER the Sadie Hawkins Day Dance my senior year. About a dozen senior girls, all with steady boyfriends, chased a cute little freshman boy in the Sadie Hawkins Day race. He was fast, but they caught him.

The poor kid never had a chance to sit down. He was on the floor for every dance, and he remembered it for years.

For our senior class trip, we traveled to Chicago. We stayed at the Hilton, visited Riverview Park, the Field Museum of Natural History, Adler Planetarium, Shedd Aquarium, the Museum of Science and Industry, Brookfield Zoo and the popular radio show, Don McNeill's *Breakfast Club*— all in about 48 hours' time. It was unforgettable!
—*Lucille Mentzel, New Lisbon, Wisconsin*

Girl Gave Up Trip to Stay with Friend

WHEN I WAS attending school in Cloud Chief, Oklahoma in the late 1950s, our school took a busload of students to Springlake Amusement Park in Oklahoma City, about 90 miles east. This was a school-sponsored "fun day", and everyone had been looking forward to it.

When we arrived, there was a sign at the gate that read, "NO ADMITTANCE TO BLACKS." We had one black student on the bus. The sponsors and teachers looked truly perplexed. What would we do?

I volunteered to stay with my black friend on the bus. The others went inside for a fun-filled day. Every now and then, someone came out of the park to check on Margaret and me.

I enjoyed just talking to Margaret, but I wonder what she must have felt. I'm glad there's less prejudice today and that I didn't contribute to it then.
—*Anna Sue Gray*
Walters, Oklahoma

NIGHT SCHOOL? Anna Sue Gray (second from left) and her friend Margaret are among classmates modeling pj's they made in home economics class in 1956.

MY BEST FRIEND, Theresa, and I had just turned 13 and were feeling pretty grown up in the summer of 1959. Our biggest concerns were boys, our hair and clothes, the latest songs and the hottest movie stars.

Our absolute favorite movie was *A Summer Place*, a story of true love triumphing over all odds. The story was set at a picturesque New England island resort, and the theme song was one of the most beautiful ever.

The movie starred Troy Donahue and Sandra Dee (below). In his first lead role, Troy Donahue was strong and handsome. Sandra Dee was innocent and beautiful. The movie advertisement showed them standing on the beach, gazing into each other's eyes. We thought the movie was incredibly romantic and saw it at least half a dozen times.

Theresa and I did our best to copy Sandra Dee's look, having our hair bleached and cut into the bubble hairstyle she wore in the film. We bought green raincoats and black chiffon scarves like the ones she wore in the rainy scenes. We plastered our bedrooms with pictures of Troy Donahue cut from movie magazines.

During the day, we played the 45-rpm record of the movie theme song until it was white with wear. At night, we tucked our transistor radios under our pillows and waited until the station played the song before drifting off to sleep.

The movie and theme from *A Summer Place* always bring back special memories of the summer of 1959.

—*Judy Kallestad, St. Cloud, Minnesota*

FRESHMEN BEANIES were standard attire at the University of Nebraska in the 1950s. Barbara Farley (right) and her friend Janie Day, Class of 1953, modeled theirs on the steps of their dorm. When they weren't attending class, the girls preferred jeans and penny loafers. That's Barbara on the right with another friend, Joni Turner.

Rules Were Strict in Nebraska Girls' Dorm

MY FIRST experience away from home was when my friend Janie Day and I started attending the University of Nebraska. Like all freshmen, we had to live in a dorm, and the rules were strict. We had to sign out whenever we left in the evening, then sign back in when we returned. Curfew was 10 p.m. on weeknights and 1 a.m. on weekends.

Males weren't permitted in the dorm except in the lobby, unless they had permission from the housemother. Any girl bringing a male guest to the dorm floors had to shout, "Man on second floor!" when they got out of the elevator.

Breakfast and lunch were served cafeteria-style, but dinner was a more stylish affair. The tables were covered with white tablecloths, and we used cloth napkins. Male students served as waiters, attired in white jackets. A hostess was assigned to each table, and we were expected to use our best manners.

Freshmen wore red-and-white beanies showing the year they were to graduate. We wore skirts with blouses or sweaters to class, and lightweight dresses in warm weather. Jeans and penny loafers were our favorite attire when we weren't in class.

Football was big at Nebraska even then, and we went to all the games. We sat in the cheering section and in the card section, helping with the large card displays during halftime.

Despite the restrictions, college was fun. We'd pile into a dorm room to tell jokes, discuss blind dates and talk about the boys in the dorms and fraternities. It was an innocent time, but I'll always remember it as a growing-up time, too.   —*Barbara Farley Bannister McMinnville, Oregon*

Clocks Were Set on Fast Time

She was surprised by the pace those city folks kept.

By Ruth Morgan, Bowling Green, Kentucky

MY FIRST DAY at college in 1959 will forever stand out in my memories. The day before, Mom had driven me and my meager possessions to Bowling Green, the college town I planned to inhabit for the next few years.

I had never been away from my family in Logan County, Kentucky for any length of time, and everybody had warnings about the big city. The most unusual one came from my Uncle Bill, who had lived up north for several years.

"You'll have trouble getting used to that fast time they have in the city," he warned.

After the long drive, a visit to the campus and the move into my rooming house, I was exhausted. To make matters worse, the band of my new graduation watch had broken and Mom had to take it back to get it fixed.

But I wasn't worried. Western Kentucky State College (now Western Kentucky University) had a clock that chimed loud enough for me to keep up with the time.

Woke Without an Alarm

The next morning, I woke up after daylight, so when the clock chimed, I asked my landlady what time it was. Imagine my surprise when she said it was 7 o'clock. Back home, I would have milked the cows and been ready to catch the school bus by then.

I fixed my breakfast, opened a book and started my new way of city living. I had barely finished my cereal when the chime rang again. Oh well, time always did fly when I started reading. I washed my dishes, straightened my room and sat down to write thank-you letters for my graduation gifts— a book from cousin Cathy and a nice fountain pen from my Aunt Elizabeth.

I was just beginning another letter when the chime sounded again. I got dressed and walked the six blocks to the post office.

I was surprised to see so few people downtown, but I was overwhelmed at all the stores as close to my room as the back of the pasture had been at home.

I was ready to do some window-shopping when the clock chimed again. I had an appointment with the college librarian about a job, so I returned to the rooming house and ate a quick sandwich when the clock chimed again.

It's Noon Already?

My, I thought, it's already 12 o'clock, and I have to be at the library at 1. I had to walk the three blocks to the college, and it might take a few minutes to find the right office.

I showered, then dressed and hurried out the door. My landlady was sitting on her front porch, reading the newspaper.

"My goodness, you sure are one busy little girl. Where are you headed before 10 o'clock in the morning?" she asked.

"Oh, I thought the clock just chimed for 12 a few minutes ago," I said.

"Oh no, child. That was the church clock. It chimes on the half hour. The college clock only chimes on the hour. I thought you were rushing around at double time for some reason this morning."

In reality, I was…but I didn't even know it!

Crossing Guard Risked His Badge for Pretty Classmate

AT THE START of fifth grade in the mid-1950s, our school in Hollywood, Florida asked for volunteers to be crossing guards. I was the first one to put up my hand. The principal seemed pleased. I wasn't one of her better students.

The real reason I joined this elite group was for the uniform. Crossing guards wore a white belt, which went around the waist and crossed the chest, with a large badge on the front. I also was given a hat, a large handheld stop sign and a whistle.

I was assigned to Filmore Street where it crossed U.S. Highway 1. There were no traffic lights on Highway 1, so I was to help students cross only on Filmore.

For the first week, everything went fine. The younger kids would listen, and the older kids would heckle me.

At the beginning of the second week, one of my prettier classmates was trying to cross Highway 1 without much luck. I should have directed her down to the crossing on Filmore, but instead I sprang into action.

With sign in hand, whistle blowing, I stopped the traffic on Highway 1 so the girl could cross. She smiled and thanked me, then walked away.

For that infraction, I was stripped of my hat, sign, belt, badge and whistle. This may have been a little harsh, but for a few seconds, standing in the middle of Highway 1 with stop sign in hand and whistle blaring, I *was* the law.

—*Sam Sinatra, Melbourne, Florida*

Betsy McCall Made Her a Real Cutup

BETSY McCALL was one of my best friends when I was a little girl growing up in Delavan, Wisconsin in the '50s. *McCall's Magazine* arrived once a month, and my mom faithfully gave me the Betsy McCall page. Betsy was a paper doll complete with family, friends and her dog, "Nosey".

A few colorful story panels told a different Betsy adventure every month. But the real treat was the paper doll and clothes to cut out that related to the story. Armed with blunt-nosed scissors, I set about cutting out every illustration on the page. A real bonus was two dolls. Some months Betsy and a friend or cousin or even her mom would appear on the page.

I especially loved Betsy's bright red dress, even though she had clothes for every occasion. Sometimes the illustrator would add a doll, a Christmas ornament, Betsy's dog or some detail from the story as an added decoration to the page. I cut those out, too. Betsy made me a pro with scissors.

My mom knew how much I played with Betsy, so she surprised me with a few extra Betsy items. One was a little etiquette book for proper little girls, another was a send-in sheet of Betsy and her younger cousin, Linda. They came with more outfits than the magazine could run on a page; I was in heaven!

A real treasure was the Betsy McCall Pretty Pac I got for Christmas one year. It was a little round zippered suitcase. It was probably made for the 8-inch Betsy doll, which I didn't have. But that was okay with me, because Betsy McCall would always be a paper doll to me.

She was the first of a lot of paper dolls I owned and always a favorite.
—*Trudi Bellin, Franklin, Wisconsin*

Girls Spent Hours Dressing Paper Dolls

ONE OF MY favorite memories of the early 1950s is of sitting on a friend's front porch, playing with our "cutouts". These were paper dolls with matching clothes, which were kept in place with paper tabs that folded around the doll.

You could buy a cutout book for about 29¢, and it was a treasure. After we cut out the clothes, we carefully stored them in cigar boxes scrounged from relatives and friends. My friends and I had so much fun dressing up our dolls. We could pass hours and hours this way on a summer afternoon. The little-girl clothes of Shirley Temple were my favorite.

Oh, my, what children are missing out on today!
—*Charlotte Shollenberger*
Port Carbon, Pennsylvania

Betsy McCall

I am your paper-doll friend, Betsy McCall.

Every month, there is a story about me in McCall's Magazine, with pretty new clothes for you to cut out.

Washing and Ironing Took Up Much of Mom's Time

I VIVIDLY REMEMBER my mother, Edna Falk, washing and ironing clothes for my siblings and me back in the 1950s in Jamestown, North Dakota. It seemed to be all she did, besides cooking.

Mom washed all our clothes in the basement with a wringer washer. The head revolved to different positions, and she had to pick up each piece of clothing and send it through the wringer to the rinse water—twice. Then she'd wring it into the laundry basket.

In the summer, she took the laundry outside to hang on the clothesline. I'm not sure why she bothered, though, because when everything was dry, she'd bring it back into the house and sprinkle it, using a 7-Up bottle with a special sprinkler head. Then she rolled everything as tightly as she could and let it all sit for a day before ironing.

Mom ironed everything—our clothes, my father's handkerchiefs, the dish towels, the sheets and pillowcases, underwear and whatever else she could get her hands on. She was always proud of her wash. Where she found time to breathe is beyond me.
—*Mary Anne Wyland*
Fargo, North Dakota

Dad Helped Him Cash in His Chips for a Prize

IN THE EARLY 1950s, when I was 11 years old, the Granny Goose Potato Chip Company sponsored a contest—buy a bag of chips, win a three-speed bike. Each bag came with a ticket. If the number on your ticket matched the one that was going to be drawn at the end of the contest, you won the bike.

My dad worked at a mom-and-pop grocery store in our town of Monte Vista, California. He was determined to help me win the prize, so whenever he sold a bag of chips, he'd ask the customers if they wanted their tickets. Many gladly handed theirs over.

In a few months, Dad had collected more than 100 tickets. The night before the drawing, we put all the tickets in numerical order. On the day of the drawing, I went to our movie theater with my future brother-in-law. The drawing would take place between the two features. I can't even remember what the movies were.

After the first movie, the manager spun a big drum, and an audience member drew out the winning ticket number. The manager read the ticket number, but no one seemed to have it. Most of the kids had checked their tickets quickly, as they only had two or three. But I had more than 100 to look through.

I frantically fumbled through the pile as the manager read the number again. There it was—I had the winning ticket! I went forward to claim my prize, but I was so nervous that when the manager asked my name, I could hardly answer.

I got to ride home in the large white Granny Goose truck with my shiny new prize. Thanks, Dad!
—*Ignatius Frank Passantino, Santa Rosa, California*

Son Got Most of His Pledge Right

OUR FAMILIES were staunch Republicans, so you can imagine our joy when General Eisenhower was elected President in 1956.

Shortly after the inauguration, our 6-year-old son came home from school and told us he had learned the Pledge of Allegiance.

He stood solemnly in front of the fireplace with his hand over his heart and said, in part, "…and to the Republican for which it stands…"

We barely retained our composure while he completed his recital. When he finished, we complimented him on a job well done, then explained that we did not believe the country had made the change and that it was Republic, not Republican.
—*Elmer Olson, Laguna Hills, California*

One-on-One Time with Dad Created Precious Memories

BACK IN the '50s, my parents didn't want a television in their Kansas City, Missouri home until we kids were grown, so we only had the radio.

On Saturday nights, Dad would make popcorn for us and fold out our sofa bed. Then he and I would lie on the sofa, eat popcorn and listen to the *Grand Ole Opry* from Nashville.

Dad worked hard all week, and I'm sure he would have preferred to do other things on his night off. But he created a very precious memory for his oldest daughter by spending that time with me. —*Dolores Adams, Gentry, Arkansas*

Fate Kept Childhood Chums Closer Than They Knew

MY FRIEND Richard and I lived on the same street in Brooklyn, New York when we started first grade in 1956. Our mothers took turns walking us to and from school, and we became good friends. We played together often at the beach and the park.

When I was in second grade, we moved away. Our family lost touch with Richard and his parents.

Some 25 years later, I was visiting my friend Sherry and saw her husband talking to a neighbor. The man looked familiar, but I couldn't place him.

Later that day, I asked Sherry who the man was. It was Richard! I couldn't believe it. He was married, had two children and lived just two doors down from my friends.

Sherry told me to ring his doorbell and introduce myself, but I was embarrassed. What would his wife think? What would I say if she answered the door? "Hi, I was in first grade with your husband," sounded a little silly.

The next day, Sherry mentioned me to Richard, and he did remember me. We got together and I met his wife, who was a very friendly and lovely woman. We reminisced, talking about all our friends from the old neighborhood.

Not long after that, Richard and his family moved to Connecticut and we lost touch again. Six years ago, I moved to Connecticut, too.

Just recently, Richard looked me up through our mutual friend, and it turns out we live just one town away from each other. And here's an even bigger coincidence: He works in an office building directly across the street from mine.

I guess some friendships are never meant to be broken.
—*Brenda Russo, Fairfield, Connecticut*

FIRST-GRADE PHOTO. "I'm in the front row, far right," says Brenda Russo. "Richard is standing in the back at far left."

Mother's Presence Made Graduation Unforgettable

I WAS A CHILD of the Depression, growing up in southern Illinois. It was impossible for me to pay for college, but a stint in the Navy during World War II entitled me to tuition and books under the GI Bill.

My wife, Imogene, didn't have those benefits. She worked at a defense plant while I was in the service. Together we saved enough for her to attend Southern Methodist University in Dallas, Texas with me. We enrolled together after I was discharged.

As our graduation approached, we wanted so much for my mother to be able to attend. She was living alone, barely making ends meet, and we were unable to help her financially. We grew desperate as the big day drew near.

About 2 weeks before graduation, we got some good news. Mom was coming to Dallas after all. My late father had a miner's pension, which Mom had been trying to get for years. The check had finally arrived—just in time for her to attend graduation. This would be a great trip for my mom, who'd never traveled more than 50 miles from home.

When we graduated, my mother was in the audience. As we walked across the stage to receive our diplomas, we saw her wiping tears from her eyes. She was so happy that we'd accomplished what we set out to do.

Afterward, we all hugged, kissed and cried outside the auditorium. It was an unforgettable day for all of us, and I've cherished the memory ever since. —*George Foster Sturgeon Bay, Wisconsin*

First Golden Arches Were Magnet to High Schoolers

FROM 1952 to 1955, I attended San Bernardino High School on E Street in San Bernardino, California—just a block away from the first McDonald's. It opened as a barbecue place in 1940 and changed to a burger-and-fries restaurant in 1948, but it was always popular with teens.

Our favorite place to hang out was under those golden arches, where there was parking for about 10 automobiles. We could buy a hamburger, fries and a malt for 50¢, and get change. What wonderful days those were!

The original building is long gone, but the structure there now houses an unofficial McDonald's museum and displays from the California Historic Route 66 Association. It's open year-round, and admission is free.
—*Esther Penkala-Reiman Canton, Michigan*

Pint-Size Car Was a Barrel of Fun

By Becky Besel, Yakima, Washington

OUR FAMILY might not have had much money while my brothers and I were growing up in Wenatchee, Washington in the '50s, but no one else did, either. What we did have was a rich life with friends and family.

Dad had an auto shop that kept us going, along with Mom packing apples in the fall. Times were tough and Dad often allowed people to trade goods for auto repairs. On oc-casion, folks couldn't pay, but Dad never turned them away; he knew they would pay their bills when they could.

Our parents, Bob and Lucille Feil, always managed to make Christmas and our birthdays an event to remember. They couldn't afford expensive items, but Dad could put his talent and stockpile of stuff to good use to accomplish magnificent things. The little sports car shown in the picture is a perfect example. That 1954 "Christmas car" was built by my dad when I was 7-1/2.

The stylish body was made of the same type of steel as a regular automobile. It stood 18 inches tall and was 5 feet long. The only control was a selector handle that operated the transmission as a brake and forward and reverse gears. A pull rope started the engine, much like an outboard motor.

Dad installed a governor so he could control the speed of the car. When my older brother, Danny, drove, it was set at 10 mph. When Dickie, 4-1/2, or I drove, it was set at 6 mph. My little brother, Tommie, was a passenger only.

Dick has the car at his house now and hopes to restore it to its original splendor.

Dad, who's turning 80, still puts in 10-hour days at the shop, which has expanded. My three brothers also are in the business.

This story is a tribute not only to my dad, but to all the people of his generation who are the backbone of the country.

I'll never forget what Dad told me when I wanted to borrow money to buy my first car.

"If you can't afford to pay for it, you can't afford to have it," he said.

Heeding his words, I got a job, then got my car.

NO HITCHHIKERS! "My brothers Dickie and Tommie (in car) ignored brother Danny and me as they enjoyed the car Dad made for us in 1954," writes Becky Besel.

Train Left Station Without Conductor

WHEN I WAS a high school sophomore in 1952, I had to take a train to get from our home in Midland Park, New Jersey to the closest high school, which was in Pompton Lakes, 10 miles away.

Every school day, about 100 students boarded trains at two depots of the Susquehanna Railroad, which we called the "Susie-Q".

One day a student decided to pull the chain inside the train, signaling the engineer to leave the station. It would have been a pretty good prank except for one "minor" detail —the conductor wasn't aware of this early departure and was left behind.

That student was suspended from school for a few days. We had many interesting experiences riding the train to school those 3 years.
—*Barbara Vriesema*
Ridgewood, New Jersey

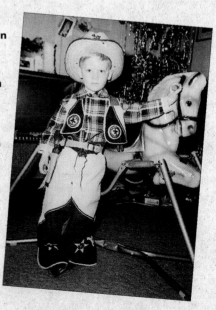

SADDLE UP! "When my son, Joe, was 3 in 1959, he loved watching cowboy shows on television, especially those with Roy Rogers and Gene Autry," writes Joe Johnson of Pasadena, Texas. "At Christmas, Santa brought him the horse in this picture, and his Aunt Lacene gave him the cowboy outfit. He was one happy boy after that. By the way, he didn't grow up to be a cowboy, but he is a deputy sheriff in Houston."

ALL DRESSED UP. "Everyone dressed up for 'picture day' at the one-room Brown Center School near Janesville, Wisconsin in 1953," says Marilyn Johnson, third from right in the front row. With four pupils, Marilyn's second-grade class was the largest in the school. "Our teacher, Miss Arnold, taught all eight grades," remembers Marilyn, who now lives in Aitkin, Minnesota. "The only help she had was when a music teacher came to the school for an hour once a week."

They Did Have a Delicious Crunch

FRESHMEN at Carthage College in Carthage, Illinois in the mid-1950s had to face freshman initiation. Since this was a Lutheran college, things didn't get too out of hand.

For one week, there was a theme for each day, such as Pajama Day or Backwards Day—that's me in the photo (left). We also endured short-sheeted beds and an initiation in the bathroom with overripe bananas and squishy spaghetti.

A group of us freshmen decided to get even, so we gave a "forgiving" lunch for the sophomore girls.

Everyone contributed a snack—mine was chocolate-covered grasshoppers that I had purchased at Marshall Field's in Chicago.

Everyone raved about the crunchy chocolate candy—until I told them what it was! —*Sandie Missioni Livingston, Texas*

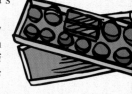

Free Pass in '55 Only Worked Once

ONE OF OUR favorite teenage haunts in the '50s was the drive-in theater in Somerset, Pennsylvania. One of the gang had a pass for a vehicle to get in free.

We decided to take advantage of that with my brother's pickup truck. We filled it with kids and seating supplies.

When the owner, operating the ticket booth, saw a truckload of kids, he couldn't believe we'd take such advantage of the pass. After our coaxing and pleading, he let us in.

We backed into the back row, then some of us sat on the cab while others arranged boards across the sides for seats. Others sat on blankets on the floor and the rest sat on the tailgate.

It was quite a sight to see, and the owner said this was the only time he wanted to see it. —*Margaret Cramer Friedens, Pennsylvania*

Teens Brushed Up on Helping Others

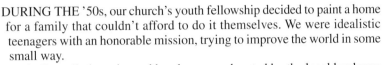

DURING THE '50s, our church's youth fellowship decided to paint a home for a family that couldn't afford to do it themselves. We were idealistic teenagers with an honorable mission, trying to improve the world in some small way.

As I recall, the paint and brushes were donated by the local hardware store. All we had to do was supply the labor.

About a dozen of us went to work that Saturday morning, putting down newspapers, scrambling up ladders, cleaning ceilings, selecting brushes, stirring the paint and distributing rags.

I can't recall a single grumble of disappointment or disagreement that morning, only harmony and enthusiasm as the dingy rooms and halls were brightened with cheery pastel colors. We even painted an old wooden toilet seat lavender to complement the bathroom's lilac walls.

Perhaps we weren't Habitat for Humanity, but helping people less fortunate than ourselves made us grateful for all we had at home—even though, in some cases, it wasn't all that much.

We were proud to be part of a team that was helping others. It was fulfilling, and it made us extremely happy. I'm sure our memories of that day lasted long after the paint had faded.

—Gardner Kissack
Chicago Heights, Illinois

Horns and Music Blared At Drive-in Restaurant

IN MY HOMETOWN of Morgan City, Louisiana, everybody hung out at Dusty's Drive-in restaurant. After you parked your car, the carhop would come and wait on you, hooking a tray on a car window that you rolled down three-quarters of the way.

Everyone would meet there, play music, blow their horns, yell at each other and just have a great time.

—Yvonne Perk, Thibodaux, Louisiana

French Cafe Scenes Adorned "Teen Town"

IN 1956, the powers that be in Centralia, Illinois decided a room in our old Community Center could be used once a week for a teen dance.

There were seven grade schools in the area, and all of the seventh and eighth graders were abuzz. None of us were allowed to date, so having a place where we could all hang out together was very exciting.

On the big Saturday night when "Teen Town" opened, my parents dropped off my girlfriends and me. Of course, we had to comb our ponytails, so we headed downstairs to the ladies' room.

To our surprise, we found that a very talented lady had repainted the restroom walls with French cafe scenes and French poodles! It was beautiful.

When I visited the building many years later, the pretty walls were still there. Seeing those pictures brought back such good memories.

I'm sorry I don't remember the name of the artist, who was such a big part of our teen dance scene. Maybe she'll see this and know how much we appreciated her work and the efforts of all the other volunteers at Teen Town.

—Janet Lusch, Vandalia, Illinois

Snakes Alive! Pick Those Berries

I BEGAN a summer seasonal job in 1950 that ran for several years—picking boysenberries for Safeway Stores.

We carried a large tray with a shoulder strap that held a flat of berries and had to weigh in at 45 pounds gross when filled. We were paid 25¢ per flat. If you were a good picker, you could make between $10 and $12 a day during the peak season.

We began picking at daylight and had to quit at noon because it got too hot to handle the fragile berries.

The most interesting part of the job was carrying a long, large stick in your free hand to poke into the berry bushes before reaching in for the berries in order to chase out the rattlesnakes that came to the irrigation ditches for water.

Fortunately no one ever was bitten. The upside to the job was being able to eat the berries that were too soft to go into the flats. As I remember, there were a lot of soft berries.

In the '50s, there was hard work all the way around, but as usual, country folk worked together…and somehow that made the work and the times a lot lighter and happier.

—Sister Anna Mary Meyer, Los Angeles, California

Polio Sapped Her Muscles, But Not Her Spirit

In 1953, life for a carefree 11-year-old took an unexpected turn.

By Carole Sauer, St. Joseph, Minnesota

IT WAS August 29, 1953 and I was 11 years old. I was cutting our farmyard lawn with the old push mower when I started feeling very weak and ached all over.

I went in the house to tell Mom how terrible I felt and she told me to lay down for a while, thinking I'd feel better soon.

By evening, the aching and weakness was so bad I couldn't even lift my head off the pillow. Mom and Dad took me to the hospital in St. Cloud.

The nurse rushed me into an examining room and wouldn't let my parents in the room. I remember being very scared. A doctor told my parents they were going to check me for polio, which would involve a spinal tap.

The procedure confirmed I had polio. They sent my parents home and placed me in an isolation room for 2 weeks without visitors or even a phone.

During that period, I was rolled up in wet blankets, as hot as I could stand them, six or eight times a day. To this day, I don't like the smell of wet wool.

The hospital was very crowded with polio patients. One room meant for two people held four to six.

Home at Last!

Because of the overcrowding, a nurse called my mother and asked if she could put on the hot packs at home. After 2 weeks of not seeing Mom or Dad, I was the happiest little girl!

I went home, but it was a lot of work for Mom. She'd roll out the wringer washer and use it after soaking the blanket in hot water. Because we didn't have running water, she had to pump the water and heat it on the stove first.

Mom put the hot packs on four times a day and helped me exercise my legs, arms and neck, too. It was all very painful.

Mom did that for 3 months and I began walking and getting better and better. After 4 months, I went back to school, although I used a cot at school to rest twice a day.

I was pretty strong for about a year and a half, but then, because of the polio, my back started growing crooked.

Now the doctor told my parents I needed back surgery, but I'd be in a body cast for about 10 months—no sitting or standing.

For the first 2 months, I was in a hospital ward, with up to 30 other girls.

There were no lights or buzzers to call for a nurse and the girl closest to the door had to call out when one of us needed something.

One bright spot was an old parrot, named "Polly", of course, in the room for company. He'd call out for a bedpan and the nurse would come running. We got some laughs from that.

Once I was able to go home, I was still in my body cast, and Mom was very busy taking care of me.

Some friends of Dad's made a cart so I could go from room to room, even outside, if someone pushed it.

Once I got the walking cast, I practiced walking, and my strength gradually came back. I wore that cast for about 5 months.

By the time I was 14, I was pretty much back to normal, although I kept going back to the hospital for checkups until I was 21.

Didn't Stop Dancing

By the late 1950s, I was enjoying life to the fullest. We had six dance halls in the area and I would put on my poodle skirt and dance every single dance wearing 3- or 3-1/2-inch heels!

When the bands took a break, they put on records and we girls would dance to that, so it was nonstop dancing the whole evening.

I'm glad my mom and dad decided to go ahead with my surgery and that they did so much for me, as well as my teacher and friends who visited me at home over many months.

The episode took 2 years out of my youth, and I'd never want to go through that again, but I was one of the lucky ones. ◖

A LONG WALK BACK. Carole Sauer recovered from her bout with polio and was able to enjoy dancing as a teenager. Check out the high heels she's wearing above left. The Christmas photo shows Carole with her father before her illness.

Schoolgirl Had Answers
For Groucho's Stumpers

IN THE EARLY 1950s, we bought our first television, a set with a 9-inch screen. My parents loved to watch the quiz show *You Bet Your Life*, with George Fenneman and Groucho Marx (right) and that crazy duck that dropped down when someone said the "secret woid" and as the show ended.

I loved the program, too, but always had to go to bed halfway through it, because it was a school night.

One evening while listening to my little bedside radio after everyone had gone to bed, I discovered that *You Bet Your Life* was on the radio before it appeared the following week on TV. I listened silently, writing down all the answers on a notepad.

The next week, when my parents sat down to watch the TV show, I got excited when especially difficult questions were asked, saying things like, "Oh, my gosh—Mom, Dad, I know that answer!" Then I read the correct response off my hidden notepad. My parents looked at me in astonishment, as if I'd miraculously become brilliant overnight.

This went on for about 8 months. Then one night, I started giggling hysterically and couldn't stop. I finally spilled the beans, and my secret was revealed. Considering that I was only 9 years old, I thought I'd been pretty clever!

—*Camille Saso-Carpenter, West Hills, California*

Brown Brothers

SCOOTING ALONG. "This is my brother, Bob Zawasky, when he got a new scooter at age 7 in Jamaica, New York about 1950," writes Mary Ann Struller of New Port Richey, Florida. "He was so proud of his red scooter that he insisted on having his picture taken."

Dad's Jury Duty Alarmed Daughter

OUR DAUGHTER, Janie Lou, started talking at a very early age. When she was about 3 years old, her great-grandmother gave her some beads and earrings, which she loved to play with in different combinations every day.

One time when her daddy was called for jury duty, she asked where he was going.

"Honey, he's going to sit on a jury," I told her.

After about 3 days of asking the same question, I said, "Now, Janie Lou, you know exactly where your daddy is. I told you before."

She folded her little arms across her stomach and said, "Well, if my daddy don't stop sitting on the jury, I'm not going to have any jury to wear!"

I guess jewelry and jury sounded the same to a 3-year-old.

—*Edna Price Cobbs, South Charleston, West Virginia*

Players Went to Bat
For Boy in Hospital

WHEN I WAS in grade school in the '50s, I became good friends with Greg Spahn, who lived about a block from our house. Greg's dad was Warren Spahn, a pitcher for the Milwaukee Braves.

One day Greg came over to play, and Mom told him I was in Children's Hospital with rheumatic fever. Greg went home and told his dad.

Mr. Spahn and Lew Burdette, who were my favorite players, asked the entire 1953 Braves team to sign a baseball and an 8-by-10 team photograph. Then they came to my hospital room and presented them to me.

I still have the baseball and photo to this day. I can't imagine ever parting with them.

—*Jim Shultis*
Aurora, Colorado

ALL AGLOW. Cathy Nash, flanked by her friends Janet and Judy, was 7 when she donned her first dance costume. "My mom made it from newspaper patterns on an old treadle sewing machine," Cathy recalls. "We were supposed to be glowworms, but we looked more like butterflies."

Studio Was Dancer's Home Away from Home

SHARON KAY'S Dance Studio in St. Joseph, Missouri was my home away from home in 1955.

We didn't dance to digital sounds from a high-tech boom box as dancers do now. Our music came from a live piano player, who tickled the keys while watching the dancers and turning pages.

Mom spent many an hour hand-sewing sequins on my various costumes. We danced bare-legged in those days.

When we began to wear tights a few years later, I had the first of many embarrassing moments in my dancing career. I proudly donned my brand-new tights and came out to the studio floor to practice.

My savvy teacher quickly pulled me aside and sent me back to get dressed again. I was wearing the tights on top of my leotard, instead of underneath! —*Cathy Nash Wilson*
Midvale, Utah

Grandpa Had a Leg Up On Bicycling Skills

I BECAME the proud owner of a shiny new two-wheeler, a maroon Huffy, in 1952. It had a basket and horn and was just about the most beautiful bike in the world, or at least in my Brooklyn, New York neighborhood.

The only problem was, it had training wheels. I was 7 and still didn't know how to ride a two-wheeler.

Uncle Fred, who was 16, tried to teach me, but I just couldn't get the hang of it. Two or three pedals, and I'd invariably fall over. To make sure I didn't fall into the street, all my lessons were held at Thomas Jefferson High School.

One spring day, Uncle Fred and I (right) were walking my Huffy the three blocks to the school yard when my grandfather decid-

ed to accompany us. During our walk, he suddenly took the bike from me and said he'd meet us at school. I watched, open-mouthed, as my old grandpa—he was 54—mounted my Huffy and took off.

I knew then and there that I could ride that bike. I had to, just to show my grandfather I could do it.

When we caught up to him, I got on the bike. With a push from Uncle Fred, I started riding across the school yard. I was in heaven. I rode across the entire yard.

Nothing could stop me…except the chain-link fence on the other side. Unfortunately, my lessons hadn't included any instructions in stopping.

I learned to ride my wonderful bike that day, but I also learned that my "old" grandfather had lots of things to teach me.

—*Alan Zeitchick*
Delray Beach, Florida

Kid Sister Swooned For "Older Man"

WHEN I WAS 16, in 1955, my older brother reconnected with a fellow he had known in the service. My brother's friend started coming around our house a lot, and I started to get interested.

But my brother and his friend were both 22, and I was only 16. At that age, 6 years is a big difference. I had to think of some way to get this "older man" to notice me.

One night when I knew he was coming over to our home in the Bronx, New York, I got all dressed up. When he arrived, I told him I had a date later. I didn't, of course.

Unfortunately, he and my brother returned to our house much sooner than I'd expected, and I had to run up to my room to keep him from seeing me. I stayed there the whole night.

Apparently I did make some sort of impression, though.

We started dating when I was a senior, got married in February 1958 and celebrated our 43rd wedding anniversary in 2001.

—*Maria Kennedy*
Stuart, Florida

Orange Grove Was Their Field of Dreams

Sunny Arizona was the backdrop for ballrooms and buzzards, safaris and scorpions.

By Gina Ledoux, Brookings, Oregon

IN 1955, our Sunnyslope, Arizona neighborhood held America's promise for families to own a home with a yard. The new pink stucco ranch house was built in the middle of an orange grove.

We couldn't wait to unpack our boxes. My brothers, sister and I each climbed separate trees and ate ripe oranges. The juice dripped down our shirts and we learned the hard lesson of consuming too much fruit in one sitting.

Once recovered, we ran through the orchards with our new neighborhood friends. We played hide-and-seek, pretended to be Tarzan and Jane, Robinson Crusoe or safari hunters.

We transformed the orchard into glittering ballrooms, or Western towns, depending on the whim of our active imaginations.

My brothers, Jimmy, 13, and John, 11, were the most entertaining. Once, to Mom's horror, they brought home a glass jar full of small *scorpions*. They were inspired partly by science, but most of all, by a cash reward of 50¢ per scorpion offered by a biology teacher.

Mom ordered the boys to take the scorpions far away from the house, back where they found them. Sadly, they never collected their fortune.

Never a Dull Moment

Once a plan was dashed, another would follow. Jimmy decided it was time to catch a buzzard. John, my sister, Karen, and I were instructed to lie like dehydrated corpses at the end of our cul-de-sac. A large buzzard began to circle. I was 8 years old and refused to be an easy meal for a gigantic bird. I ran away, the bird flew off, and Jimmy was as mad as a hornet. As far as my own carcass was concerned, he would have to find some other bait.

We were too young to understand why Jimmy could not play outside when his asthma left him wheezing and weak. He read constantly, played chess and wrote stories when bedridden. When he felt better, he and John became door-to-door doughnut salesmen with great success. Neighbors would open the door to see two smiling, blue-eyed, dimpled kids with powdered sugar on their upper lips.

The boys safeguarded their wealth in a locked safe, and only they knew the combination; not to imply that they didn't share. The treat of the week, was buying a 45 record. Rock 'n' roll was new on the scene and we adored the beat. I remember Fats Domino, Elvis and Jerry Lee Lewis were favorites. One Saturday, *Blue Suede Shoes* turned on the plas-

LITTLE SAVAGES. In 1956, the author (second from left) and her siblings, Karen, John and Jimmy Savage, left their orange grove playland behind briefly to dress up and pose for a picture.

tic turntable and we all swayed and gyrated to the music.

Caught up in the moment, Jimmy kicked off his shoe and it sailed through the front window. Several weeks' record money went toward window repair.

Karen, at age 12, received her first kiss in that neighborhood. Bobby White, her own personal "dreamboat", was our version of Ricky Nelson with wavy brown hair and black eyelashes. Karen, with dimples and blue eyes, was hands down the prettiest girl in Sunnyslope.

I can see the great influence the orange grove days had on us. At play, the worlds of business and science belonged to Jimmy and John. My sister was the baby-sitter, volunteer crossing guard and model. I was the storyteller, secretary and homemaker.

We didn't feel a destiny inside us, but it was being created as we played and worked in our childhood.

Future Foretold in Childhood Orchard

Today John is a commercial contract superintendent; he has a small apple orchard on his property. Karen works in human resources and creates flower arrangements; she also modeled. I am a homemaker and writer. Tragically, Jimmy died at 16 of complications from his asthma.

Now I look out my window onto oak and pine trees. My grandson, James, and I discovered an immense oak tree and we built a tree house, where he climbs up to his make-believe world.

He told me he spotted a dinosaur and a dragon that threatened his castle, and he shares with me his pirate adventures aboard his great sailing ship. His destiny remains a secret, but I know it's being created. Little James plays until he tires, then begs for a story. He smiles as I tell him a story about Great-Uncle Jimmy, his namesake.

"He wanted to catch a buzzard," I say.

The greatest gift of those early years is the dreams and imagination of children who were free to explore and climb trees.

In my case, it was in an orange grove.

PROUD POPPS. "The lady on the left, Mrs. Popps, and her husband, the owners of Popps' Coffee Cup in Roscoe, Illinois, hired a photographer to take this picture in May 1954," writes James Butts (third from right) of Kenosha, Wisconsin. "The Popps were very nice people, and they were so proud of us when we graduated from eighth grade on the way to high school. We hung out there all the time and they kept us out of trouble. The other three graduates are Roger Gable, Paul Bolander and Chuck Townsend. Standing behind us are Bob Mutimer and my brother, Jerry."

BIRTHDAY SMILES. "This photo of my first-grade class was taken during a birthday party during the 1950-51 school year," writes *Margery Strang Hillman of Homedale, Idaho,* the pigtailed girl second from left in the back row. "This was our last year in our old brick schoolhouse in the country. The following year, we moved to a new school in Marsing, Idaho. Note the fire escape under the window—during fire drills, we left the basement classroom by clambering out the window."

"Candy Stores" Crowded With Teens at Lunchtime

MOST OF THE KIDS at our high school ate lunch at one of the two "candy stores" behind the school.

These were little family businesses that offered made-on-site hamburgers and sandwiches as well as Cokes, candy and ice cream.

One candy store had a separate room with a jukebox, benches around the walls and a small space for dancing. This was where the popular crowd gathered.

The other store was very small, crowded and noisy. That's where the more daring, somewhat rebellious types hung out. Since I belonged to neither group, my friends and I usually took our lunch back to school and sat on the stone wall to eat and gossip.

—*Sharon Hickman, La Luz, New Mexico*

School Lunches Were Good, But No Match for a Grill

By Marthe Hildreth, Sarasota, Florida

"NO POTATOES, please!" I chirped to the cafeteria ladies as I entered the school lunch line in 1955 in Liverpool, New York. Potatoes were the only part of the lunch that I avoided. Whatever the entree was, I was sure to like it.

In fact, I enjoyed eating the school lunch so much that Mom suggested eliminating the potatoes to cut my calorie intake. But that didn't stop me from putting a dime in my penny loafers for an ice cream sandwich. After all, the school's idea of "dessert" was fruit cocktail.

Our brand-new cafeteria was one result of the federal school lunch program launched in the mid-'50s, when I was in second or third grade. Before then, we'd carried our lunches to school in metal lunch boxes painted with cartoon characters, or in a brown bag, and bought our milk for 10¢ a day.

The only time my bag lunches were memorable were when Dad made them, because I never knew what to expect. Sometimes it was a sandwich of leftover pork roast with mustard and butter. Other times he sent meat loaf, Lebanon bologna (a kind of summer sausage) or whatever interesting food he found in the refrigerator.

Treat from Dad Was a Surprise

Once Dad tried to surprise me with a treat—Coca-Cola in a thermos bottle. I was surprised, all right. Coke sprayed all over my face and down my jumper, much to the delight of everyone else at the table.

My favorite lunches during that time didn't even take place at school. A couple of times a month, Dad would pick me up at noon and take me to a wonderful place called Tarbe's. It was the best place ever for hamburgers. I loved going there and always ordered the same thing—cheeseburger with ketchup and onions, fries and a soft drink.

I liked to stand at a counter in front of the kitchen and watch as one of the Tarbe brothers put a ball of ground beef on the grill and pressed it flat as a pancake. Every sizzling burger was so big that it overlapped the bun.

The only problem was, Tarbe's was the neighborhood bar. Mom didn't mind if Dad took me there, but I wasn't supposed to tell anyone at school. Mom was one of the teachers, and she didn't want the superintendent or school board to find out her child sometimes went there for lunch.

Mom must've breathed a sigh of relief when the school lunch program started and she could just hand me a quarter every day and tell me to skip the potatoes. But I missed those Tarbe's lunches, sipping my orange Nehi while Dad teased me about the onions on my cheeseburger.

Her Kingdom for a Kiss

DURING my senior year at Washington High School in Phoenix, Arizona in 1957, I was elected the homecoming queen.

I was so excited that night. A handsome football player named Mitch was chosen to be my king.

During the football game, I was a cheerleader, cheering our team on. At halftime, the outgoing homecoming queen put the crown on my head and Mitch was crowned by the outgoing homecoming king. We were supposed to kiss, but because Mitch was shy, he didn't move. Everyone watched and held their breath.

I finally told him under my breath, "Either you kiss *me* or I'm going to kiss *you*!"

That worked, and he gave me a quick kiss.

—Joanne Vaneenenaam, Phoenix, Arizona

GOOD GRUB. Marthe Hildreth (right) loved going out for lunch with her father, Robert Colvig (left), when she was in elementary school in the mid-'50s. Also in the photo are her mother, Lois, and sister Melissa.

Eskimo Yo-Yo Came to a Chilling End

By Linda Fletcher, Gresham, Oregon

ONE SUMMER morning in 1958, as I poured cereal into my bowl at the breakfast table, an advertisement on the box caught my eye.

For only five box tops and 50¢, it said, I could be the proud owner of an Eskimo yo-yo!

I'd always wanted one of those odd-looking things: A jump rope handle with a short piece of rope coming out of each end, and a rubber ball, about the size of a child's fist, at the end of each piece.

The object was to get one end going around and around, then try to get the other end going in the opposite direction.

I'd seen them on TV and they'd made it look easy. The demonstrators could even throw it up in the air, catch it and keep the whole works going.

Yes, indeed, I wanted an Eskimo yo-yo in the worst way!

As I ate breakfast, I did

NO YO-YO YET. Author (on left) and her sister, before the Eskimo yo-yo arrived.

some calculating. If Mother kept buying this cereal, it wouldn't take long to save up the required box tops.

Excitedly, I showed the ad to my mother and told her my idea. Slowly, she nodded. Yes, she would buy the cereal, but I would have to eat it.

Oh yes, I promised, I'd eat it all by myself if I had to. And yes, I would use my allowance for the 50-cent fee.

I ate the same cereal every morning, day after day, week after week.

At first, my brothers and sister were happy to help out with the eating part, but after the second or third week, I was pretty much eating it by myself. I hung in, though, and was finally rewarded with a small stack of box tops.

Proudly, I mailed my order and waited.

I waited patiently for a long time. Summer turned to autumn and school started, but nothing came.

I had actually forgotten about it when I came home one day and there was the package for me.

I tore it open and

there it was—my Eskimo yo-yo had finally come! Quickly, I hurried outside to try it out. My sister and younger brother came, too.

Time to Try It

They watched for a few minutes as I tried to get it going. I was doing pretty well with it when my sister cried out, "Oh, let me try it."

With a fair amount of skill, she managed to get it going in two directions at once. Then it happened!

Imitating the demonstrators on television, she threw the yo-yo up in the air and, a split second later, it was wrapped around a telephone line.

I stood there and stared helplessly at my new toy, the one I'd worked so hard to get and finally owned—for a grand total of 5 minutes.

My sister felt bad about it, but there was nothing either of us could do.

The following summer when Dad was trimming our trees with one of those long pole-like tree trimmers, he cut off the two rubber balls that still dangled from their ropes so we could throw them for the dog. The rest of my Eskimo yo-yo remained wrapped around the telephone line.

That was the end of my Eskimo yo-yo, although it lives on in my treasure chest of memories.

Silly Putty Has Left a Lasting Impression

JAMES WRIGHT, a scientist working for General Electric in New Haven, Connecticut in 1943, was seeking a synthetic rubber substitute when he mixed silicone oil and boric acid, creating what would become a classic toy—Silly Putty.

The resulting blob didn't measure up for its intended purpose and languished for several years as GE searched for a scientific use, according to Binney & Smith Inc., the makers of Crayola crayons and, for the last 24 years, Silly Putty.

Peter Hodgson, an out-of-work New Haven advertising copywriter, came across a sample at a party at the home of a Harvard physicist. Also at the party was a toy store owner. Along with Peter, he decided to put a description of the silly stuff in the next toy store catalog.

Peter saw the putty's potential as a toy for adults and children alike and went to work. Silly Putty burst onto the national scene in 1950 after he took small portions of

the material and sold them in plastic eggs because the Easter season was approaching.

Its unique properties—high bouncing when rolled into a ball, breaking in two when quickly pulled apart, ease in shaping and the ability to pick up color comics and then change the shape of the characters as you stretch the putty—have kept it in stores now for more than 50 years.

It recently was added to the National Toy Hall of Fame. Since the first egg was filled, more than 300 million have rolled off the assembly line—about 4,500 tons worth, or enough to fill the Goodyear blimp.

'Holstein' Sheets Left Dad with Egg on His Face

By Dorothy Behringer, Cameron, Wisconsin

MOTHER had to start washing clothes early in the morning back in the early 1950s. With 11 kids to clothe, it took her all day to finish the chore.

I was in the fifth grade in Fairdale, North Dakota when we got our first washing machine. Dad was always fixing it. Its gasoline motor made lots of noise, and even though there was an exhaust hole in one window, it seemed the fumes came right back in the room.

When we came home from school, we'd see clothes hanging everywhere—in the house and all over the lines outside. Even the fences sported overalls of every size.

One day when Mother had so many things hanging outside, a man going into town stopped and asked her if she ran an orphanage. "It just could be, it sure feels like it," she replied with a chuckle.

Mother sure liked to see her white sheets hanging and blowing free in the breeze. She said the sun bleached them whiter and they smelled so fresh when she brought them in.

One day, before she realized it, it got dark and she decided to leave the sheets hanging outside all night. It happened to be Halloween night. In the middle of the night, after all of us kids had returned home from playing pranks and settled down, Dad was awakened by a lot of noise outside. He told Mother it must be those "Halloween kids" again.

The temperature had dropped below freezing, he noticed immediately as he stood outside in the dark in his long johns. He yelled at whoever was out there making all the racket to leave, but the noise continued.

Mud Would Chase Away Revelers

He thought some kids were trying to tip over our outhouse. Standing on the porch with few clothes and no shoes on, he decided to throw chunks of near-frozen mud in the direction the noise was coming from. He tossed several chunks, but the noise started up again, Disgusted and cold, he went back inside, telling Mother the revelers would tire and go home soon.

In the morning, frost was covering everything. When Mother looked outside, she let out a terrible scream. We *never* heard a scream come from her before.

She called Dad so loud that it hurt our ears. When Dad got up to see what she was having such a fit about, all she could do was point.

The sheets that she'd worked so hard on had big dark spots all over them. They looked like Holstein cows to us.

Dad couldn't believe his eyes. He knew exactly what had happened. The noise he'd heard was her sheets as they froze and snapped, swished and scraped against each other.

Dad had really done in all Mother's hard work. The tears ran down her face.

She got so mad, she was just fuming. Dad just turned around and walked out of the room. We'd never seen such an expression on Dad's face before either.

He was never allowed to forget what he had done. This was Dad's worst day, week, month or year.

And you know, he never ever said another word about it to anyone. Not one word! ◣

GO TIGERS! "I met Judy at the start of her junior year at Ironton (Ohio) High School," says Pete Harris of Florence, Kentucky. "This picture from 1950 or '51 shows her doing a split in front of the old Tiger stadium in Ironton. She was a Girl Scout camp leader after graduating from high school. We were engaged in 1954 and have been very happily married for 45 years."

Teens Formed Bond That Would Last a Lifetime

PEGGY AND I met as teenagers, when her family moved to Utah from Colorado. We grew up together, sharing all the aches and pains of those teen years. We knew we'd be best friends forever.

Peggy was stricken with polio at 17 and had a long stay in the hospital in Salt Lake City. The polio settled in her throat and neck, and she couldn't swallow or speak. I went with her parents almost every night to see her.

When Peggy finally got out of the hospital, she had to learn how to speak all over again. I went with her to speech therapy several times.

After high school, Peggy and I both attended business college, then went our separate ways and began raising our

FRIENDS FOR LIFE. Janell Blake (right) and her pal Peggy Small were best friends when above photo was snapped of them in 1955...and they're still close today (left).

families. Life has taken us in different directions and we've both moved around the country, but we've stayed in touch. Though we rarely see each other, the bond of friendship will always be there.
—*Janell Blake, Richfield, Utah*

DIGGING IN. Joan Meyer and her brother Jimmy didn't waste any time digging into the bounty under the Christmas tree in this cherished holiday photo. "We both received globe banks that year, and we still have them," says Joan, of Grand Rapids, Michigan. "Jimmy also got John Deere farm toys, as always. He got a different implement every Christmas and on his birthday." Joan's favorite toy was the metal dollhouse in the background, which she's now trying to refurnish. Jimmy kept all the John Deere toys, too. "Those toys survived not only Jimmy, but his three sons," Joan says.

Washday Was Always a Wringing Experience

THE CLAMOR of our wringer washer filled the entire house on Monday mornings. Washing clothes was a noisy, time-consuming process—and with no electricity, the chore was a far cry from what it is today.

Mom first had to haul water to a large oblong copper boiler on top of the stove. Once heated, the water was transferred to the washing machine—a precarious operation at best.

On a good day, one or two tugs of the cord would start the washer. The gas engine labored under the washtub, driving the agitator back and forth.

Since the wash water would be used more than once, Mom started with white loads and gradually moved on to darker colors, saving the darkest fabrics for last. When the wash was done, the water was drained into a pail and carried outside.

The best part of washday was helping Mom wring out the clothes. We kids stood on a chair, wooden spoon in hand, to fish wet garments out of the tub and feed them

through the rolling wringers perched above. It was fascinating to watch the excess water squish out and run back into the tub as the clothes fell, ribbonlike, into a pan.

Sometimes we tried to put too much through the wringer, and the emergency release would pop to relieve the tension. That was fun, too. It gave us a reason to pull a lever to reverse the direction of the rollers and pull the laundry back through so we could try again.

While I enjoyed helping with this task, I was cautious. When I was 2, I'd been left alone with the washer for just a minute and decided to examine the rollers more closely. The rollers grabbed my fingers and pulled my arm in all the way up to the shoulder.

I hollered, but not from pain—I don't remember any, probably because the wringers were too worn-out to squeeze my arm very hard. What did make me yell was the fear of being totally consumed by that monstrous machine!

Mom quickly came to my rescue and took me to the village doctor. There were no broken bones, but I had a new respect for our wringer washer after that.
—*Elaine Fehr*
Fox Creek, Alberta

Parents Spirited Them Away
For Surprise Trips

THERE WASN'T a lot of extra money when I was growing up, but somehow my parents found enough to make a few days very special for my three siblings and me.

Once a year, Mom and Dad (below) would surprise us by showing up at our two-room country school and taking us away for the day. The destination was top-secret, which only added to the intrigue.

One time we went to the Royal Ontario Museum in Toronto, about 60 miles from home. There

was so much to see! I was mesmerized by the mummies wrapped in their dusty shrouds, ancient artifacts from all over the world and especially the huge totem pole. Our guide said it had to be lowered through the roof due to its great size.

I will always treasure the memories of those wonderful family excursions. They taught much more than just history. They were a lesson in the joy and happiness derived from being part of a loving, caring family.

—*Ruth Lee, Troy, Ontario*

Wyoming Teens Enjoyed
Surroundings Without TV

I GREW UP in a small Wyoming town in the early '50s and attended a high school with 280 students. Thermopolis is in a valley surrounded by easy-to-climb ridges, with a blue river to float or fish in, and one of the world's largest mineral hot springs, which feeds three warm-water swimming pools.

We had so much to keep us busy that the most trouble we got into was stealing watermelons or getting a jalopy stuck as we explored the surrounding hills.

I feel sorry for today's youth missing the fun of a country dance. We had Friday night "mixers", a harvest moon dance, Sadie Hawkins Day, sock hop, junior prom and snake dances around a bonfire at homecoming games.

The dances were held at our country schools, and town and country kids danced and played together—no cliques here. We square-danced, jitterbugged and two-stepped, then had a late-night snack furnished by the local Grange wives.

Since TV hadn't arrived, we hung out at the drugstore, drinking sodas and blowing straw covers at the ceiling, trying to get them to stick.

Transportation consisted of old jalopies, Jeeps or used pickups, but you had to work odd jobs to pay for them yourself. My first job was at a local pool for 35¢ an hour. I saved a good share of that salary to buy school clothes.

A favorite spot for young lovers was a hill above town called Snider's Point. There were so many cars parked there, and so much teasing and honking back and forth, that there was little time left for smooching.

The best part is that most of us who grew up during that time are still friends. It's a unique bond. I've run into people from my hometown in far-off cities, and we still greet each other with hugs and giggles.

—*Bonnie Jo Blakesley*
Thermopolis, Wyoming

Plastic-Factory Rejects
Made Indestructible Toys

MY MOTHER worked in a plastics factory in Dayton, Ohio that made Aunt Jemima and Uncle Moses salt and pepper shakers, pitchers and cookie jars. The company also made Ben Franklin and Roy Rogers drinking mugs, many of the plastic toys packed in cereal boxes and a multitude of other household items.

Mom's job was spray-painting the plastic figures. Even though it was a typical factory setting, the ladies in her department all wore dresses or skirts. Mom was a trendsetter—she wore blue jeans.

Mom often brought home items that were defective. We kept them in a box, and my cousins and I would dump them on the floor and play with them for hours. They were just plastic, so we threw them around with abandon.

Those toys are long gone in some junk heap. But if you're lucky, you can still pick up a set of those "just plastic" salt and pepper shakers at antique shows for $60 a pair. —*Billie Zappone, Mason, Ohio*

GREAT TOYS. Author's mother (left) worked in a plastics factory and brought home imperfect plastic premiums, such as the Aunt Jemima salt and pepper shakers (below). They made wonderful toys because they were nearly indestructible.

ALL POMPED UP. Gary Hill (left) and his buddy "Red" show what a good hair day was like in the 1950s. Gary's carefully styled pompadour looked good—before the sun began playing havoc with the styling goo.

Boys Had Bad-Hair Days, Too

Heavy goo held pompadour in place—until it melted.

By Gary Hill, Fresno, California

WHEN I started high school in Fresno, California, I decided to leave my "little-boy" haircut behind and go for something a little more "hep". Only nerds still wore their hair with a part on the side, and I wasn't smart enough to be a nerd.

The athletes sported flattops or butches. The cool guys who drove hot rods had pompadours with ducktails in back, or "boogies"—hair flat on top, with long sides combed into a ducktail.

I wasn't big enough to be a jock, and I had sort of a pinhead and a thin neck, so that ruled out the butch or flattop. My only choice was to try to be cool.

The biggest difficulty in acquiring a pompadour was getting rid of the part Mom had put in my hair 15 years before. If I wanted my hair to look like Elvis', the part had to go!

After a few minutes of combing, my pompadour would look pretty good, but before long, it would flop to the side and the miserable part would reappear.

I found the solution at Stillman's Drugstore. It was called Dixie Peach. I'd put a big glop of that sweet-smelling goo on my hands, smear it into my hair, style it with my ever-present comb and be ready to go. The entire process only took 15 to 20 minutes if everything went well.

There were a couple of problems with Dixie Peach, though. It was so heavy that if you had a skinny neck like mine, it tended to make your head flop forward or to one side, which made it much harder to look cool.

The other problem was the heat. When you went outside in summer, the goo started to melt. Dixie Peach would trickle down your forehead, and your pompadour would go into a serious sag. The scent attracted bees and flies, too.

Dad and I were often squabbled about my hair. He wore a butch and thought everyone else in the world should, too, including my mom and sisters.

Dad would walk me into Joe's Barbershop, next door to the grocery store we owned, and tell Joe, "I want this hair cut off!" After he left, I'd tell Joe, "Just a trim, please, not too much."

Poor Joe didn't know what to do—trim it gently and incur my dad's wrath, or cut it aggressively and risk dealing with a sobbing teenager. He always tried for a happy medium, leaving enough hair so I could comb it back, but trimming enough so Dad could see my hair had been cut, and that he hadn't wasted $2.

All of us wanted to look like James Dean, Ricky Nelson, Frankie Avalon and Fabian. Why? Because all the girls wanted guys who looked like that.

But no matter how hard we tried, we never even got close. I could almost make my upper lip curl like Elvis', but when I managed it, the girls just laughed. They said I looked like I'd just smelled some bad cheese. ◄